# Psychoanalysis and Social Theory

P62157-B1(C)

# Psychoanalysis and Social Theory

## IAN CRAIB

*Department of Sociology, University of Essex*

## HARVESTER WHEATSHEAF

NEW YORK   LONDON   TORONTO   SYDNEY   TOKYO

First published 1989 by
Harvester Wheatsheaf,
66 Wood Lane End, Hemel Hempstead,
Hertfordshire, HP2 4RG
A division of
Simon & Schuster International Group

Printed and bound in Great Britain by Billings and Sons Ltd, Worcester

British Library Cataloguing in Publication Data

Craib, Ian
  Psychoanalysis and social theory: the limits of sociology
  1. Social psychology
  I. Title
  302

ISBN 0–7450–0139–4

1 2 3 4 5   93 92 91 90 89

For Ben

# CONTENTS

# PREFACE

This book is intended as a textbook; I have used it rather selfishly to try to explore some of my own thoughts and feelings about the nature and possibilities of sociological explanation. I am not sure that the two sit easily together, but I hope they do not get in each other's way.

As I worked on the Conclusion, I became preoccupied with the idea of therapy and theory as play. Now I am left with two images. The first is of my son's room before and after I have tidied it. Before, it is a jumble of strange things and unconnected toys; after, it is a collection of piles of strange things and unconnected toys. When my son tidies his room, he, of course, makes a better job of it. The first draft of this book was a jumble of unconnected ideas, repetitions and loose ends. I think I have succeeded in dividing them into piles and throwing some of them out. I comfort myself with the hope that the repetitions will be useful for the reader, the contradictions and loose ends stimulating.

The second image comes from John Mortimer's autobiography, *Clinging to the Wreckage* (Harmondsworth, Penguin, 1983). Writing of his education he comments:

> Ideas are clapped on us as top hats were once set on the grizzled heads of African chieftains; they make us all look more or less ridiculous. (p.54)

I am now about to cavort in front of the world in a top hat I've put together myself from various, perhaps sometimes rather bizarre, materials. I can only hope that some of my contortions will be entertaining and some instructive.

This book has grown from the day-to-day activity of teaching sociology and social psychology, and training and then working as a group psychotherapist. I owe much to students, patients, teachers and colleagues who provide a fertile soil that I feel I can never exploit to its full potential. I am particularly grateful to the Fuller Bequest Research Fund, administered by the Sociology Department at Essex University, for supplying a grant which enabled a comprehensive search of relevant literature, and to Helen Crowley for the efficient and intelligent way she carried out that search. I am indebted to Christopher Badcock for some very pertinent comments on a late draft. I am especially grateful to Dr John Walshe, Consultant Psychotherapist at Severalls Hospital, Colchester. He has given me a great deal of time, reading drafts and discussing ideas in a way I found constantly stimulating and encouraging.

None of these people is responsible for the fact that I complete the task standing in the middle of a jumbled toy room wearing a ridiculous top hat.

Ian Craib

# 1

## TAKING PSYCHOANALYSIS SERIOUSLY

Sociology . . . dealing as it does with the nature of people in society, cannot be anything but applied psychology. (Freud, *New Introductory Lectures on Psychoanalysis*, p.216)

This book has two aims: the first is to provide the student of sociology or psychoanalysis with a reasonably intelligible and fairly elementary introduction to different attempts to bring the insights of the two disciplines together. The second is to develop a criticism of these attempts and to suggest an alternative way of looking at the relationship between individual and society. In the last analysis, I am interested in the ways in which, if we take psychoanalysis seriously, we have to modify and limit the ambitions of sociological explanations.

I start with the assumption that Freud was wrong: that sociology is more than and different from applied psychology, that one cannot be reduced to the other. I shall be directly concerned with the implications of the difference for sociology, since, if sociology is not psychology writ large, then psychology is not sociology writ small. This means that we cannot derive a knowledge or understanding of how individuals and groups act from a sociological understanding of the structure and processes of society.

The label 'sociologist' often seems the only thing that its bearers have in common. It is a notoriously pluralistic discipline and while some sociologists might be happy with Freud's statement, others would reject it. It seems to me that Freud is right only in the sense that, if we are to understand social organisation and processes, then we have to know how the individual psyche is constructed and how it operates. It does not follow that the social world is made up *only* of individuals and their relationships. There are phenomena that, though related to individuals, have an existence over and above individuals. A language, for example: many people speak English but the English language is not the product of individuals. It has a structure and involves rules of which many of its speakers are unaware and it has a history which does not depend upon any one individual or group of individuals. It is an external reality we each have to accept if we are to be part of the world around us. There are many such social phenomena, social institutions or social structures within which individuals are placed and their relationships develop. Strictly speaking, perhaps, sociology ought to concern itself with the former, psychology and social psychology with the latter. It is as if sociology deals with the framework of the theatre and the stage, psychology and social psychology with the actors and the play.

Discussion of the relationship between the disciplines, however, hides the more important and real problem of the relationship between what they study: society on the one hand, and individuals and groups on the other. For sociologists this is a tediously familiar starting point. Less familiar is the attempt to approach it through psychoanalysis, although such an approach has undergone occasional fashionable upswings, most recently in connection with the development of feminist theory. It is a project that has proved capable of generating exciting ideas, yet one which has remained marginal to both disciplines. In the case of psychoanalysis, this is largely because practising analysts, often in the face of criticism in the wider intellectual community, have confined themselves to clinical practice and issues of treatment, although there is little direct objection to using psychoanalytic theory to look at wider issues. In the case of sociology, however, the use of psychoanalysis is something which has to be justified. There is suspicion not only of its relevance, but of its intellectual respectability. The first question to ask, then, is why take psychoanalysis seriously?

## WHY PSYCHOANALYSIS? THE UNCONSCIOUS

On one level, this book as a whole ought to be taken as a justification for sociologists to take psychoanalysis seriously: I shall be trying to show that it opens up ways of dealing with issues that can barely be approached from other directions. The dominant sociological emphasis tends to be on the rational and cognitive aspects of human behaviour, on what people consciously think rather than on what they feel and on what might be unconscious aspects of their actions. We find, in sociology, very little work on the complexity and conflicts of people's emotional lives, on the profound ambiguities of motivation and meaning, or on the strange and often difficult relationships we each of us have with our bodies. Psychoanalysis plunges straight into these areas, as well as having much to say about the conscious and rational aspects of our lives. It deals with the irrational, the 'crazy' side of human life, the peculiar and frightening world which underlies much of our everyday existence. It does this more directly than sociology and, I think, with what is eventually greater respect for the integrity of individual experience.

If there is one central idea in psychoanalysis that captures all of this, it is the idea of the unconscious. As Freud himself pointed out, it is not a new idea. We can find it in some form or another throughout literature and in much philosophy. It is also present in a common-sense form even among those who know little or nothing of Freud. There is a simple use of the term, referring to those things of which we are not conscious all the time. I know what I had for breakfast this morning, but I have not thought about it, been conscious of it, all day. Most people would accept this use. Beyond this, most of us have the experience of discovering something new about ourselves, a new talent or ability, a new motive or desire, and realising that it must have been present all along even though we were not aware of it; and we are rightly suspicious of those who claim to know themselves completely. The psychoanalytic use of the term is, however, more systematic.[1]

This is clearest in Freud's work as part of what is known as his 'metapsychology', an admittedly speculative theory of the general structure of mental life.[2] He talked of three levels or 'structures': the 'id' or 'it', those basic drives we have by virtue of being human, of which sexuality is the most important; the 'ego' or 'I', the central organiser of our mental life; and the 'super-ego', something we can for the time being think of in terms of a 'conscience'. Each has an unconscious aspect, but the id is commonly thought of as comprising the core of the unconscious. These basic drives aim at immediate satisfaction but it is in the nature of the world that all our drives cannot be satisfied – it is, after all, a dangerous place and resources are scarce. Consequently, we can be seen as developing our consciousness as a sort of protective screen between ourselves and the world. Consciously, we can stand back and judge what is and what is not dangerous, safe, possible, etc. Unconsciously, we would be the fools that rush in.

Unconscious drives are part of our mental life; as we shall see, they involve ideas and feelings that influence conscious thoughts and actions. For example, I might not be conscious of how scared of my father I felt as a young child, yet that fear may influence my reaction to men in positions of authority in my adult life. I might react in a nervous or submissive way, or be arrogant and bloody-minded, a gut reaction that I do not connect with how I felt about and reacted to my father. Nevertheless, that original and now unconscious experience influences my present behaviour. This way of talking about the unconscious involves the idea of repression. I do not allow myself to remember my original fear of my father, perhaps because I was so scared. I thought he would destroy me and that thought was unbearable.

Given that the dominant Western philosophical tradition has regarded the conscious mind as the source of knowledge and the originator of action, it is not surprising that the idea of the unconscious has not always been very popular. Criticism has often focused on the idea of *the* unconscious, a sort of 'thing' determining our behaviour, and it is true that psychoanalysts sometimes talk of the unconscious as such a 'thing'. At other times it seems to be a place in the mind, or even an 'inner person' battling it out with those other internal inhabitants, the ego and the super-ego. Sometimes it is identified with the instincts, genetically patterned forms of behaviour about which we can do little. In this case, Freud is criticised as a biological determinist, for claiming that everything stems from our biological make-up.

Although 'instinct' is a fairly common term in psychoanalytic writing, I think it would be a mistake to attribute to it the same meaning it has in biology. Freud himself often spoke of drives, a combination of physical and mental components. The unconscious is composed not of biological instincts but of the mental representations we attach to these instincts. I am perfectly conscious of my sexual instinct, while I might repress the thought that I can satisfy it in relationships with members of my own sex. I have repressed my homosexuality. In such a case, the energy attached to my homosexual ideas becomes attached to something else, perhaps to building close, but not sexual, friendships with other men. Freud called this process sublimation. Further, a feature of human life is that an instinct such as the sexual instinct is not directed at any one object, but has to be socially channelled, in our society usually towards members of the opposite sex. The attribution to Freud of a simple biological determinism is mistaken. It is none the less true that psychoanalysis lays great stress on the body and its functions, but this is best understood as looking at the way in which our bodies and bodily functions become models for our relationships and actions in the world. This is especially true for the most sensitive areas of the body: the mouth, the anus and the genitalia. This is not a startling idea: we often use bodily metaphors to describe relationships. We talk about people 'looking good enough to eat', people can be 'greedy' for love, knowledge, money and many other things. We can 'suck up' to others. We can suffer from 'verbal diarrhoea'. We can be 'shat upon', 'screwed' or 'fucked up', not to mention 'buggered' and 'eaten alive', without any of the physical events described actually taking place.

Even if Freud's theory is not determinist, it is sometimes useful as a metaphor to think of the unconscious as a thing, a place or even as a sort of internal person. As a thing, it captures the way we sometimes seem to be taken over by forces over which we have no control; 'it' takes charge of our behaviour. As a place it is where things happen behind our backs, only to be discovered later by our conscious selves; the place, for example, where I first take the decision to fall in love. As an internal person, it is a participant of the many internal conflicts that we all experience, but a secret participant, constantly surprising us. It does not follow, however, that the usefulness of thinking about the unconscious in these ways means that it should actually be regarded as *being* any of them. My own view is that the most useful general way of thinking about the unconscious is in terms of unconscious actions, attempts to satisfy desires that we cannot allow ourselves to recognise, attempts to relive past experiences in order to reach some more satisfactory conclusion, and the hiding of feelings that are, for one reason or another, too dangerous.[3] For example, my submissive attitude to men in authority might be an unconscious attempt to hide the murderous rage I feel at the fact that anybody should have authority over me; it might even be an unconscious attempt to seduce the other person into a homosexual relationship. As well as a conscious, more or less rational life we also lead an unconscious life. It is a fairly simple idea: at the same time as I am trying to get on with my boss, I am also, unconsciously, trying to get on with my father. Inevitably, this unconscious activity gets in the way of the conscious, rational task. One of the peculiarities of our unconscious life is that although it is not readily available to our conscious selves, it is by no means always entirely *un*conscious. It appears as inexplicable, often compulsive feelings, as anxiety, as repetitive patterns in our lives. We are conscious of the effects of our unconscious on our feelings and behaviour.

Psychoanalysis, then, offers a way of making contact with this dimension of our existence. It is a difficult dimension in two senses: it is hard to understand and it is hard to tolerate. Our unconscious life is the most dangerous part of ourselves in that it seems that, if we allowed it into consciousness, we would face destruction – physical and/or psychological and/or social. In the history of psychoanalysis, there are various theories of the unconscious that posit different types of threat. For Freud, the crucial pressures were a combination of internal and external needs to control and direct sexuality. A stable social organisation which continues from generation to generation requires human beings to be by and large non-incestuous and heterosexual. Since human sexuality is diverse and not genetically patterned and directed towards members of the opposite sex, it has to be limited and pointed in the requisite direction. This is achieved through the infant's developing relationships with its carers – in our society usually the biological mother and, to a lesser extent, father. Certain sexual choices are made and others repressed; the repressed sexual desires make up the core of our unconscious life and are felt to be personally and socially threatening.

As his work developed, Freud formulated a theory of what he called the 'life' and 'death' instincts, *Eros* and *Thanatos*. The fact that he endowed them with names from Greek mythology is perhaps a sign that the term 'instinct' is not to be taken literally. The death instinct is best thought of as our destructive desires, directed at others and ourselves. The idea was developed in the work of Melanie Klein, where much of what is repressed and avoided is seen as our destructiveness and our fear of it. A third view, based on the development of Klein's work and drawing out another aspect of it, moves away from the idea of innate destructiveness. Instead, the central proposition is that the infant's dependence on its environment, its helplessness during its early years, involves fears for its physical and psychic survival, fear for its growing yet still fragile sense of self. What is repressed and avoided in this case is the experience of helplessness and psychic disintegration and, often, our fear of them.

I shall be elaborating on all these approaches later. They are not always mutually exclusive and there seems no reason to have to choose between the three. They will be most important in my argument, although there are others. I do not think that they involve any radical modification of what Freud had to say about the workings of the unconscious. Here, the irrationality of our unconscious life stands out. This life is timeless; it does not develop and mature. Some part of us remains forever the demanding and insecure baby, seeking immediate gratification. The laws of logic do not apply to the unconscious. It is also true that they do not always apply to our conscious life, but generally we try to achieve some sort of coherence in our thoughts and actions. Unconsciously, however, we might desire entirely contradictory things. A common-sense intuition of this is the oft-remarked proximity of love and hate. At the same time as I remained submissive to my father, it is conceivable that I harboured murderous desires based on my resentment of his power, and an intense love, connected with the care and protection he offered me. In our unconscious life, we are as contradictory, impulsive and devious as any infant.

It should be clear from my examples, as well as from my argument, that psychoanalysis reaches places that sociology does not reach. Why, then, are so many sociologists (and others) suspicious of psychoanalysis? If the examples have perhaps seemed rather odd, then you are already beginning to understand the suspicion.

### PSYCHOANALYSIS: FRAUD OR SCIENCE?

To read many commentators one would think psychoanalysis to be a sort of witchcraft, perhaps even a deliberate confidence trick, which, if it made any difference at all, only served to damage already unhappy people. There is an ambivalence in the way Freud's work has been absorbed into our culture. On the one hand, there seems to be a general, if vague, acceptance of his ideas about infantile sexuality, and the idea of an unconscious mind. At the same time, there is a refusal to accept some of his ideas: they seem outlandish and absurd. From this point of view, it is obvious nonsense, if not downright evil, to say that a young child desires, sexually, one or both of its parents. Some acquaintance with the psychoanalytic interpretation of people's actions leads to the objection that if you want to, you can say anything about anything, and psychoanalysts usually do. Who, for example, could take seriously Freud's suggestion that a patient's habit of squeezing his blackheads symbolised masturbation and castration?

This ambivalence is reflected in the intellectual culture. On the one hand, there is a vast body of work that treats psychoanalysis as a serious intellectual and practical pursuit, building up a body of established knowledge and technique. For a number of reasons, including the often self-defeating need to establish respectability in the face of external hostility, much of this is rather narrow, focusing on the 'clinical evidence' that comes from psychoanalytic treatment, and isolated from the wider intellectual community. On the other hand, there is a body of work that claims to demolish psychoanalysis as a respectable enterprise. Occasionally, the two sides become locked in a battle that resembles the more absurd dimensions of marital conflict: each partner's abuse seems precisely judged to prove the other right. Opponents accuse psychoanalysis of being a sort of totalitarian religion, its theory no more than dogma, its organisation as exclusive and concerned with heresy as the medieval church in which initiates (and patients) are subjected to a process not unlike brainwashing. If the treatment fails, it is the patient's fault, a result of irrational resistance. The psychoanalytic response, when it comes, confirms the accusation: nobody can talk about psychoanalysis unless they themselves have been analysed, and the only reason to launch such a virulent attack is a fear of and irrational resistance to the ideas of psychoanalysis. The accuser's response is then so violent that one suspects the analyst is right.

I do not believe that we need get caught up in this battle, since it is possible to sort out the significant issues from the surrounding straw targets and unanswerable questions. The crucial arguments are around problems in the philosophy of science: how do we acquire knowledge and how do we know that it *is* knowledge? Psychoanalysis has become a happy hunting-ground for various philosophies of science and it must be borne in mind that what disappears in the various arguments is the very thing which, for me, makes it interesting: what it has to say about the irrational, the crazy aspects of human life. It seems to me possible to argue that although some aspects of psychoanalytic work and theory can be seen as scientific, other aspects cannot. I shall try to make this clear as I look at the various arguments.

The central argument is around testability; to be acceptable as knowledge, a theory must be tested against an external reality. Many psychoanalytic claims, for example, that civilisation is based on the repression of instincts, are too general to be tested. Beyond this, since the unconscious is thought of as having contradictory desires, we cannot derive any reasonable prediction to test, and there is no way in which we can say that the result of a test disproves the theory. If I both love and hate my father, any action can be explained. In any case, the evidence for testing comes from clinical work within the privacy of the consulting room and hence cannot be confirmed by independent others and is open to all sorts of unacknowledged influence by the analyst.

The psychoanalytic reply is that any science rests on more than testing its propositions against reality. Psychoanalysis, like many 'respectable' scientific theories, covers a number of different areas and works with a number of explanatory levels. It is a theory of sexual development, emotional development, mental illness, motivation and the structure of the mind, to name only a few. One would expect that in some areas it would develop more rapidly than in others, and that in some it might prove entirely inappropriate. For example, I shall be arguing in this book that it tells us very little about social structures despite the fact that Freud thought it was also a social theory. It is, therefore, not really appropriate to think of there being any one test, or even a series of tests, that would lead to the rejection of the theory as a whole.

Psychoanalysis also moves through levels of explanation. For example, my anger with my analyst might be explained in terms of my reproducing feelings that I have towards authority figures in the outside world, perhaps originating with my father. This in turn can be explained by a theory of neurosis which posits a tendency to reproduce unsatisfactory or traumatic relationships and events in early life as an attempt to solve or come to terms with past problems. Also useful at this level is the theory of defence mechanisms which would suggest that I am using my anger as a defence against feeling powerless. These explanations in turn presuppose one or the other of the various theories of the unconscious – in this case, that the feeling of powerlessness was so awful that I repressed it.[4] Like many other scientific theories, psychoanalysis tries to explain observable phenomena – in this case my anger. In the course of the explanation, it conceptualises unobservable phenomena such as defence mechanisms and the unconscious. We cannot test our ideas about these phenomena directly against the external world, but only indirectly in terms of what we expect their effects to be. This leaves problematic areas of explanation where other factors might intervene, and we might expect that the more general the level of explanation, the more problematic it will be. Thus, perhaps, the widest theoretical differences between psychoanalysts appear in theories of the unconscious.

A slightly different way of saying much the same thing is that, like the other human sciences, psychoanalysis cannot create a closed experimental situation in which all the relevant factors can be isolated and controlled, as can sometimes be achieved by the natural sciences. There have been attempts to do this, but it seems to me to be impractical simply because one cannot control a person's past, and the results of such attempts are usually, and predictably, ambiguous.

Psychoanalytic theory is not, therefore, as some of its critics have claimed, a monolithic myth but a complex theory. It has developed in various directions. Some elements have been abandoned, the classic example being the way Freud abandoned his early theory that neurosis is the product of childhood sexual abuse; many have been modified and there are many debates still continuing. It is clear that many of these debates and developments are based on clinical evidence and, therefore, that the theory does have contact with and can be changed by a contact with an external reality – in this case the patient and his/her progress through the analysis. The fact that access to such evidence and its interpretation depends upon a psychoanalytic training and the integrity of the psychoanalysis is not, I think, a major difficulty. One has to be trained as a physicist to be able to identify and interpret what counts as evidence in physics. The difficulties again centre on the difficulty of controlling variables and the impossibility of creating a closed system, which would in turn enable reproducible experiments.

These, then, are the reasons to take psychoanalysis as a serious intellectual and perhaps scientific, or potentially scientific, pursuit. There is, however, another issue at stake in the attacks on psychoanalysis. There is a traditional psychoanalytic reluctance to define a 'cure', which makes it difficult to test the effectiveness of psychoanalytic treatment; and given that other forms of therapy seem to achieve cures despite radical differences from psychoanalysis, there is no reason to grant any particular validity to the approach. Although there is plenty of room for debate about the studies of effectiveness, what is clear is that they do not present anything like a conclusive case for psychoanalysis. This leads us into the area where, I believe, psychoanalysis ceases to be 'scientific' and comparable with other sciences. In the first place, it has something to say about what, in everyday terms, we call human nature. The assumption is that, whether we are dealing with individual or social life, there is inevitably conflict and irrationality and, as a result of this, there will inevitably be repression. I think that most psychoanalysts would also accept that there is an inevitably destructive side to human existence, which, like conflict and irrationality, must be lived with. Most scientific activity, in both the natural and the human sciences, sees itself as problem-solving; psychoanalysis claims that there is no solution to our troubles. We might ease them; but they will not disappear.

Secondly, psychoanalytic theory implies a morality, a view of how people might best live with their conflicts and problems. It does not offer an ideal to be lived up to, nor does it presuppose that human beings are 'naturally' good or moral beings. Rather, it tries to say something in between. It is customary for social scientists to concern themselves with the origin of moral beliefs, but it is not usual for them to address moral problems.

Finally, psychoanalysis is concerned directly and intimately with what what we might call human creativity, with the ways in which our unconscious affects and often inhibits the way we live, but also with our ability to use it to produce something new: new ways of living, realising our potentialities, perhaps in artistic terms. The analysis of dreams reveals much of the nature of this creativity, and one way of looking at psychoanalytic treatment is as a way of freeing our imagination and emotions, so that we are no longer governed by them but are able to use them. This is summed up in the words of one patient reported to me: 'Before my feelings had me, now I have my feelings.'

In other words, crucial aspects of psychoanalysis are concerned with areas of human life that are often manifested in art, literature and religion. The fact that these concerns are intimately bound up with something much closer to rational scientific investigation makes psychoanalysis fascinating to philosophers and scientists, but often a fascinating anathema. For the present writer, this combination is what makes it attractive. In general, sociology has little to say about what used to be called the 'soul', yet for all human social animals that word or its equivalent still has some meaning, whether it arouses fear, hostility or interest.

Here we can see the reasons that psychoanalysis has difficulty with the idea of a 'cure'. It is a crucial plank in the arguments of critics and a thorn in the side of apologists. It would follow from what I have been saying that 'mental illness' is a condition that haunts us all, and there is in that sense no such thing as a cure, perhaps only alleviation. Freud himself spoke of returning people to normal human misery. The disappearance of symptoms, the usual and for some people obvious criterion for a cure, becomes, in this light, problematic. Symptoms can disappear, they might be alleviated, or might simply be borne with less misery. Some psychoanalysts respond to this issue by arguing that the treatment is not concerned with symptoms but with a long-term restructuring of the personality. There is something to this, but it too has its problems. My own preferred way of thinking about it is in terms of healing rather than curing. We cannot, nor should we try to, cure the human condition. Rather, we can perhaps strengthen aspects of the personality which contribute towards growth and creativity. The conflicts of our situation wound all of us. We can help the healing process, but not remove the trace or scar of the wound. I shall return to these issues again in Part IV, when I look at modern, clinically-based psychoanalytic theory.

THE PLAN OF THE BOOK

So far, I have tried to offer a *prima facie* case to interest the sociologist in psychoanalysis: its concern with the irrational, the emotions, its understanding of the complexity of the personality, and its concern with the nature of creativity and morality. I have also tried to suggest that if we are not rigidly strict in our conception of science, and are willing to recognise that there are other than scientific aspects to the understanding of social life, then psychoanalysis can take its place among respectable intellectual pursuits. The rest of this book will be concerned with exploring ways in which that interest has been and can be developed.

In Part I, I shall look at various attempts to build a social theory on the basis of Freud's work, attempts to develop a sociology as an applied psychology. I shall argue that in each case such development involves underestimating or denying the importance of social processes and structures that do not have their origin in psychological processes. In Part II, I shall look at a number of attempts to use psychoanalysis as an adjunct to social theory – to see psychology as a product of social processes and structures. Here I shall argue that what is lost is a sense of the irrational and a grasp of individual creativity. In both cases, we lose an ability to understand the individual and the group's contribution to social processes and are left with generalisations that mask very real differences between people.

In Part III, I shall attempt to use modern psychoanalytic theory particularly that developed from Melanie Klein's ideas and the British 'object-relations' school, to explore a different way of looking at the relationship between the individual and society. I shall argue that, in some ways, this approach can add to a sociological understanding, but more importantly, that it shows the limits of what can be understood through sociological analysis and enables us to look at the wider significance of the irrational side of our existence. I shall try to take the argument even further. If psychoanalysis enables us to look at the irrational aspects of human behaviour, at unconscious meanings and motives, then we need to ask not only how such meanings and motives affect the subject matter of sociology but also how they affect the enterprise of sociology itself. Sociologists too are human and have unconscious drives and motives. A sub-theme which will emerge in

Parts I and II will be a psychoanalytic interpretation of sociology as a human enterprise and the unconscious meanings that it might carry; this will come to the fore in Part III in terms of a critique of sociology that tries to go beyond its limits.

## NOTES

1. Wollheim (1971) presents a useful introductory discussion of Freud's conception of the unconscious.
2. We can find another model in Freud's work, involving a distinction between the unconscious, the preconscious and the conscious. The preconscious consists of ideas that are capable of becoming conscious; the unconscious, on the other hand, cannot be allowed into consciousness.
3. On this, see especially Schafer (1976, 1978).
4. On this sort of explanation, see Will (1980).

# REFERENCES AND FURTHER READING

There are many introductions to the work of Freud, but hardly any basic, inclusive introductions to the wider range of psychoanalytic theories. Those I have found most useful, both for teaching and for my own benefit, include:

A & Z (1979) *Freud for Beginners*, London: Writers and Readers Publishing Cooperative.

Bettelheim, B. (1983) *Freud and Man's Soul*, London: Chatto and Windus/ The Hogarth Press.

Wollheim, R. (1971) *Freud*, London: Fontana.

I shall include introductions to other areas of psychoanalytic theory when appropriate. Of the three above, I prefer Bettelheim, although unlike the other two it does require some previous knowledge of Freud's work. It might first seem like an essay on translation, but in fact it is an exciting humanist interpretation of Freud's work.

One recent polemical attack on psychoanalysis which covers most of the arguments is:

Gellner, E. (1985) *The Psychoanalytic Movement*, London: Paladin.

More reasoned philosophical critiques include:

Cioffi, F. (1970) 'Freud and the idea of a pseudo-science', in Borger, R. and Cioffi F. (eds) *Explanation in the Behavioural Sciences*, Cambridge: Cambridge University Press.

Grunbaum, A. (1984) *The Foundations of Psychoanalysis: A Philosophical Critique*, Berkeley: University of California Press.

Popper, J. (1963) *Conjectures and Refutations*, London: Routledge and Kegan Paul.

For critiques of the idea of the unconscious, see:

Archard, D. (1984) *Consciousness and the Unconscious*, London: Hutchinson.

MacIntyre, A. (1958) *The Unconscious: A Conceptual Analysis*, London: Routledge and Kegal Paul.

For reasoned philosophical defences of Freud, see:
Collier, A. (1981) 'Scientific realism and the human world', *Radical Philosophy*. 29, pp.8–18.
Farrell, B.A. (1981) *The Standing of Psychoanalysis*, Oxford: Oxford University Press.
Schafer, R. (1976) *A New Language for Psycholanalysis*, New Haven, CT: Yale University Press.
    (1978) *Language and Insight*. New Haven, CT: Yale University Press.
Will, D. (1980) 'Psychoanalysis as a human science', *British Journal of Medical Psychology* 53, pp.201–12.
Wollheim, R. and Hopkins, J. (eds) (1982) *Philosophical Essays on Freud*, Cambridge: Cambridge University Press (particularly Hopkins' introduction and the essays by Cosin *et al.* and Glymour).

For a case by a practising analyst, see:
Edelson, M. (1984) *Hypothesis and Evidence in Psychoanalysis*, Chicago: University of Chicago Press.

On the testing of Freud's theories, see:
Eysenck, H.J. and Wilson, G.D. (1973) *The Experimental Study of Freudian Theories*, London: Methuen.
Fisher, S. and Greenberg, R.P. (1977) *The Scientific Credibility of Freudian Theories*, New Haven, CT: Yale University Press.

For a defence of a non-scientific reading of Freud, see:
Ricoeur, P. (1970) *Freud and Philosophy: An Essay on Interpretation*, New Haven, CT: Yale University Press.

The best general introduction to Freud and sociology is:
Bocock, R. (1976) *Freud and Modern Society*, Walton-on-Thames, Surrey: Nelson.

# PART I

I am not going to set out a systematic account of psychoanalytic theory; there are many good accounts already available. Rather, I shall move directly to Freud's speculations about society, introducing the relevant psychoanalytic ideas where appropriate. I shall be returning to many ideas over and over again, each time taking them a little further or looking at them in a slightly different way. At this stage, it is simply necessary for the reader to hold on to the idea of there being unconscious aspects of human behaviour that influence our conscious lives, the idea that these unconscious aspects are in some way related to what Freud called 'drives' and the idea that human sexuality is not genetically determined but has to be socially directed.

Opening his chapter on 'Civilisation and Society', Richard Wollheim argues that there is no coherent social theory in Freud's work, as he himself recognised. I agree with this, but Freud is full of paradoxes and his speculations do offer a basis for a social theory; in fact, for three social theories. The first has to do with the necessity to control and direct the drives – not just the sexual drives – if social life is to be possible at all. Society, from this point of view, is based on the repression of 'instinctual' processes. The second is closely connected to the first, but concentrates on the social organisation of the sexual drive; this focuses on family relationships and the development of childhood sexuality as the basis of social organisation. The third concentrates on the sort of interpersonal relationships that are formed in the course of the first two processes.

When I thought about the organisation of this book, it seemed it would be fairly easy to divide the approaches I discuss in Parts I and II: the former would deal with theorists who see society as a product of individual and collective psychological approaches, the latter with theorists who see psychological processes as a product of social processes. By no means the least paradoxical aspects of Freud's work is that it can be interpreted in both ways and the division is a difficult one to make. On the whole, the approaches I look at in Part I *tend* towards the psychologistic, i.e. they see society as a result of psychological processes; and they *tend* to look at social organisation in Freud's terms of a conflict between drives and civilisation. But in each case it is only a matter of emphasis. Perhaps their clearest common feature is that they are more closely related to Freud's writings than those considered in Part II.

One other point remains to be made here. In the Introduction, I went to some pains to argue that the use of the term 'instinct' is metaphorical, and that perhaps the use of the term 'drive', combining the idea of both instinctual energy and psychic representation, is more useful. As is often the case, I find myself wanting to make two contradictory points: to emphasise that Freud, and psychoanalysis generally, are not offering a theory based on biological determinism, and to emphasise that none the less, we are biological entities and that that is important if we are to understand human action and social life. Consequently, I shall move between talking about instincts and drives depending on what I want to emphasise. On the whole, I shall follow Chodorow (1985) and refer to 'drive theory' when I am talking about a general approach that we find in Freud, since it is this part of his theory that is most often, and undeservedly, labelled biologically determinist. When I want to emphasise the biological aspect of drives, which usually has connotations of energy and immediate satisfaction, I shall tend towards 'instincts'.

Chapters 2 and 3 cover the first two of the three approaches that can be drawn from Freud's work. I shall look at the basis for each approach in Freud and then look at modern developments. In Chapter 4 I shall outline the third approach, which I think is quite different from the first two and leads on to the concerns of Part IV of the book.

# 2

## THE BALANCE OF MISERY:
## INSTINCTS AND FREEDOM

The first link to social theory that we can find in Freud's work presents a conception of social organisation that is especially loaded with ambivalence. What he calls 'civilisation', the ability of people to live together in a harmonious and productive way, to achieve economic and cultural progress, is a hard-won and often tenuous achievement, involving considerable cost. It is hard-won because it involves a battle that cannot, strictly speaking, be won at all, since the enemy is always there as a part of our make-up as human beings. This is our unconscious, our drives and instincts.

A source of intellectual pleasure that I regularly find in Freud's writing is his ability to combine, unexpectedly, very different approaches. In his account of the conflict between civilisation and the instincts we can find a 'social contract' theory and elements of its opposite, a 'noble savage' theory. By a 'social contract' theory, I mean that he concentrated on the problem that sociologists would call the 'problem of order', the Hobbesian problem of how, if we are all selfish, concerned with our own satisfaction, is it possible for social order to exist at all. This way into the study of society supposes that, somehow, people come to agree that it is better to renounce their own personal advantage so that others might do the same, and life will not be a risky battle of all against all. It follows that such an approach is often conservative: the emphasis is on social order and the alternative is seen as chaos, disorganisation. The 'noble savage' theory can be summed up in the famous statement of Rousseau to the effect that man is born free but is everywhere in chains. Human beings are restrained by social organisation from a free and good expression of their drives. Through its oppression, society forces people into neuroses and psychoses. This approach is frequently taken up by radicals, emphasising the restrictive and oppressive nature of social institutions. As we shall see, there have been both conservative and radical developments of Freud's work.

Before looking at these aspects of his social theory in more concrete terms, I want to look at the background, at his theory of the life and death instincts in the development of civilisation.

## THE LIFE AND DEATH INSTINCTS AND THE GROWTH OF CIVILISATION

The ambivalence in Freud's analysis, society as liberator and oppressor, corresponds to his theory of the life and death instincts, an ambivalence in human beings themselves. In the Introduction, I warned against taking the concept of instinct too literally, particularly in this grand summation of drives that Freud developed as his work progressed. The idea of a death instinct is particularly difficult for people to accept; in my experience it arouses hostility among analysts and non-analysts alike. However, it seems to me that it is reasonable to assert as normal or in the widest sense 'natural', a human aggressiveness, which might depend on some instinctual quality, or, more likely, might result from the overall requirement of renouncing the immediate gratification of our desires. There is a range of phenomena which seems to require such an assertion if we are to make sense of them, from a baby's apparent and inexplicable refusal to take perfectly good feeding, through to what seems to be a near-universal fear that people have of unprovoked attack. Such a fear is clearly present when strangers come together in an unstructured situation, at the first meeting of a new therapy or experiential group for example. It is also a fairly common phenomenon for people to experience unprovoked attacks even when no such attack has taken place: in everyday interaction we have all had experience of a remark being 'taken in the wrong way'. The fact seems to be that unprovoked attack, a 'pure aggression', is somehow in the air in people's day-to-day reality and, like all unpleasant things, we prefer to see it in other people rather than in ourselves. Freud has a particularly interesting explanation for this, and my reason for taking it seriously is that I have come across no explanation that is quite as subtle and manages to link such a range of phenomena.

The death instinct, aggressiveness, Freud roots in biology, and eventually in physics, as a tendency to return to a static state; in human terms, it might be seen as a desire to return to the womb. It is put to the service of the life instinct when it is directed outwards against some external human or natural enemy. Freud's analysis of the super-ego draws on the death instinct. I said in the Introduction that we could regard the super-ego as something like a conscience. This is only a rough approximation. The super-ego has rational components and irrational components; in everyday terms, we might think of some of the workings of the latter as the workings of the conscience. It is the irrational aspect of the super-ego that makes us suffer, sometimes out of all proportion to any misdemeanour we might have committed, sometimes even without any wrong deed being carried out at all. The super-ego is the internalisation of external control which demands the renunciation of instinctual satisfaction in order that society might be formed and maintain itself. The infant experiences aggressive feelings towards this initially external authority which forbids instinctual gratification; when that authority is internalised, the aggression becomes attached to that internalised part of the infant's psyche and is turned against the other parts. The child deals with its aggression by turning it inwards.

It is important to remember that the aggression comes from the child and not from the external authority. What is interesting about this is that, however rational, kind and sympathetic our parents, we all develop to some extent a fear of a punitive irrational authority which we turn against ourselves. Despite an absence of physical punishment, my own child at the age of three asked me not to beat him when he had been naughty; many parents report similar experiences. Here, then, is another aspect of the ambivalence of civilisation, of the way in which its necessity causes suffering. It is easy to see how this can be developed into ways of looking at real or imagined social authority. For Freud, the process on a social level is clearest in our conceptions of the Almighty. Perhaps the social equivalent of the punitive super-ego is the stern God of some forms of Protestanism, the God who has condemned or saves us independently of what we do. One feature of this irrational, punishing part of the super-ego is that it does not distinguish between the thought and the deed. If I feel like murder, but do not kill anyone, I can still punish myself as if I had.

In the last analysis, my attitude towards the idea of the death instinct is that it is difficult to find a theoretically or philosophically adequate explanation for its existence, yet it seems to me easy to accept as an experienced fact, whether the destructive aggression is directed towards others or the self. If destructiveness were the product of environmental frustration, then one would expect it to be comparatively easy to find empirical links between destructiveness and frustration, and one feature that emerges clearly, even in my own limited clinical work, is that there is no such clear link. Destructiveness might stem from a blanket necessity for frustration in general, rather than from specific frustrations, but if that is the case, it is something to which we are all subject, and we might as well treat it as innate.

The life instinct has similar aims to the death instinct, at least in so far as it aims at a release of tension and a return to stasis, but it pursues these aims in a different way, through the formation of social relationships and the creation of future generations. Freud talks about what he calls the 'pleasure principle'. It is in the nature of human beings to avoid suffering and seek pleasure. There are many ways to avoid suffering, most of them involving some denial of internal or external reality (among these we can place religious belief). There are many courses by which we seek pleasure, and in both cases it is for each individual to choose his or her own way. In *Civilisation and its Discontents*, he points out the obvious fact that despite the various ways of seeking pleasure and avoiding suffering, it is very difficult to succeed. There are three reasons for this. The first is our own weakness in the face of external nature. Although today we have achieved even more control over nature than was the case in Freud's day, we still have to work within its limits and we cannot abolish floods, droughts and earthquakes. Our very control over nature generates new restrictions and dangers: witness acid rain. The second restraint on our pleasure is our physical make-up, our bodies, which are part of nature. We must grow old and die, and our physical powers are limited. Thirdly, there is the way we organise our communal life, our social order. Against our reluctance to acknowledge this, Freud argues that we are forced to think of our civilisation too as a cause of our failure to achieve happiness. He draws a parallel between the growth of civilisation and the growth of the child. Just as we associate such things as order and cleanliness with the achievements of civilisation, so too do we regard them as achievements of the growing child. Adults no longer routinely shit in the street; by a certain age the child must be taught to use the toilet. The demands of civilisation and of maturity are such that we have to forgo immediate satisfaction, often at the expense, in this example, of physical discomfort, but also of a sense of dirtiness and shame about something that is indisputably natural.

This parallel between the development of the individual and of society is an important one for Freud, involving what I can only call a 'metaphysical' notion of human development. Freud suggests that there is an identity between the development of the individual and the development of the species and of society. Each individual travels the whole course of the evolution of the species. We pass through the pre-historic stages of evolution while still in the womb: we all start off as fish and emerge as human, in the same way that the human species itself once emerged. From here, each of us passes through a series of developmental stages that society as a whole has already passed through. This idea is usually described as the identity of 'ontogeny' (individual development) and 'phylogeny' (species development). For present purposes, what is important is that for society, as for the child, this development can be seen as the development of the rational elements of the super-ego and ego to the point where they are stronger than the irritational, punitive, magical infantile elements. In society, this development can be seen through the evolution of religious beliefs.

We can now see the problem of civilisation. The death instinct, human destructiveness, must be contained and where possible direc-ted in useful ways; and the search for pleasure must be restricted and socially channelled. The history of civilisation is the history of such containment and channelling; the stages through which it moves are also the stages through which each of us moves as we grow up to be more or less acceptable members of society. Just as each individual can run into difficulties, so can society. The ambivalence is pervasive: the search for pleasure can be destructive; human destructiveness can be channelled in constructive ways. Society enables us to achieve pleasure without danger but at the same time can deny us pleasure and put us in danger.

## THE PROBLEMS OF SOCIAL LIFE

When Freud talks about death, in his discussion of the meaning of war, he talks about our desire to eliminate anybody who gets in our way, and our inability to accept that we ourselves will die. If we are to live in anything like a reasonable way, then that desire to kill has to be repressed. It is not that we are likely to go blindly murdering everyone in sight as a result of our biology. It is a matter, rather, of being aware of the world, of desiring some form of satisfaction, and finding that satisfaction blocked by another human being, whom, consequently, we want to remove from the scene altogether. It presupposes less biology, more the existence and recognition of social relationships and a desire to change them to our advantage. It is an infantile desire, appropriate to the baby or young child who cannot tolerate frustration. As we grow, we must learn to tolerate frustration, otherwise we shall eliminate those very people in whom we physically depend: our parents. That is why infantile anger is often so frightening when recalled or re-experienced in later life.

The desire to kill anyone who frustrates us thus becomes unconscious, but none the less remains. The unconscious is the infant within us, demanding immediate satisfaction. We make the repression easier by developing ideas of the soul, life after death and original sin, or neurotically, for example, in the exaggerated concern about loved ones. Freud seems to believe that sometimes these desires are simply overlaid and suppressed through fear of social punishment. Sometimes our destructiveness can be directed against nature, as an enemy which threatens us; sometimes against an external human enemy. Sometimes it is transformed and incorporated into our culture and personality as ethical and religious systems prohibiting the acting out of our unconscious desires. Similarly, our infantile belief in our own immortality matures into the adult's recognition of the possibility of his or her own death, and this encourages restraint. Both civilisation and the individual have the task of internalising such restraints in a way that enables them to operate effectively. In situations such as war, where the community relaxes its prohibitions as far as outsiders are concerned, the unconscious desire surfaces and is acted out. Most of the time, some compromise is reached, albeit at a cost because the frustration of our desires involves unhappiness and that unhappiness emerges sometimes in the form of neuroses – an obsessive fear of one's own death, of others' deaths, or an unusually strong and punitive reaction to those who do kill. Sometimes it emerges as jokes or slips. Freud quotes the husband who is supposed to have said: 'If one of us two dies, I shall move to Paris.'

Love, with its origins in sexuality, can be equally threatening to social order. When we look at crowd behaviour, Freud argues, we can see that some of the usual restraints are removed. The intellect becomes weaker and emotions stronger; crowds seem particularly open to suggestability, and the way we can understand that suggestability is through love or, more accurately, through sexual desire which has been transformed into feeling close to the others around us. There is a sense of identity and we can experience in ourselves what the other experiences. It is with love that the ambivalent and paradoxical nature of all this becomes most apparent. In the formation of society, love is important in two senses: sensual love aiming at sexual satisfaction and what Freud calls 'aim-inhibited' love – the love we feel for our children and our friends, where the desire for sexual satisfaction has been modified:

Both . . . extend outside the family and create new bonds with people who before were strangers. Genital love leads to the formation of new families, and aim-inhibited love to 'friendships' which become valuable from a cultural standpoint because they escape some of the limitations of genital love, as, for instance, its exclusiveness. But in the course of development the relation of love to civilisation loses its unambiguity. On the one hand, love comes into opposition with the interests of civilisation; on the other, civilisation threatens love with substantial restrictions. (Freud, 1985: 292)

The conflict arises because love also keeps one away from the community; it isolates people, perhaps into family groups, or in its most intense sensual form, into couples. Society, therefore, has to place restrictions on love, in particular sexual love, demanding of everybody a single kind of sexual life, irrespective of differences. This is one of the paradoxes and it take us immediately to the second – the relationship between sexual desire and the issue I opened with: aggressiveness. Society must insist on stemming and sublimating sexual desire in order to 'libidinise' the relationships between all its members: we must 'love our neighbours as ourselves' – a commandment which, as Freud points out, is thoroughly irrational and against our individual interests. What this means is that we must not only give up the satisfaction of our sexual desire in order to live peaceably with our neighbours; we must also give up the satisfaction of our aggression, or some measure of it.

Whatever desire we repress, however, there is for Freud a permanent dilemma that human beings have to face: to satisfy some needs we have to renounce the satisfaction of others. To produce sufficient food, or the comfort we want, we need to co-operate with others and that involves renouncing our desire to be the first and only, to have it all. While we might have progressed a long way in exploiting nature to our own benefit, we have not progressed so far in understanding our own human nature. Freud is renowned as a pessimist, and he saw discontent, human misery, as a necessary concomitant of civilisation, the main question being the point at which the misery caused by instinctual renunciation in favour of civilisation came to outweigh its benefits. Hence the title of this chapter. The 'noble savage' aspect of his approach, the view of human beings as restricted and enslaved by society, is there, but it takes second place. Any social organisation will require some instinctual renunciation, and will therefore entail some misery.

Although I have portrayed Freud as a theorist of the irrational, in so far as he saw a way of handling these conflicts it was through the development of our rational understanding; this distances us from our emotions, our instinctual drives. In many ways Freud was much more of a rationalist than many modern therapists who would see the healing process in terms of a greater toleration of instinctual drives and an ability to distinguish between having feelings and acting on them. Freud was concerned with the overcoming of instinctual drives. In his speculations about society, this emerged as a rationalist critique of religion. Religious belief, for Freud, was essentially an illusion. It continued into adulthood, for the whole culture, as a phantasy which properly belongs to infancy: the possibility of being all-powerful and all-knowing, of being omnipotent. Further, it offered an illusory rationale for instinctual renunciation in this world – that all would be perfect in the next. If people were to renounce satisfactions in this world, Freud thought, it should be for the this-worldly reason that life would otherwise be impossible. Freud himself, with a full sense of the complexity and ambivalence of what he was talking about, can, I think, best be described as a pessimistic liberal. He was well aware of the sometimes tenuous hold that civilised behaviour has over people and he was also aware of the suffering imposed and brought out by civilised behaviour and the damage that can be created by too strict a social regime.

### THE FOCUS ON THE SUPER-EGO

As an understanding of the relationship between individuals and society, the central focus of this aspect of Freud's work is the super-ego and the ego – the rational aspects of the super-ego being taken over by the ego. It provides the link between individual and society, and explains why it is difficult to distinguish between psycho-logistic and sociologistic versions of the approach: the former start from individual development, the latter from social development, but the concluding point for both is similar. This perhaps explains why Freud's writings prove so attractive to some sociologists. There has always been a tendency in social theory towards grand, all-inclusive schemes and the neat, unitary vision of the world that can be derived from Freud's theory is very seductive. The individual's development follows the development of the species, and the development of societies that of the individual. The major divisions within social theory are therefore bridged.

I want now to look at two attempts to build this approach into a social theory. The first, a conservative version, remains very close to

Freud and reveals some of the problems of regarding sociology as applied psychology; the second is a radical development of his work which illustrates the difficulties of basing a social theory, and especially a radical social theory, solely on the conflict between civilisation and the instincts, and reveals the limitations of 'instinct' or 'drive' theory.

### *The personality, authority and the social order*

I shall look first at the work of a contemporary British writer, Christopher Badcock, concentrating on two books: *The Psychoanalysis of Culture* and *Madness and Modernity*. I have reviewed these books in a different context but I want to make the same points again here. Badcock takes up Freud from the point of view of defending society against the instincts. Unlike other sociological psychoanalytic thinkers discussed later, he maintains the idea of conflict between civilisation and the instincts and he takes absolutely literally the identity between individual and social development. He is on the side of the rational parts of the ego and the super-ego, over and against both the instincts and the irrational, punitive aspects of the super-ego that come from the very earliest period of life. Following Freud, he argues that the social equivalent of the super-ego is the religious systems developed by different types of society. He does not hesitate to equate maturity in the individual with the replacement of religion in society by psycho-analysis as a basis for education and culture. If this happens then the rational will have triumphed.

The social super-ego develops in stages parallel to the individual super-ego. The earliest stage of development, the starting point of civilisation, is the primal horde. This is approximately equivalent to the narcissistic stage of the infant's development. In our common-sense usage of 'narcissistic', it applies to people who are in love with themselves, who are perhaps vain, arrogant, who see themselves as the centre of the world. It carries clear overtones of selfishness. The psychoanalytic use of the term carries other connotations, but for the present it is that idea of selfishness that we need to hold on to. Freud talks about 'His Majesty the Baby', the young infant's inability to make a clear distinction between itself and the rest of the world and its imperious demands for satisfaction – a satisfaction which it assumes it produces for itself. What stops the primal horde falling apart as each seeks satisfaction is that one – a male – comes to dominate, holding the group together through his own strength, in particular by monopolis-ing the women. The religious beliefs that accompanied this primitive organisation were animistic: people see divinity everywhere, just as the baby can only see itself in the world.

The next stage, in religious terms, is totemism. This is marked by the overthrow of the autocratic father and the institution of joint rule by his sons. It is realised that a combination of individuals is more powerful than one strong individual. Each member of the group places restrictions on the others and accepts restrictions on himself to keep this state of affairs in existence. In terms of individual development, this is equivalent to the oedipal stage, which, as we shall see, is when the infant or, strictly speaking, the little boy – for it is the boy that Freud is talking about most of the time – gives up his desire for his mother after a period of competition with his father; he gives up the desire under threat from the superior force of his father, and the implicit promise that when he comes of age, he will receive a woman of his own. One of the effects of the overthrow of the autocratic father is that the males share out the women in the tribe between themselves.

The next stages in individual and social development involve the repression of the needs that aim at immediate satisfaction, the repression of narcissistic needs that led to the overthrow of the primal father and the focusing of energy on learning the skills necessary for an orderly social life. For Badcock, the social expression of these stages is monotheism and then the development of Catholic and then Protestant theologies. Each marks a new stage in social maturity, and the final stage would be the abandonment of religious beliefs altogether, with their traces of the primitive autocratic father and infantile omnipotence, encapsulated in the idea of an all-powerful God and an idyllic after-life.

I have used the term rational fairly loosely so far and there are very different conceptions of what is rational. In the book under discussion, rationality seems to involve accepting reality and all its restrictions and accepting authority. When Badcock comes to look at current social problems, these are seen in terms of a failure to accept and internalise the authority of the father. Rebellion against authority involves a reversion to the irrational phantasies of an arbitrary, punitive parent; the strengthening of the state, particularly in socialist societies, is seen as prohibiting the development of mature, rational individuals, and encouraging the development of dependent, pliable, amoral people. In such societies the state takes over the functions of the super-ego, a recurrent theme in much Freudian social theory. Both tendencies – rebellion against authority and the strong state – encourage the return to consciousness and its expression in action, of what should have been repressed in the interests of civilisation. Examples of such a 'return of the repressed' include both terroristic policies used by strong states against dissidents and the insistence of some groups of dissidents to self-expression, the fulfilment of their needs and immediate happiness, and the dissident resort to terrorism. There is another conception of rationality, which emphasises individual moral responsibility over and against authority. Badcock is also aware of this and makes it clear in a later work, *Essential Freud*.

I think there is something in Badcock's argument, but I do not think that it involves the political implications that he draws from it. However, the usefulness of looking at the relationship between state and super-ego is outweighed in Badcock's work precisely by the assumption of an identity between individual development and social development. *The Psychoanalysis of Culture* is a history of civilisation in a few hundred pages, and it rests almost, but not quite entirely, on the work of psychoanalysts who have dealt with evolution and historical development. There is comparatively little independent evidence and this is enough to make one suspicious of the enterprise: clear knowledge of even single historical events, from whatever point of view, is difficult enough to maintain when the evidence is considered – a problem Marxists regularly rediscover. When most of that evidence is omitted and we are talking about the whole of human history, one would have to be very daring to embrace it. The whole exercise is a vast over-simplification, from which one might draw an occasional useful insight but no more. The individual is sufficiently complicated, society immensely complicated and our understanding of the latter can only be modelled on our understanding of the former at an immense cost.

The most important difficulty, however, is analytic, concerning the way we assess cause and effect, and the relationship between causes. The following quotation illustrates well what I want to say:

> We have seen that the decisive adaptive advantage in big-game hunting was in large part economic, that hunting was so much more effective a way of getting food compared with foraging. But it would be quite wrong to imagine that material forces operate in some occult way, as proposed by Marx, and that economic systems and the technology that go with them have any other origin than the mind of man. (Badcock, 1980: 67)

We can see here the dangers of seeing society as a product of the psyche. It is acknowledged that economic factors have some significance, a causal role, but we are then told that somehow these things all originate in the human mind and this leads into a criticism of Marxism.

Yet what is it exactly that Badcock suggests originates in the human mind? To the extent that he is talking about big-game hunting, then one can accept his argument; in order to go big-game hunting, somebody has to think of the possibility: I imagine that everybody would agree that it is not a product of our genes, nor a revelation from God. But he is also talking about big-game hunting being a more effective way of getting food. That does not come from the human mind: it is a fact of the world, rather like jumping into the sea is a more effective way of getting wet than looking for a puddle in the Sahara. One imagines that it is this fact of life that persuades people to opt for big-game hunting. There is, admittedly, a choice, but a proper explanation of the development of big-game hunting must presumably refer to the fact that somebody thought of it, and that it was more effective economically. In other words, two factors, one to do with the workings of the internal world and thought processes, the other to do with the nature of the external world, are at work. Both have to be taken into account; and there is no *a priori* reason why one should have priority over the other. One can think of instances where ideas have been more effective than economic benefit, and vice versa.

The main point here is that any historical event or situation involves a number of processes that have some sort of causal influence, and sometimes it might be possible to give priority to one, sometimes to others. The dominant mono-causal theory in social science, Marxism, has from the 1920s been regularly forced to limit and revise its emphasis on the priority given to economic relationships. It is a paradox to find an anti-Marxist turning to an equally rigid mono-causal position.

This does not, however, involve an abandonment of this particular version of Freud's approach to society and civilisation. It does involve saying that at best we need to regard the positing of a unified course of development in the species, in society and in the individual as a metaphor, particularly when relating the latter two, and although it might occasionally be suggestive, it is no more than that. It also means that perhaps the dynamics identified by Freud are operating but in conjunction with a range of other factors yet to be specified. This begins to emerge in the work of Herbert Marcuse.

### The id and social freedom

I want to turn now to a more radical and interesting attempt to use Freud's theory to construct a social theory – that of Herbert Marcuse.

I have fond memories of Marcuse's book *Eros and Civilisation*: it was influential on the student left in the 1960s and seemed to provide a way of combining a socialist critique of capitalism with a thorough-going critique of morality and the quality of everyday life. He took the opposite side of Freud to Badcock, emphasising the repressive nature of social organisation and managing to maintain some of Freud's rich ambivalence. He was more optimistic about the possibilities of social liberation than Freud ever was.

Marcuse's Marxism is the humanism of Marx's *1844 Manuscripts*. For Marx the crucial feature of the human animal, its 'species being', involved the fact that human beings work co-operatively to transform their environment, and in doing so transform themselves; other animals, by contrast, adjust to their environment without transforming it. Marcuse modifies this notion of a 'human essence' to include what Freud called the pleasure principle. What human beings seek is the satisfaction of their desires, instinctual gratification, they seek happiness. He accepts Freud's perspective of the identity of the history of the individual and the history of the species, and he sees this history in terms of the unrolling of a fundamental and three-sided conflict between the pleasure principle which seeks immediate gratification, and the reality principle, the scarcity and dangers of the external world which have to be dealt with and adjusted to, and the 'Nirvana principle'. This is the idea that all life progresses towards stasis, a stable and unmoving state, the aim of both the life and death instincts.

We have already seen that the disturbing tendency of the two instincts to merge is overcome by the fact that they seek their aims in opposite ways. The life instinct, in particular the sexual drive, seeks to reproduce life, and to produce lasting human units, constantly to hold back the death instinct and delay the descent towards stasis. The death instinct can become subordinated to the life instinct, and human existence becomes a struggle between the two. When the death instinct dominates and directs the life instinct, we have, according to Marcuse, a situation similar to that described by Marx under the heading of alienation. For Marx, the creative human ability expressed in work can become distorted and transformed against human beings. People can become enslaved to the society they have produced, with a reversal of all 'the natural' processes and features of humanity. In capitalist societies, for example, work, the most fundamental and creative of human capacities, becomes transformed into an unpleasant chore, a daily grind, which, if possible, people shun like the plague. In people's assessment of pleasure, work, the most human, takes second place to food and sex, our most animal needs.

Freud, on the other hand, shows the humanness rather than the naturalness of human sexuality: it is not somehow given, but must be socially channelled. For Marcuse, this social process is subject to alienation. We must work to survive and in order to achieve some pleasure, if not all the pleasure we desire. In this process, the means become the end. Our energy becomes focused on the organisation of work for its own sake. We become slaves to labour and lose sight of pleasure. Capitalist society, if not modern industrial society as a whole, becomes dominated by 'practical reason' or 'instrumental rationality'. Everything is seen as a tool, a means of doing something not only to nature but also to human beings. Everything becomes manipulable, to be used in the service of material interests. Sexual enjoyment is not an animal need but the truly human need which we (and Marx) come to regard as 'animal' because it gets in the way of work. For Marcuse the reality principle does not merely force a compromise but diverts the instincts away from their aim of gratification. This enables the death instincts to predominate and turn inwards, energy being directed not to the struggle against nature but to the struggle of human beings against each other. The clearest manifestation of the death instincts in our society is the existence of nuclear weapons capable of destroying the species altogether.

There is an inbuilt contradiction in this process which goes beyond the conflict between the life and death instincts. The direction of human energy towards work has the effect of reducing, or perhaps even overcoming, the restrictions placed on us by nature. With the advent of advanced industrial society, we are in a position to produce immense wealth and, argues Marcuse, overcome scarcity altogether. The contradiction is that in achieving this, civilisation has produced human beings who are suited only to work, whose bodily capacity for sexual gratification (originally immense, in that the human is 'naturally' polymorphously perverse) has been restricted and minimised to genital sexual activity for the purposes of procreation. The super-ego is the internal mechanism that enforces this, ensuring the dominance of past sacrifices over present possibilities for pleasure.

Marcuse's real development of Freud's work comes when he introduces several new concepts. The first is what he calls the 'performance principle', the particular socio-historical organisation of the reality principle. Work has not been organised in the same way throughout history, and different ways of organising work require different levels of instinctual repression. He argues that this enables us to differentiate between the general level of repression required by civilisation *per se*, and the particular level required by particular forms of civilisation. This enables him to make a distinction parallel to Marx's distinction between necessary and surplus labour, which Marx used in order to understand profit. In Marcuse's case, it is the distinction between necessary repression, 'necessary' for civilisation to exist at all, and 'surplus repression', that degree or amount of repression which exists at any one time over and above what is necessary at that particular stage of social development. What this adds to Freud's work is an ability to distinguish the independent role of social organisation: it is not simply a matter of a universal conflict between instincts and civilisation: different forms of civilisation require different levels of repression and some enforce unnecessary levels of repression.

It follows that in modern society there is a great deal of surplus repression, constantly made more and more unnecessary by industrial and technological development. A new vision of a liberated society becomes possible in which the pleasure and reality principles can be reconciled. At present the social system deals with this possibility by 'repressive desublimation': allowing an alienated gratification in a way that serves the system rather than the pleasure of the individual. Consumption, rather than the body, is 'sexualised' (naked women draped over cars) and the stricter sexual mores of the nineteenth century are relaxed, but in 'safe' directions: 'swinging' and increased sexual freedom for adolescents, etc., actually serves to direct energy away from any fundamental change. David Held sums up the new possibilities succinctly:

> Given specific preconditions – the abolition of scarcity, the transformation of relations of production, the cultivation of faculties – sexuality, he argues, can create 'highly civilised human relations'. Under the altered conditions there could be a reactivation of all erogenous zones and a resurgence of pregenital polymorphous sexuality . . . the 'organism in its entirety' would become the substratum of sexuality. Sexuality would be integrated with the order of work and play. (Held, 1980: 124)

'Polymorphous perversity' was for Freud the starting point from which the human infant had to develop into a more or less hetero-sexual adult. Marcuse sees it as the aim of social development. Since the whole body would be an erogenous zone, activities now not considered sexual at all (for example, sitting at a word processor trying to come to grips with Marcuse's thought) would become a source of direct libidinal satisfaction. This would enable what Marcuse seems to think of as the final defeat of the death instinct. Tensions would be released through instinctual gratification and would no longer feed human aggression. The core of the attraction of Marcuse's thought to radicals in the 1960s lies here and is summed up in the not quite accurate slogan 'Make love not war' – not quite accurate since, for Marcuse, practically everything we do, and not just sexual relations, would become a way of making love. He gives a new social and progressive importance to polymorphous perversity and to the death instinct. Both are opposed to the performance principle, the former because it aims at sensuous enjoyment, the latter because it aims at stasis: the death instinct is not in favour of work. He therefore finds in what Freud regarded as the most dangerous aspects of human nature, the hope for a different and better future.

It should be clear that Marcuse overcomes one of the objections I made to Badcock: he does not assume that sociology is only applied psychology. He is able to introduce, at least implicitly, other causal processes into his conception of society, and employ psychoanalytic theory to elaborate on this wider conception of social development. What is important is the interrelations of psychological, economic and social organisation. However, this still leaves us at a very general level of analysis, and he does not really leave the area of speculative theory: he tends to reduce our psychological history to a play of instincts. Juliet Mitchell (1975) argues that he tends to retain the determinist aspects of both Marxism and psychoanalysis.

### AN INFANTILE UTOPIA

In an intelligent critique of Marcuse, and of the use of drive or instinct theory to build a social theory, Nancy Chodorow makes an important point which has much to do with my theme of over-generality. Marcuse's Utopia carries the idea of an almost mystical union and absence of difference between people, a universal polymorphous perversity. Nowhere does he have anything to say about procreation and child-rearing, except in a critical sense, and he has little or nothing to say about women. Chodorow argues that, in fact, he is presenting a masculine vision of Utopia which depends on the use of women as objects. It is worth quoting her argument at some length:

> The argument against adult genitality and procreative sexuality – the rejection of 'normal Eros' – amounts implicitly to an argument against

relations with women, a rejection of women. Marcuse . . . idealise[s] Narcissus who chooses himself rather than a woman. Marcuse in addition idealises Orpheus, who loves only boys and whose unfortunate end occurred when 'he was torn to pieces by the crazed Thracian women' . . .

Like the argument against 'normal' sexuality, the denial of intersubjectivity involved in the narcissistic vision implicitly argues that women constrain, and denies women as subjects. It is of course the mother who is experienced as a narcissistic extension of the child and who imposes drive organisation and modification. The mother's subjectivity is the reality principle for the child and the mother requires that the infant separates from her and give up its primary narcissistic relation to reality. The narcissistic refusal to accept separation from the libidinous object is not refusal to separate from just any object or subject. A woman directly enforces the primary restraints that seem to be the essence of unfreedom from the perspective of drive liberation and limitless narcissism.

Only by assuming that the mother is an object and emphatically not a subject can we envision narcissistic union and the complete satisfaction of pregenital demands and desires as progressive social principles. (Chodorow, 1985: 298–9)

It is often the case that Utopias hark back to some previous golden age. Marcuse's is explicitly in the future, but Chodorow's argument is that implicitly, unconsciously, it is a desire to return to the golden age of infancy, when the world is experienced as being there for one's own satisfaction, when needs are met by others (a woman) before the painful business of growing up into one's own individuality has begun. In fact, the conceptual structure of Freud's drive theory means that a radical interpretation must involve a return to such a stage, before the suffering of civilisation emerges. Chodorow goes on, as I shall do, to explore the possibilities of object-relations theory as a basis for radical social criticism.

Marcuse's utopianism, the idea that the discontents of civilisation can be eliminated, is by itself a good reason for caution. If we confine ourselves to the reductionist level at which Marcuse himself works, I think it can be demonstrated that he is wrong. The life and death instincts for Freud imply each other, and indeed at the most general level they are united with the same aim: Nirvana. They are both dynamic: they do not rest until they have achieved eternal rest, which presumably would be the end of humanity. It is true that for social relations, civilisation, to develop, the death instincts must be more or less subordinated to the interests of the life instincts, but both must remain in existence and, therefore, in conflict. The removal of the conflict presupposes Nirvana. In earthly terms, the improvement of our lot might make it easier for the life instincts, but to imagine a world without conflict, renunciation and suffering is to imagine Nirvana. The evidence is, and it is in fact a central part of Marx's humanism, that as we transform our environment, we transform ourselves and develop new needs, hopes and ambitions, and, therefore, new conflicts. This is what makes us human. Marcuse's Utopia seems to involve the adjustment to an (admittedly very pleasurable) environment which takes us back from humanity.

Utopianism always seems to me a difficult issue. There is no doubt that things could be better than they are, and Marcuse restored a radical tradition to psychoanalysis that had tended to disappear as it established itself as a respectable profession. However, it is always necessary to maintain a sense of the possible. An unrealistic utopianism can be self-destructive. It is a commonplace that very intelligent students can become unproductive and blocked by their ambitions. Nothing is ever good enough. Utopian ideals, whether for personal ambitions or social organisation, can feed a punitive super-ego, which is always ready to say: 'Because you are not perfect, then you are nothing.' A government (or a revolutionary movement) which can be, metaphorically at any rate, thought of as taking the role of a punitive super-ego can easily become tyrannical. There need perhaps not be so much suffering, but the important message of Freud's work on civilisation was that it goes hand in hand with some suffering. And anyone who has engaged, as a patient or as a therapist, in clinical work must know that suffering and growth go together.

Radical interpretations of Freud often employ one version or another of instinct or drive theory. Nancy Chodorow also develops an intelligent argument against deploying Freud's theory of the instincts in this way. She points out that given what Freud had to say about instincts turns a radical interpretation of Freud into a radical individualism. Civilisation for Freud involved the formation of lasting relationships and the continuing of life through the creation of family units and the production of children. The radical vision is implicitly or explicitly critical of these truly human relations and in favour of a world in which individuals seek to satisfy and gain pleasure for themselves as individuals rather than for the human group – family, community or species – as a whole. Despite the fact that these thinkers are building a sociological theory and critique on Freud's work, it was Freud the psychologist who had a clearer conception of real human relations and their difficulties. Marcuse is not concerned with clinical evidence, suspicious of it because it limits the radical possibilities of Freud's thought, yet it is in clinical practice that we meet real human relationships.

My argument against building a social theory on the conflict between instincts or drives and civilisation, then, has two parts. Politically, at least in its radical form, it can lead to tyranny. Conceptually, it leaves us working at too general a level; an assumption of the identity of ontogeny and phylogeny loses sight of important and complex social processes; and even when the assumption is not rigid, it seems from Marcuse that we can only deal with very general social processes. Concrete social relations, as well as concrete human relations, are lost from sight. I shall develop this criticism as I discuss the use of Freud's oedipal theory to produce social analysis.

# 3

## WOMEN, MEN AND THE
## FOUNDATIONS OF CIVILISATION

The second potential social theory in Freud's work has become
particularly clear under the impact of modern feminism, although it
was always there. It focuses on the way in which the child develops
from polymorphous perversity into a more or less heterosexual adult,
gaining pleasure from the genital area and concerned with reproduction. This development is intimately bound up with the nature of social
order: some would argue that it is the foundation of the social order.
This approach too is concerned with the repression of drives, but with
a specific set of drives: our sexual desires directed towards our parents.

### SEXUALITY

To begin with, I shall confine myself to Freud's account of the
development of sexuality during childhood. One of the most frequent
common-sense criticisms of Freud is the importance he gave to
sexuality: some people regard it as an attempt to explain everything in
terms of the sexual drive, and it follows that it, therefore, explains
nothing at all. Various commentators have pointed out that this is not
the case. It is true that he extended the concept of sexuality. In the first
place he emphasised the existence of infantile sexuality – something
which many of his contemporaries were reluctant to accept, but which,
as he pointed out, 'every nursemaid knew'. In the second place, he
argued that sexuality was at the root of a number of phenomena
despite the fact that this was not obvious: he was concerned with the
ways in which sexuality manifested itself in apparently non-sexual
behaviour. I think it is this that leads to the impression that a Freudian
can find a sexual meaning behind everything. But as Freud himself is
reported to have said, 'A cigar is sometimes just a cigar'. It is best seen
as a matter of context. Squeezing blackheads is a quite reasonable
activity, especially in front of the bathroom mirror: they are unsightly

and can repel other people. Systematic squeezing of blackheads on the analyst's couch might well be symbolic of masturbation. It could also symbolise other things – perhaps an obsession with cleanliness or an unfocused anxiety, which, depending on context, could be more important.

Beyond this, Freud was well aware that a single explanatory factor is, in fact, no explanation at all. As he explains in *Civilisation and its Discontents*, what gives sexuality its causal effectiveness is the way it interacts and conflicts with the other instincts. His elaboration of the death instinct enabled him to avoid claiming that sexuality is the cause of everything. Juliet Mitchell (1975) argues, rightly I think, that in defining sexuality and its relation to the other instincts, he developed a more precise and systematic, but not an all-inclusive, conception of sexuality.

From a modern point of view, Freud's most radical innovation in relation to sexuality was to question and undermine popular ideas about the naturalness of heterosexual, genital intercourse. We know now that there is a considerable proportion of homosexuals in the population, and a much larger proportion who will engage in homo-sexual acts at some point in their lives. We also know that homo-sexuality (male and female) involves attractions and actions that are common to heterosexuals and that sometimes take priority in hetero-sexual intercourse: activities such as sucking, looking, anal intercourse and masturbation. Sexual activity does not *just*, or even necessarily, involve heterosexual genital intercourse even amongst heterosexuals. We are faced with a vast range of human sexual activity that would be difficult to explain if heterosexual genital intercourse were natural. Freud argued that heterosexual attraction and intercourse involving the penetration of the vagina by the penis is the product of a long and complex development. We are, at the very least, born bisexual, if not 'polymorphously perverse' and we have to develop, or not develop, towards heterosexuality.

SEXUAL OBJECT AND SEXUAL AIM

It is useful at this stage to introduce a distinction, which can be found in Freud, between the sexual aim and the sexual object. This will become increasingly important in this book. A crude and inaccurate, but temporarily useful, way of describing the distinction is in terms of the aim referring to what you want to do, and the object to whom or which you want to do it. When I discussed the identity of individual and social development in the last chapter, I mentioned narcissism, which is a stage in object-choice – we all start by loving ourselves – and the oedipal stage, which combines issues of sexual aim and object choice.

## The development of the sexual aim

It is common to talk about this development in terms of stages, but this is misleading in so far as it carries the idea that each stage is passed through and left behind. Rather, each is a particular organisation of sexual energy (the libido) and persists in various relations to the others right through adult life. The important point in understanding Freud's account is to see it as related to certain vital physical areas of the body. In principle, any area of the body can become an erogenous zone, but nature gives us three such areas that are particularly important because of their sensitivity and their connection with a vital 'somatic' or physical function. The first area is the mouth, essential for life from the moment of birth; the second is the anus, also essential for life, but in addition one of the first areas over which we gain autonomous muscular control; and finally the genitalia, organs through which we eject waste fluid but also those by means of which we reproduce ourselves.

There are three significant levels of organisation prior to the oedipal stage. At the first stage, the oral, Freud argues that the sexual instinct attaches itself to the newborn baby's need for self-preservation, for food. He likens the baby settling back to sleep after satisfaction at the breast with the adult settling to sleep after sexual intercourse, with 'flushed cheeks' and a 'blissful smile'. He spends some time talking about thumb-sucking as a substitute for the breast, arguing that it is clear that this activity is a source of great pleasure. The significance of thumb-sucking is that it replaces the breast with the baby's own body – it signifies what Freud calls 'autoeroticism', the attempt to satisfy desire through one's own body. He argues that it is this tendency that develops into masturbation. The mouth, of course, remains important in adult sexuality.

The second stage is the anal stage. The anus is often an area of pleasure in adult sexuality – 'normal' adult sexuality, that is – and it is a source of pleasure (as well, often, of pain) in its natural function; as the child gains control over its muscles, the anus becomes weighed down with meaning in the parent–child relationship. Refusing to shit in the right place or at the right time can become a sign of rebellion; shitting in the right place and time can be a sign of compliance; shitting can be a gift to the parent or an attack. Freud suggests that, unconsciously, the faeces themselves become associated with the penis and with babies, and with having babies, through the unconscious construction of metaphor that I discussed in the opening chapter.

Finally, there is the phallic stage, involving organs of a similar sensitivity and something clearly recognisable as masturbation. Strictly speaking, the phallic stage is, for Freud, the same for both sexes; the physical difference in the central organ – for little boys the penis, for little girls the clitoris – is secondary. The pre-genital stage follows and is closely involved with the oedipal stage. This brings us back to object-choice.

Before going on to look at the development of object-choice, I want to say more about how we should regard these stages, or, as I would prefer, levels of organisation, of sexuality. There is, I think, an understandable tendency, sometimes encouraged by Freud, to regard them exactly as stages that are left behind, at which we might become fixated, or to which we might regress. Associated with this is a tendency to link personality types with each stage. Somebody fixated at or regressed to the oral stage, for example, might have eating problems, talk a lot, smoke or drink a lot, be an expert in kissing, or have a special or even overriding fondness for oral sexual acts. Somebody fixated or regressed to the anal stage might be obsessively clean and ordered in their lives (keeping away the shit) or mean (where there's muck, there's brass). I find this way of thinking about it unhelpful, if not misleading. It tends towards encouraging a mechanistic view of human growth and the attribution of problems to identified or hypothesised childhood events: I smoke too much because I was deprived of the breast as a baby, or over-stimulated orally as a baby. I have self-defeating, obsessive work patterns because my toilet-training was too harsh. It is rarely, if ever, as simple as this. Although there might be some temporal sequence in their development through early childhood, we can see each level of organisation as present from birth and actually variable in its relations to others throughout life. This comes closer to accounting for the variability in adult human sexuality. We can couple this with the idea that, for most of us, the level of genital organisation has some priority. Why this should be the case leads forwards to the oedipal stage.

### *The development of object-choice*

Freud had comparatively little to say about the development of object-choice, although as we shall see, it has become a central area for much modern psychoanalysis. We can find in his work reference to three stages, the first two of which have already been mentioned. The first is autoeroticism: the child experiences itself as the centre of the world and responsible for its own satisfaction through its own body. It does not yet have any sense of a separate, outside world. As such a sense emerges, it becomes aware of the mother as a separate person and of its own body and self as separate. This leads to the second stage: narcissism, when a primitive sense of self develops and is taken as the first love-object. Once the child gains this sense of separation and of self, it is able to recognise objects in the world that are similar to itself. The most important of these is the mother and through a process of identification, of recognising and experiencing the similarity between self and mother, the mother is taken as the first external love-object. This process is the same for the little boy and the little girl.

So far I have used the term 'object' as if it were unproblematic, although many people might be wondering about it. I am, after all, talking about people, not about objects. The term 'object' is appropriate in the sense that I am talking about the object of a desire, something the infant wants to possess. The full recognition of another human being comes much later; it must be remembered that the baby or infant is still demanding immediate satisfaction, it has not yet been able to surrender or postpone its satisfaction. This comes at the oedipal stage. Later, I shall discuss other reasons for using the term 'object' in this context.

## THE OEDIPAL STAGE

The oedipal stage is where men become men and women women, or, more accurately, little boys become future men and little girls future women. Up to the phallic stage Freud thought that the development of little boys and little girls followed much the same course, and that there was for each a fundamental bisexuality. He often thought of this bisexuality in terms of active (masculine) and passive (feminine) drives. This distinction is established at the anal stage: in relation to the parent the infant can either submit or rebel – the struggle of toilet-training. For the oedipal stage, however, Freud took the little boy for his model and, despite his many women patients, it is fair to say that he tended to derive his view of what happens to the little girl from what happens to the little boy.

So far, then, we have a bisexual infant with active and passive drives who has taken the mother as its first love-object. Freud argues that the development of infantile sexuality reaches a peak with the phallic and oedipal stages, around the age of three to five. For both little boys and girls, the object of desire is the mother. If you think this is far-fetched, think how many times you have heard a child, especially perhaps a little boy, announce that he is going to marry his mother when he grows up; or how many times you said it, or your mother can remember your saying it. The frequent reply is to the effect that when the little boy grows up, he will find a woman of his own to love and to love him, and they will marry. This sums up what happens to the little boy during the oedipal stage: he learns to give up his desire of his mother and wait. The mechanism that enables or persuades him to do this is the fact that his desire for his mother brings him into conflict with his father. Paternal jealousy of the child is an oft-noted occurrence, from birth onwards: suddenly the child gets all the attention and love that the father used to experience as his own. In the child's internal life, perhaps, but not necessarily unconsciously, this jealousy, the competition between father and son, becomes a sexual competition. The threat is perceived, again not necessarily unconsciously, as a threat to his sexual organs: the phantasy is that the father will secure victory by cutting off the little boy's penis. If childhood masturbation has been handled by the threat to 'cut it off', the experience is likely to be intensified, but such a threat is not necessary. The vulnerability of the male genitalia is easily experienced, especially in a sexualised situation. Again this can be seen in normal experience, from the way they become a target in fights through to the physical reaction of men if castration is portrayed in a film of play. The crossing of legs is audible.

With the carrot of a woman of his own in the future and the stick of the father's victory, which is inevitable given his superior strength, the little boy acquiesces. The threat is so powerful, Freud argues, that in fact he undertakes a mammoth repression of his sexual desire and enters a period of latency which lasts until the onset of puberty, when it all erupts again in a different form. This repression accounts for the fact that we cannot remember our childhood sexual feelings and that adults often find the idea difficult to accept.

What the little boy does not give up is his active desire for a woman; he postpones it. Freud also talks of a 'negative' oedipal complex in which the little boy identifies with his mother and desires the father in a passive way. In 'normal' progress through the oedipal stage, this passive desire is subordinated to the active and the little boy becomes a future heterosexual man. This stage is particularly important for the development of the super-ego, since the little boy undertakes an identification with the father, internalising the father's threat and controlling his own behaviour. Here too the internalisation of the father can become part of the child's ego-ideal – a sense of oneself as one would like to be; and if the fathering is wisely handled, then the basis for a rational super-ego and strong ego is laid. The little boy has, after all, accepted a rational attitude to a real situation: he is too immature to possess his mother, so he must wait and then look for somebody else.

Still following Freud's map of development, it can be seen that the little girl's course is different and also much more difficult. To begin with, she has to transform her object-choice if she is to become a heterosexual woman. She must cease to desire her mother and desire her father or, rather, father-substitute. Again, the mechanism by which this is achieved involves the idea or phantasy of castration. Only this time, the little girl discovers that she is already castrated. She has no alternative to identifying with the mother since she cannot actively possess her. She desires her father in a passive way; the centre of physical attention moves from the clitoris to the vagina. At the same time, there is resentment at her castration – the notorious idea of 'penis envy'; in 'normal' development, this is transformed into the desire for the father's penis, then another man's penis and then a baby, preferably a male baby.

OBJECTIONS TO THE OEDIPAL THEORY

I imagine that most readers feel a stirring of uneasiness at all this, even if they are sympathetic to Freud. My experience in teaching Freud has been that there are two main bases for objection: common-sense reactions to the idea of childhood sexuality, and feminist objections to the implications that the theory has for women. I shall consider these in turn.

While people are often willing to accept some notion of childhood sexuality, the detailed account of the oedipal conflict seems to go too far. Interestingly, spontaneous objections to what Freud says about the little boy are much less frequent, and tend to centre on the idea that he might desire his mother: 'I certainly don't fancy *my* mother'. I have already pointed to the common-sense evidence in support of Freud, and his explanation of this reaction would be to point to the massive repression that takes the little boy into latency. Even so, I suspect most men can remember developing a flirtatious and protective relation to their mother at some point during adolescence – a resurrection of the old infantile desire. In the case of little girls, the usual objection is this: how does the little girl know about penises if she has never seen one, and, beyond this, why on earth should she want one? This can be dealt with in terms of her already possessing a phallic organ, the clitoris, which receives little or no recognition. One might imagine that fantasies of having a larger organ, of penetrating the mother, and therefore fantasies of what mother does with father are built into the physical make-up and family situation of the child. Why she should feel inferior is rather more difficult. One argument put forward by Freudians is that the penis becomes associated with the power of men, and this can easily be taken up by anti-Freudians: why can we not just deal with male power without bringing in the possession of a penis? My own guess is that the male bias in Freud produced two difficulties: first, he did sometimes write as if the woman were biologically and socially inferior because she did not possess a penis (Nancy Chodorow (1978) catalogues some of his more outrageous statements); and second, he did not recognise the reverse side of the coin, what is usually called womb envy. Envy can and usually does arise from any physical difference; if we can accept this, then we can look at the way in which penis envy is overlaid with all sorts of meaning by power differences in the wider society and, as we shall see later, how womb envy might be a foundation of those structures. We can look at the social without abandoning a significance for the biological. However, this is not a full answer and I shall return to these issues when I look at the feminist objections to the theory.

Whatever their individual validity, I suspect that behind these reactions there is an ambivalent attitude to children which has its origins in a cultural ambivalence about innocence and guilt: an envious desire to deny the possibility of innocence coupled with an urgent need to find purity. The existence of incestuous desires in children can be dealt with in a fairly straightforward way. It is normal for adults to have sexual fantasies which express sadistic or masochistic or whatever elements of their sexuality; most people can distinguish between these fantasies and reality, and recognise that it would be dangerous or damaging to themselves or others to act them out. The young child is in the process of learning to distinguish between fantasy and reality, and it is clear that if he or she is provided with the opportunity of acting out sexual fantasies, the result may be damaging. There are good reasons for prohibiting sexual relations with children that do not require the idea of childhood innocence.

A further range of common-sense objections consists of variations on the question: what about one-parent families, particularly father-headed families? I shall deal with this later when I look at the social role of the oedipal complex. I want to turn now to the feminist objections to the model, which, on the face of it, are very strong, especially if we follow the little girl's development in more detail.

Feminist objections to and interpretations of psychoanalysis will run through this book as a major sub-theme. I shall, paradoxically, show the force of feminist objections to the oedipal theory by outlining an account of its implications for women which has been developed by a feminist psychoanalyst, Juliet Mitchell. I have already mentioned her a number of times, and *Psychoanalysis and Feminism* was, in its context, a revolutionary book, the first to try to appropriate psychoanalysis for feminism rather than attacking and dismissing it.

I said that, prior to the oedipal stage, there was already a division in the infant's sexuality between active and passive drives. In the little boy's case the active drives come to predominate over the passive drives. In the little girl, the opposite occurs. We can see the difference if we compare the male and female displays that in our culture are still conventional. In adolescent males, especially, there is a showing-off, a sort of peacock strutting, which carries a feeling of strength. The man wants to be looked at – a passive drive – but this is put to the service of the active desire of possessing a woman. In the girl's case, the feeling of strength is absent; the activity which goes into making herself attractive takes second place behind the passive display of attraction. In the little girl, there is a physical counterpart to the subordination of active to passive drives: a shift in the erogenous zone from clitoris to vagina. Mitchell outlines the three possible routes that the little girl can take into adulthood. The first is to accept her lack of a penis, identify with the mother and displace her desire for a penis on to another man and, eventually, a male baby. This, in Western society at any rate, would be 'normal femininity'. The second is to refuse to acknowledge the absence of a penis, give way to unrestrained penis envy, identifying with her father and becoming a 'masculine' woman, competing with men at male activities. The third is the little girl's refusal to give up her mother, her first love-object, and, in adulthood, this is likely to emerge as lesbianism. Whichever way she goes, she is likely to have a raw deal.

Mitchell goes on to discuss what she calls the 'marks of woman-hood', of 'normal femininity'. Freud remarked how often his patients produced a dream or phantasy in which 'a child is being beaten', usually by the father or a father-figure. This has rather different meanings in men than it does in women; for women it is associated with the transition from active clitoral sexuality to passive vaginal sexuality: 'beaten' can mean 'caressed'. It can also involve the desire for punishment, turning against oneself a desire for a particular type of pleasure (incest) which arouses feelings of guilt: '[it] . . . typifies the feminine predicament. It expresses the wish to submit to castration, copulation or childbirth and to get erotic pleasure out of painful experiences' (Mitchell, 1975: 114). Mitchell goes on to point out that 'feminine masochism', as Freud called it when distinguishing it from other forms of masochism, is present in both men and women. However, it is a crucial part of normal femininity, together with the passivity I have already mentioned.

The 'normal' woman is narcissistic. Mitchell deals with this as vanity, jealousy and a limited sense of justice. Vain through the passive desire to be loved, the woman pays great attention to her body, which becomes a beautiful, phantasied substitute penis. Penis envy also produces a greater sense of jealousy. Generally, both men and women can deal with envy and jealousy by developing demands for justice and equality. These act as a protection both against the unrestrained pursuit of one's own envious goals and the envy of others. The strength of a woman's envy, Freud argues, inhibits the development of a sense of social fairness. Beyond this, it is less socially necessary (since she has already 'been castrated') for a woman to repress her desire for her father than it is for the boy to repress his desire for his mother. Consequently, she does not need to internalise as strong a super-ego as do men, and consequently her attachment to the wider society is less. She represents the private, the familial, as opposed to the public and social.

It is easy to see why feminists, and non-feminists, object to all this. Freud seems to be saying: this is how women are and they are like it because they do not have a penis. They are condemned by biology. At the very least, he is justifying a patriarchal culture that involved the systematic oppression of women; at the worst, he is simply expressing his own hatred of women. There are some Freudians who might still maintain that not only was Freud right in his analysis of the development of femininity, but that he was also right in his occasional implication to the effect that women are inferior because they do not possess a penis. It seems to me that this is so clearly wrong that it is not worth arguing about; it also seems to me that there are places in Freud's work which justify attributing this clearly wrong view to him. But there is also a way of maintaining Freud's theory without its implicit justification of patriarchy or its overtones of misogyny. Mitchell makes two points. The first is that it is possible to separate a theory from the theorist. The theorist might hate women, and traces of that hatred might become apparent in the theory, but it does not follow that the theory is simply and only an expression of a hatred of women, that it does not have any knowledge of the outside world to give us. The theory has a logical cohesion and a field of application that stand apart from its producer; it is open to development and criticism by others, and this public nature can enable the manifestations of individual quirkiness (or even general cultural values) to be eliminated. Secondly, Freud is describing and analysing what happens; it does not follow that he is prescribing it. In fact, Freud might have prescribed it, but for us, it does not follow that because a certain situation exists, it ought to exist. Mitchell takes this latter position: what Freud is describing is the way patriarchy operates; such a description is not necessarily a prescription.

## THE FOUNDATIONS OF CIVILISATION

The question of the origins of civilisation seems almost as fascinating as the question of the origin of life itself, perhaps for the same reason: that we can never have an answer. A combination of Freud, modern anthropology and modern feminism has produced a series of speculations that place the oedipal stage at the very centre of the beginning of ordered social life. At its simplest, the argument is that since human beings are not genetically patterned to heterosexual intercourse, the survival of an ordered social life depends on the social patterning and directing of the sexual instinct. This is what is happening at the oedipal stage, witnessed by the fact that some sort of incest taboo seems to be a universal feature of social life. The speculations are more complex than this.

The starting point is Freud's own speculation, what he called his 'scientific myth', intended to give some idea of how it all began. I touched on this myth in the last chapter. At the beginning was the primal horde, a group dominated by the strongest male, the original father. This father held a monopoly of the women in the group. To break this monopoly, the sons rise up and kill the father, and divide the women among themselves. There then follows the guilt that results from killing a loved figure, and the need to make sure that the situation cannot occur again. Rivalry has to be limited, restraints imposed on instinctual gratification. The authority of the original father is internalised by the sons in the form of the super-ego. The element of this scientific myth that appears in modern anthropology takes up the idea of the women being shared between the men in the group.

## THE CIRCULATION OF WOMEN

Both the prohibition of incest and the channelling of human sexuality away from polymorphous perversity towards genital heterosexuality are seen as governed by social needs, as necessary for the continuation and preservation of any society. It is important, if a society is to survive, that a sufficient number of adults experience heterosexual desires for a sufficient length of time to reproduce enough replacement members. As Gayle Rubin (1975) points out, this means that there must be some way in which we can distinguish between the sexes, that men and women have to be different. We often tend to think of the two as being opposites; we talk of the 'opposite sex'. Freud's theory entails a symmetrical opposition: in men, the active desires predominate over the passive; in women the opposite is the case. In Rubin's startling language, this difference is not given in nature:

> In fact, from the standpoint of nature, men and women are closer to each other than either is to anything else – for instance, mountains, kangaroos or coconut palms. The idea that men and women are more different from one another than either is from anything else must come from somewhere other than nature. Furthermore, though there is an average difference between males and females in a variety of traits, the range of variation of those traits shows considerable overlap. There will always be some women who are taller than some men, for instance, even though men are on average taller than women. But the idea that men and women are two mutually exclusive categories must arise out of something other than a non-existent 'natural' opposition. Far from being an expression of natural differences, exclusive gender identity is the expression of natural similarities. It requires repression: in men, of whatever is the local version of 'feminine traits'; in women, of the local definition of 'masculine' traits. (Rubin, 1975: 179–80)

It is convenient here to introduce a familiar sociological distinction between sex, the biological structure of the human being, and gender, what society builds on to sexual difference. Rubin is talking about the necessity for gender differences and she goes on to give examples of societies where individuals are allowed to move from one gender to another – women, for example, are allowed to become fathers, men mothers – to make the point that although the characteristics of men and women may vary from society to society, what is common is that there are clearly different gender roles. One must be either a man or a woman, irrespective of sex; one cannot be both. This is true even in the case of physical ambiguity. The difference helps to reinforce and secure heterosexuality; one of the ways it does this is by making sure that an economically viable unit must contain members of both genders. The division between the genders is a fundamental form of the division of labour.

So, we need contrasting genders and heterosexual adults. Incest is a threat, but less a biological threat than a social threat. To allow incestuous relationships would be to allow society to fragment into small self-contained groups. Mother–son incest is particularly danger-ous because it is unlikely to lead to the production of a new generation. By the time the son is old enough to reproduce, the mother is likely to be nearing or at the end of her child-bearing life. Daughter–father incest is not such a threat (and correspondingly, it seems that generally its incidence is much higher – here is another reason why the repression of oedipal feelings is less necessary in the little girl than in the little boy). This is where modern, structuralist anthropology comes into the story. Claude Lévi-Strauss's version of the beginnings of civilisation involves the idea that kin groups become dependent on each other through relying on each other for marital partners.

Lévi-Strauss's argument is that all primitive kinship systems, excluding hunting and gathering societies, involve the systematic circulation of women between men. The basic family unit is not, as we often assume, the primary biological unit of man, woman and child, but includes another partner: the woman's brother. This last figure is vital. It is he who gives the woman away to the man from another group in the knowledge that, based on the kinship rules of that society, he or one of his descendants will receive a woman in return from that group. The separate groups are all given an equal stake in the society: it ensures the supply of women and avoids the inequality and paternal terrorism of the primal horde. In some societies the role of the maternal uncle is clear and vital, and in relationship to the child, symmetrical to that of the father. If the father has prime disciplinary responsibility for the child, then the maternal uncle has a friendship role. If the father has the friendship role, then the maternal uncle has the disciplinary role. In our society the importance of the extra figure is encapsulated in the way the father 'gives away' the bride during the wedding ceremony.

The next question is: why is it that women, rather than men, are exchanged, and why does it seem to involve their subordination to men? As Lévi-Strauss points out, the subordination of women does not follow from the act of exchange. There are several possible answers. The first is to speculate that the reproduction of the population depends upon the number of women of child-bearing age who are available to bear children. The circulation of women enables the control of this number, which in absolute terms is contingent – it is 'accidental' how many girls and boys are born in a particular generation, and the numbers can be transformed by natural or human disaster. Kinship rules enabling the circulation of women also ensure that if there is a shortage of women of child-bearing age, then those available are enabled to bear children, since they are assigned to a husband; and if there is a surplus, then some will lack husbands and there will not be a population increase which would strain the resources of the society. The second answer is that women, because they give birth, are perceived as closer to the state of nature than men, and a consequent threat to a newly established society. Consequently, their natural functions of childbirth, menstruation, etc., have to be restricted or surrounded by taboos. The exchange of women becomes the basis for their subordination. Such taboos continue into modern society (think of 'the curse'). A third answer is that men are afraid of female sexuality: women are capable of more and faster orgasms than men; therefore, again, women have to be controlled and the exchange of women provides the basis. Fourthly, women are more essential to reproduction than men – a society could not survive with a few women of child-bearing age; but it could survive if most men were eliminated and a few kept in a cage somewhere. Again, women have to be controlled and circumscribed: the whole system can be seen as built upon womb envy on the part of the inessential male.

Given the set of social requirements that lead to the circulation of women, Freud's theory of the oedipal stage can be seen as describing how the circulation operates on a psychic level: how parent–child and sibling incest is forbidden, and men and women become ready for each other, rather than choosing members of the same sex.

## THE IMPORTANCE OF THEORETICAL FANTASIES

I want now to look at this approach in the same way that I looked at the theory of society built upon the idea of the repression of instincts. It is a matter not of adopting or rejecting it *in toto*, but of sorting out where and how it is useful. The starting point must be its speculative nature. It is always tempting and nearly always interesting to embark on such speculation. We all, as children, have fantasies of how we come into the world. Freud was particularly interested in these and used them in his developmental theory. We all, perhaps at a later age, have fantasies about the sexual act, frequently developed, elaborated and passed on by word of mouth in the school playground. I remember one particular version of the sexual act involving male masturbation and rubbing the sperm into the outer areas of the female genitals, rather as one might apply sun-tan lotion. It is tempting to follow this analogy through a little further. The fantasy I have just described could be seen as a result of ignorance, at least conscious ignorance, of the vagina and penetration. Alternatively, it could be seen as an attempt to deny penetration because of an unconscious fear – after all, putting a vital and vulnerable organ in somebody else's body is a risky thing to do. The theory of Rubin and Lévi-Strauss, taken up by Mitchell, is based on ignorance and is an attempt to fill that gap; I also suspect that it is fulfilling unconsciously an infantile desire for omnipotence: after all, if we know how all this came about, we can have control over it and no longer feel ourselves in the grip of some nature about which we can do nothing.

It follows that we should be suspicious of the approach for two reasons. The first is the good empirical reason that we can never know whether the theory can be believed. Short of time travel, the evidence will never be available. Secondly, it is likely that in some way or another the theory will be a form of wishful thinking. One way of approaching it is as a theory that is trying to say something about the present situation. The sexual fantasy from my playground days about the onset of puberty was saying something about the real possibilities of sexual activity that were open to me, i.e. masturbation. It was making masturbation more than it in fact is, but none the less recognising its existence, doing something to remove feelings of abnormality or wrong-doing, even sin, which can be attached to it, and asserting its importance. In the absence of a sexual partner and a better theory, it was acceptable.

If we look at the sociological version of the oedipal theory, it does make reasonable use of available evidence. Lévi-Strauss's massive study of kinship, for example, is available for criticism, discussion and further research. The oedipal theory itself is more problematic. It is assumed that the oedipal complex is a universal one and this has always been a matter of fierce debate. I suspect that it is true to say that not many anthropologists would now accept that universality, even if they accept the existence of such a thing as the oedipus complex in Western society. On the other hand, as Paul Kline (1977) shows, there is some support from cross-cultural studies for the existence of an oedipal conflict in very different societies. The classic refutation of Freud came from Malinowski in the 1930s. He assumed that Freud's theory was appropriate only to the nuclear biological family of Western Europe, and concentrated on the significant role of the maternal uncle in the societies he studied. The version I outlined above catered for this sort of criticism by suggesting that the nuclear family as we know it in Western society is one derivative form of a more fundamental basic family unit. Mitchell's argument is precisely that there is a range of cultural situations in which the oedipal conflict is resolved, and the nuclear family of modern society produces particularly acute contradictions in its resolution. In other words, Freud's theory was dependent on the limited case of nineteenth- and early twentieth-century middle-European society, but he none the less identified something common to all societies. This approach also caters for the argument that the personality structures of men and women vary a lot from society to society, but the account of the oedipal stage only allows one outcome: the personality structures common to modern Western society. It allows for this by emphasising the importance of gender difference over and above the content of the differences. It is important that men and women be different, whatever the difference. The differences could then be accounted for by looking at possible courses that can be taken through the oedipal stage. This in turn would involve looking empirically at differing child-rearing methods and different patterns of child–adult relationships. Another way of extending the theory and protecting it against the criticism of its limited application is to see the basic family structure as a set of positions – maternal uncle–sister–husband–child – which does not necessarily have to be filled by the biologically appropriate figure, in the same way as a child does not *have* to be parented by its biological mother. This could cope with the issue of single parent families I mentioned earlier. My own experience as a child in a single parent family was that my mother attempted to combine both maternal and paternal roles (with some resulting confusion for both of us). This makes the model much more flexible.

So far, then, I have suggested that the theory that kinship systems are based on the circulation and subordination of women is a respectable theory open to debate, and that we can extend the theory of the oedipal stage to overcome most of the objections. The latter exercise is rather disreputable, leaving me open to the accusation that I cannot be proved wrong. My excuse lies in the usefulness of the playground fantasy: there is nothing better at the moment and it recognises the universality of gender differences, the cultural variability of masculinity and femininity, the necessity for heterosexuality and what seems to be the universality of patriarchy, of women's subjection to men. It speculates about the origin of civilisation, but we need not take this as more than a speculation, a more elaborate 'scientific myth', which enables us to do these other things. In all this, it must also be borne in mind that, like the playground fantasy, it has to be abandoned if something better comes along. We might be confined to masturbation at the moment, but it does not follow that masturbation is our only option for the rest of our lives.

Overall, then, the sociological extension of the oedipus theory opens up a possibility of looking at these issues.

THE PLACE OF OEDIPUS

Those feminists who have employed this approach have not, on the whole, been as exclusive in their claims as Christopher Badcock: it is not argued that this is a general theory of society. At least as far as modern society is concerned, it is claimed that it is a theory of part of society. Juliet Mitchell, for example, wishes to integrate the theory with Marxism, and in this context psychoanalysis supplies a 'regional' theory of ideology, telling us about the construction of gender differences which are then taken up and 'used' by different economic systems in different ways. For example, in capitalism, women supply domestic labour and form an important part of the 'reserve army of labour' on the labour market. There is no *a priori* reason why women should fulfil either of these roles; rather, they do so because of their position in an (ideological) patriarchal structure which preceded capitalism. The fact that women were already subordinated to men enables their subordination to particularly unfavourable positions on the emerging labour market.

The advantage of Mitchell's approach is that she does allow for the importance of other *social* processes, and an understanding of different gender characteristics in different societies. In this, I think she takes us beyond what is offered by Badcock. On the other hand, since she is still talking about the foundations of society, her analysis remains caught at a very general level, leaving one with the peculiar feeling that everything is known but nothing can be done.

One sign of this is the generality of her politics. She offers an interesting account of the present situation of the family, which bears certain similarities to Durkheim's outline of the move from mechanical to organic solidarity (Durkheim 1933). Society is no longer dependent on the kin group as the only or the prime basis of social cohesion; rather, it is the division of labour and economic interdependence that is important. Consequently, a loosening of the necessity to exchange women, of the incest taboo, can take place. At the same time, the economic structure of capitalism has isolated the nuclear family in such a way as to increase the pressures to incest. Indeed, our parents, children, brothers and sisters are the only people we are supposed to love and they are the only people with whom we are barred from having sexual relations. In our society, then, there is a crucial contradiction between the aims of the oedipal conflict, which are to prohibit incest, and the social setting in which that aim has to be achieved, which encourages incest. Presumably, this can be seen as a root cause of the difficulties the family seems to face in modern society, as well as of the sexual and women's liberation movements.

Patriarchy for Mitchell is not the rule of men, but the rule of the father, originally, in the terms of Freud's useful myth, the autocratic, all-powerful father. What we internalise during the oedipal stage is the demands of the father, the rules he would have us follow. Modern society makes this no longer necessary: 'The capitalist economy implies that for the masses demands of exogamy and the social taboo on incest are irrelevant; but nevertheless it must preserve both these and the patriarchal structure that they imply' (Mitchell, 1975: 409).

At first sight, then, it seems that Mitchell believes that demands for change should involve a campaign against exogamy and incest taboos. One can imagine what sort of success such a campaign might have. Sensibly she offers a different vision, which would have the same result. I shall consider this shortly.

There is a second aspect to the over-generality of Mitchell's approach: like Marcuse, she does not provide us with the means of understanding concrete human relationships. While she does leave us with the idea that the general processes described by Freud have specific social and cultural resolutions, the complexities of cross-gender and cross-sexual identifications as they are played out in marriages and friendships and as they appear in the psychoanalytic consulting room, cannot be understood. Her approach does not enable us to understand individual resolutions to the oedipal stage. A range of possibilities is combined within each individual. We all maintain our bisexual constitution, even if we resolve the oedipal stage as practising heterosexuals. We all have to find something to do with our homosexuality. Each woman will carry all three solutions outlined by Mitchell within her, in some combination, and in the world of external reality, in which there are many courses of action open and many other different people with whom to form relationships, there are many more than three ways of being a woman. Freud offers not a causal theory that says that every time this happens, so the other happens. Conditions are always too varied for this. Rather, he offers a general map on which each of us occupies a specific place. Mitchell's level of analysis is rather like defining a particular group of people as a nation, and then assuming that they occupy the same geographical spot, perhaps standing on each other's shoulders.

Despite the fact that she allows other social processes a determining role, there is also in her work a psychologism. It is not the whole of society that is seen as a product of individual psychology, but patriarchy is seen as a product of the psychological processes and relationships of infancy. She assumes that because the growing child internalises the rule of the father, then society must be ruled by fathers, by men. I want now to suggest a series of distinctions that will be important for the remainder of the book. The first is now a fairly conventional one in some feminist work: a distinction between hetero-sexuality, or more importantly, sexual differences and inequality. It is conceivable that there could be a difference in personality structure between men and women, but not a difference in social status, nor a differential distribution of power. One does not follow from the other. The reasons suggested for the subordination of women in exchange are no longer applicable in modern society, and we can conceive of a resolution to the oedipal conflict that does not result in large-scale social inequality. One can also imagine that in a rational society the jealousy and envy arising from simple physical difference can be dealt with without the subjection of one group by another. On the whole, I prefer to regard penis envy as one manifestation of a general envy, and I shall talk about this in more detail when I look at the work of Melanie Klein. Envy is a universal human characteristic and, notoriously, the one that people find it most difficult to recognise in themselves. In the case of penis envy, when the issue is bound up with very real social inequalities and prejudice, it is not surprising that it raises violent or defensive emotions. Even Michelle Barrett (1980), who objectively must have very little reason to feel defensive, finds it necessary, in her discussion of Mitchell, to point out that her own intellectual ambitions can be interpreted as penis envy, and wonders whether this interferes with her judgement. What is interesting is that people do not find these feelings rising around other childhood experiences. When my son was three, he imagined that he would be able to jump, without danger or damage, from the top of a ten-storey building, and he declined to accept my arguments to the opposite, despite, in the reality of jumping off walls and furniture, having a very good sense of his physical capabilities. He no longer believes that he can make such a jump. His sense of his own omnipotence has been transformed into more realistic ambitions. Now, at the age of five, it is quite possible that he imagines that I might castrate him; if he still believes this at the age of thirty-five then there will be something wrong. By then his desire for his mother will have become something else, as will his fear of me. I cannot understand why exactly the same thing should not be true of penis envy. At the age of five, the little girl might feel she has been castrated and feel highly envious of the male possessors of penises; if, at the age of thirty, she has transformed this into intellectual ambitions, then why does it matter that these honourable and socially useful ambitions might have originated in penis envy? If these oedipal experiences do continue to become the basis of dominance in society at large, then we could regard it as a form of pathology rather than the inevitable result of the oedipal stage.

In so far as we see it in terms of Freud's useful myth, then, such a society would still be patriarchal, the child would internalise the rule of the father and the fear of castration, and penis envy would still be experienced; in so far as we see it in terms of the distribution of power and rights it would not be patriarchal. Similarly, in so far as the internalisation of the super-ego takes place through a conscious or unconscious threat of castration for the boy and for the girl, as part of turning away from the mother, a society is patriarchal. If the super-ego and ego can strengthen their rational parts, that patriarchal organisation need be only a moment in the history of each individual, not something that governs social life.

Next, I want to suggest another and wider conception of the role of the super-ego beyond that offered by concentrating on the oedipal stage. The super-ego is a means by which we become attached to society in a much more general sense than controlling our sexuality. It also involves the internalisation of consideration for others, a sense of obligation and duties, and, if all goes well, the internalisation of a morality we can use to govern our relations with others and an ability to think rationally and make decisions in an independent way. It is arguably the basis for a free and independent individual who can co-operate with others and, where necessary, put others first. It is, in other words, the basis of a reasonably free community. For Mitchell, what is important is the internalisation of paternal authority; the possibility that paternal authority provides a basis on which can be built independent rational judgements, a precondition for social freedom, is not considered by Mitchell, and remains secondary for Badcock to the acceptance of authority.

I ought to say that I am speculating here, and I believe there are more secure ways of arriving at the same conclusions. I shall look at these in Part III. For the moment, I want to point to the dangers of Mitchell's position by returning to her political solutions. She takes the organisation of war-time Britain as an illustration of what is possible:

> Taking Britain as an example, we can see that in the period 1940–45 the family as we present it in our dominant ideologies virtually ceased to exist. In wartime the industrial employment of women was once more predomin-ant but fathers were absent. For the first time there was planned alternative social organisation to the family. Compulsory education was extended, pre-school creches were provided, large scale evacuation of children was organised, the state took care of food rations and ensured the basic necessary nourishment of small children and provided communal restaur-ants – all tasks normally left to the nuclear family. (Mitchell, 1975: 410–11)

It would be unfair to suggest that Mitchell wants to campaign to bring back war-time conditions. But the drift of her proposition is clear: there are other ways of fulfilling the tasks presently undertaken by the nuclear family. This can be accepted. I am less sure about the assumption that the state is the agency to take over. If, as I have suggested, the basis for a rational and free society lies in the internalisation and development of a rational super-ego and ego, then we return to Badcock's point that if such a super-ego is not internal-ised then the state must enforce social cohesion. The alternative is a strong state on which people become dependent taking over the role of the primal father in a much more authoritarian way than the millions of biological fathers who inherit his power. Wartime Britain, of course, saw a very strong state. This does not preclude the possibility that there might be other, co-operative and grass-roots ways of organising work currently carried out by the nuclear family which would alleviate or remove the strains imposed on it.

Some support for my argument comes for the sort of social changes that have been registered by modern psychoanalysis. Here, as in most of the above discussion, I am anticipating the arguments of Christo-pher Lasch. I shall discuss these in Part II. There is evidence that different resolutions of the oedipal stage are taking place in the second half of the century from those general in the first. The change in the clientele of psychoanalysts, away from obsessive neurotics and towards 'borderline' narcissists, is one indication. In fact, it is an indication that change is proceeding in the way Mitchell would like, since the former category is the product of too strict an enforcement of the rule of the father, and the latter the result of a very inadequate enforcement. It is a pity that it also results in much misery and that misery provides the strongest argument against Mitchell. A further indication of change is the datedness of her summary of the 'marks of femininity'; although there is certainly some resonance both with the way women experience themselves today and with modern social conceptions of women, the very existence of a significant feminist movement, which has influenced, if not actually recruited, large numbers of women, indicates that resolution of the oedipal complex for women is not necessarily the same as it was when Freud was writing, even though the rule of the father is still passed on.

Mitchell's argument, then, is too general precisely because it bases itself on a speculative theory of the foundations of civilisation. The theory might or might not be true, but to undertake to change that basis is, to say the least, ambitious. We are still left with no means to grasp concrete human relationships. There is also a degree of psychologism in that she assumes that the oedipal stage is responsible for male dominance in the wider society. I have argued that this need not necessarily follow.

# 4

## CODA: REAL HUMAN RELATIONS

Part of the greatness of Freud's work is that he is aware of the difficult and often mundane task of maintaining some sort of balance: of maintaining civilisation without building up the pressure on individuals to the point where they become too ill to function; and of enabling instinctual gratification without threatening the fabric of society, the very thing which, in the final analysis, makes instinctual gratification of any sort possible for the majority of people. He is also aware of the difficulties in maintaining a balance in our sexuality, of the partial and often tenuous nature of what we regard as 'normal' heterosexuality. I have argued that when these insights alone are used as a basis for social theory, we end with a very general overview and a neglect of complex social and individual processes. His work on society does give us a warning and an attitude of mind which we might bring to social theory and analysis with profit: life is difficult and complex: it is not going to be perfect, but neither need it be barbarous. However, this work, generally, does not have the subtlety and detail of his clinical studies.

There is, however, one point in his study of *Group Psychology and the Analysis of the Ego* where he does offer the beginning of an understanding of real, day-to-day human relations. It is here that we can find what, in the context of this book, is a preliminary approach to object-relations.

### FREUD ON THE GROUP

I have already mentioned Freud's 'scientific myth' of the primal horde and the primeval father, the most elementary form of social organisation. It is held together by the father, the original patriarch, who, perhaps by virtue of strength, holds a monopoly of power, including a monopoly of the women in the group. The sons, resenting this power, rise up against and kill the father; consequently they are beset by guilt and, as it were, collectively assume his role, sharing the women between them. We can find here the origins of the punitive element of the super-ego, the internalised primeval father. In his analysis of group processes, Freud has much to say about the role of the leader.

When Freud writes about groups, he is concerned not only with the renunciation of instinctual desires and the control of sexuality (although both are involved) but with looking at what goes on between people in a group. A group is formed through diverting the sexual instinct from direct expression (which would leave us with a couple) to a sublimated expression which unites group members to each other and to the leader, the latter being most important. When this is broken, perhaps because the leader is killed or his competence is brought into doubt, the organisation becomes chaotic. He cites as an example what happens to an army when its leader is lost. This means that something significant is occurring between group members and the leader.

What this is, is analysed by Freud in terms of three types of relationship we may have with other people. The first is governed by self-interest and is hostile to any sort of group cohesion. In a group it has to be replaced by something else. The other two are identification and love. The difference between them is that identification involves wanting to be like the object of desire, while love involves wanting to possess the object of desire. Identification is seen as more 'primitive' in the sense that in the child's development it comes before love. It is through identifying with the mother that the child becomes human, a person itself; it is in recognising his or her separation from the mother that the child is able to love another person. This is the move from narcissism to the choice of the mother as the first love-object. The process of identification is also closely linked to the development of an ego-ideal: the little boy wants to be like his father because that is a good thing to be. However, like love, the development of an ego-ideal, the choice of somebody one wants to be like, goes beyond identification with that person: it recognises a difference. Freud suggests that the primary tie between group members is that they replace their ego-ideal with the group leader; they then share something as part of themselves. They do not identify with their leader: if every Conservative party supporter tried to be Mrs Thatcher, the world would soon be a ridiculous place. Rather, they identify with each other through their leader and this produces the heady sense of solidarity, of living in a shared world, as well as the often-noted suggestability that goes with group membership. It is reinforced by the necessity to repress instinctual individual selfishness: notions of loyalty and equality have their roots at least in part in the desire to displace one's fellows.

Freud makes some further points about the group by returning to his 'just-so' story of the primal horde:

> The psychology of such a group . . . – the dwindling of the conscious individual personality, the focusing of thoughts and feelings into a common direction, the predominance of the affective side of the mind and of unconscious psychic life, the tendency to the immediate carrying out of intentions as they emerge – all this corresponds to a state of regression to a primitive mental activity, of just such a sort as we should be inclined to ascribe to the primal horde. (Freud, 1985: 114–15)

He does this to emphasise the ambivalence of feelings towards the leader. In the primal horde, each member feels himself not so much as equally loved by the leader as equally persecuted by him. The feeling of being equally loved is an idealisation, a defence mechanism which hides the persecution (a defence Freud termed 'reaction formation'); it is the hidden feeling of persecution which leads to the oft-remarked manipulability of groups, their 'thirst for obedience'. The group actually *wants* to be controlled by a strong leader. The group ideal is, in fact, the primal group leader. There is no reason why we should not regard this ambivalence as part of the human condition that is associated with our need for other people if we are to survive and the resentment we feel because we have to restrict our own desires in favour of co-operation.

What we learn from this is a description of what today we might call the 'mob', although Freud does not intend it to be applied simply to face-to-face groups, as his examples of the church and the army show. It seems to me that the role of the leader, the shared identification with the leader, the importance of the feeling of being equally loved by the leader, and the corresponding fear of and willingness to obey the leader, are phenomena which appear directly, or are close to the surface, in both organised and comparatively unorganised groups. In the classroom situation, for example, it emerges in the way students will paraphrase and reproduce lectures in their essays, on the resentment often felt and expressed against a student who appears to be a favourite, and the anxiety that rises rapidly to the surface when the teacher sits and waits for the students to speak. The same sorts of identification, fear and hope can be directed towards, say, a political leader who remains comparatively hidden, certainly from direct contact with supporters. Freud offers us a way into the experience of a variety of group situations. From the preceding argument, however, it should be clear that we cannot regard this as being in itself the sole constitutive factor of the group. If we take the teaching situation, for example, the experience of the relationship between student and teacher takes place in a setting that does not determine and is not determined by the experience. The setting has to do with the requirements of the labour market which needs education to take place in the first place; it is a result of the political mediation of that structure (is the education system selective, for example?); and what goes on depends upon the syllabus, the exam requirements and any number of other factors. Freud is talking about the emotional accompaniment to this structure, and the interesting question is the relationship between the two.

There is a further experiential complication that Freud points out but does not develop: each individual has a network of group identifications, from family through to nation, to being a human. Presumably, all these are to a greater or lesser extent active in any one situation. We can agree with Paul Roazen (1968) that the simple model of primal father/horde or leader/group is not sufficient for understanding societies of any complexity whatsoever, even if we do not take into account their structural features.

If we abandon the idea that social processes and structures grow out of psychic processes and take up my suggestion that Freud is talking about the emotional accompaniment to social structures, we gain a clearer idea of what psychoanalysis might help us to understand about social relations. If we take as an example issues of power, we look to the bases elaborated by sociologists: organisational requirements, the ownership of property, and so on. But these relationships, which have their basis elsewhere and their own structure and dynamics, can be seen as becoming coloured by the internal structure of the psyche, the need for leadership, the nature of the super-ego and the ambivalent feelings of love and hate that accompany it. To go back to the example I used in Chapter I, it is as if we see the outside world through the lens of the inside world. If, within our psyche, we have a strong, irrational, punishing super-ego, then we might see external authority as manifesting all these properties and act towards it accordingly: we might be servile or angry and rebellious, as I described in my early example. We are projecting our internal dynamics on to the outside world, just as we do when we identify our ideal ego with a leader. The process is most clearly revealed when we discover the ordinariness of a feared authority figure: 'Well, he or she is really quite human after all!' For people who commit themselves to permanent opposition, this discovery may be quite difficult.

## OBJECT-RELATIONS THEORY AND INSTINCT THEORY

It is now possible to elaborate a little on object-relations theory. In his account of groups, Freud draws on instinct theory: group relations are a result of the transformation of instinctual drives. But he moves from this to looking not just at the way in which group members *perceive* each other and the leader, but the way they *internalise* each other and their leader, in particular the different ways in which they may make the leader part of themselves, through identification and through incorporation of the leader as an ego-ideal. He mentions as well the possibility of love. Here we come to another reason why we talk about object- rather than interpersonal relations. It is not just a matter of choosing an external object of desire, but of internalising something into the psyche, producing an internal object world which has no one-to-one connection with the outside world. My internal father is not the same as my external father. It is here that we begin to approach the complexity of Freud's clinical and psychological work which deals with individual uniqueness. Nancy Chodorow, in her criticism of Marcuse, points this out and seems to be in favour of abandoning instinct or drive theory altogether. I do not think this is necessary as I shall try to explain.

The first reason why I think drive theory should be retained is that, as I have pointed out several times, it does grasp the paradoxical nature of living in society. Beyond this it has an intuitive correspondence to our everyday experience of social relations, the way in which our need for others, if we are to achieve any sort of fulfilment, is always combined with a resentment that can move to hatred at the sacrifices we have to make to keep others. Balancing out these conflicting needs, and the loneliness, love, anger and hatred that they imply, seems to be a central task of modern living, making the conflict even more apparent than perhaps it was in simpler historical societies. It also has something to say about the complexities and failures of modern politics, the place and dangers of idealism coupled with pointers to the possibilities of real reforms.

My second reason for wanting to keep some place for drive theory is that it seems to me that it does have clinical manifestations. This is, in fact, very clear in Freud's work where this aspect is constantly manifested in interpretations which play a central role in therapeutic treatment. Indeed, I suspect any analyst who has experienced the envy of a patient, directly or indirectly, or, especially in a group situation, watched the conflict for attention and time, the very primitive needs and hatreds that emerge, might have difficulty in denying drive theory. This does not mean that people do not do things with drives, that they are not agents; it simply means that they are agents with drives. Interestingly, if we abandon drive theory, we are left with a sociologistic argument the difficulties of which I shall show in Part II.

There is, I think, a theoretical reason why we should hold on to drive or instinct theory. Instinct theory offers an explanation of what object-relations theory enables us to interpret. The latter enables us to understand how, and within fairly strict limits, why somebody acts in a particular way, and it enables us to make sense of the way in which they experience the world. The former is concerned with the why in the most general sense, and this, of course, is a necessary level of explanation. There might be all sorts of criticisms of Freud's instinct and oedipal theories, but the necessity of something like them is clear. Kalin (1974) is helpful when he suggests that we should think of the instincts as 'inferred entities': this way it seems to me that we can avoid identifying them with instincts in a sense acceptable to the biological sciences, but still recognise the validity of Freud's theoretical speculation, which is no different in principle, as far as I can see, from the theoretical speculation of 'inferred entities' in physics. It is, however, important to remember that we are operating at two different levels. Just as, in the clinical situation, interpretations at the explanatory level are often less useful or effective than those at the more surface level of object-relations theory, so attempts at social analysis which keep to that level miss a great deal in their oversimplifications, and do produce, often against themselves, a mechanistic view of social reality.

As an example, I shall discuss a group I led consisting of young men in their late adolescence and early adulthood. What was common to all of them were oedipal difficulties with their fathers, or, by this stage in their lives, with their internalised father figures, which they often had considerable difficulty in distinguishing from the real men. Many of these difficulties were focused and acted out on myself as group leader. Over one period of two to three weeks there was something like an acting-out of the murder of the primal father. I do not believe, incidentally, that it was a modified re-enactment of a primitive rite which has survived in the collective unconscious, as some might believe; I just find it a *very* useful metaphor for this sort of event. I came under strong and universal attack: I did not take enough care of them, did not participate in the group, and when I did participate, what I said was worse than useless. The attack was generalised: my teaching too was, by all reports, no good. My presence was a threat, they wanted me out of the room.

During this period, the interaction between them changed. It became much more self-directed. There had been for a long time a strong competitive theme in the group, one they had often noted in terms of competing for group leadership, but it was at root a competition for the group's attention and for my attention. When no one member succeeded in capturing me, they had individually or collectively regressed to dependence, feeling and expressing powerful needs for my love and approval. Now they competed for power without me: it was very much an attempt to establish a pecking-order between themselves.

At first sight, the scientific myth could make sense of all of this but there was more to it. Each of them reacted to me in a different way from the others. One would urgently need my approval for his positive actions and would battle with me to get it; one would give up on me, assuming that I had an immense power that could not be challenged; one began to plumb the depths of anger that he felt at the apparent indifference of misrecognition by his own father. The room was always full of different fathers. These varied reactions cannot be understood either by instinct theory or by the theory of the oedipal complex in their most general forms. Those theories have to do with what is common to us all, our fundamental humanity and inhumanity; they explain the existence and form of the conflict I have described. To understand the content, the peculiar individual reactions, we need to understand the inner object-world of each, the particular identifications each has made, the specific ego-ideals each has set up, and that has to do with the specific and particular way in which each of us becomes the one human being that we are, and this is where object-relations theory comes into its own. That too has its general and more specific levels, but it offers the possibility of grasping individual complexity. Freud's general theory always tends towards reductionism.

I have done no more than give a very general introduction to object-relations theory here, sufficient I hope to make further references more intelligible. In Part IV, I shall elaborate on it at length.

# REFERENCES AND FURTHER
# READING

As with all further reading, I am not aiming at an exhaustive list, but including
the books and papers I have referred to in the text and adding items that I or
others have found particularly useful and that will take the reader into more
detail and more complex arguments than can be found in this book. The
reading is divided up into the topics covered in Part I.

## FREUD'S WORK ON THE PSYCHE AND SOCIETY

On the conflict between the instincts and civilisation and the death instinct, the
most useful texts are:

Freud, S. (1985) 'Thoughts for the times on war' and 'Death, civilisation and
its discontents', both in the Pelican Freud Library. Vol. 12, *Civilisation,
Society and Religion*, Harmondsworth: Pelican Books.
  (1984) 'Beyond the pleasure principle', in the Pelican Freud Library,
Vol. 11, *On Metapsychology: The Theory of Psychoanalysis*, Harmondsworth:
Pelican Books.

On the origins of civilisation and religion:

Freud, S. (1985) 'Totem and taboo' and 'Moses and monotheism', both in the
Pelican Freud Library, Vol. 13, *The Origins of Religion*, Harmondsworth:
Pelican Books.
  (1985) 'The future of an illusion', in the Pelican Freud Library, Vol. 12,
*Civilisation, Society and Religion*, Harmondsworth: Pelican Books.

On sexuality, the central text is:

Freud S. (1977) 'Three essays on the theory of sexuality' in the Pelican Freud
Library, Vol. 7, *On Sexuality*, Harmondsworth: Pelican Books. (The other
papers in this volume are also well worth reading.)

On group psychology:

Freud, S. (1985) 'Group psychology and the analysis of the ego', in the Pelican
Freud Library, Vol. 12, *Civilisation, Society and Religion*, Harmondsworth:
Pelican Books.

For useful general accounts of Freud's work on society, see:

Bocock, R. (1976) *Freud and Modern Society*, Walton-on-Thames, Surrey: Nelson.

Gabriel, Y. (1983) *Freud and Society*, London: Routledge and Kegan Paul.

Roazen, P. (1970) *Freud: Political and Social Thought*, New York: Vintage Books.

Wollheim, R. (1971) *Freud*, London: Fontana, Chapter 8.

The work of Christopher Badcock discussed here:

Badcock, C.R. (1980) *The Psychoanalysis of Culture*, Oxford: Basil Blackwell.

(1983) *Madness and Modernity*, Oxford: Basil Blackwell.

For his more recent views, see:

(1988) *Essential Freud*, Oxford: Basil Blackwell.

For an extended version of some of the critical points made here, see:

Craib, I. (1987) 'The psychodynamics of theory', *Free Associations*, 10, pp.32–56.

On Marcuse, the central text is:

Marcuse, H. (1969) *Eros and Civilisation*, London: Sphere Books.

Useful discussions of his work can be found in:

Held, D. (1980) *Introduction to Critical Theory*, London: Hutchinson, especially Chapter 8.

Leonard, P. (1984) *Personality and Ideology*, London: Macmillan.

Poster, M. (1978) *Critical Theory of the Family*, London: Pluto Press, especially Chapter 2.

On Marx's theory of alienation:

Marx, K. (1973) *The 1844 Manuscripts*, London: Lawrence and Wishart, especially the section on alienated labour.

The critique discussed here:

Chodorow, N. (1985) 'Beyond drive theory: object-relations and the limits of radical individualism', *Theory and Society* 14, No. 3, pp.271–320.

On the feminist interpretation of Freud:

Mitchell, J. (1975) *Psychoanalysis and Feminism*, New York: Vintage Books.

In this context I also mention:

Durkheim, E. (1933) *The Division of Labour in Society*, New York: Macmillan.

For her attempt to combine Marxism with psychoanalysis, see:

Mitchell, J. (1984) *Women: The Longest Revolution*, London: Virago.

I also mention a book which will be considered at greater length later:
Chodorow, N. (1978) *The Reproduction of Mothering: Psychoanalysis and the Sociology of Gender*, Berkeley: University of California Press.

On the history of the psychoanalytic approach to women, see:
Chasseguet-Smirgel, J. (1970) *Female Sexuality*, Ann Arbor: University of Michigan Press, Introduction.

For a survey of modern feminist interpretations of psychoanalysis, see:
Sayers, J. (1986) *Sexual Contradictions: Psychology, Psychoanalysis and Feminism*, London: Tavistock.

Critical discussions of Mitchell can be found in:
Barrett, M. (1980) *Women's Oppression Today: Problems in Marxist Feminist Analysis*, London: New Left Books.
Leonard, P. (1984) *Personality and Ideology*, London: Macmillan.
McDonough, R. and Harrison, R. (1978) 'Patriarchy and relations of production';
Kuhn, Annette (1978) 'Structures of patriarchy and capital in the family'; both in
Kuhn, Annette and Wolpe, A.-M. (1978) *Feminism and Materialism*, London: Routledge and Kegan Paul.

On the circulation of women, the clearest exposition is:
Rubin, G. (1975) 'The traffic in women: notes on the "political economy" of sex', in Reiter, R. (ed.) *Toward an Anthropology of Women*, New York: Monthly Review Press.

The basic work of Lévi-Strauss is:
Lévi-Strauss, C. (1969) *The Elementary Structures of Kinship*, Boston: Beacon Press.

Malinowski's critique of Freud can be found in:
Malinowski, B. (1927) *Sex and Repression in Savage Society*, New York: Humanities Press.

On the universality of the oedipus complex, see:
Kline, P. (1977) 'Cross-cultural studies and Freudian theory', in Warren, N. (ed.) *Studies in Cross-Cultural Psychology*, London: Academic Press.

For an approach which contrasts Freud and Marx, and which offers a useful way of thinking about the instincts, see:
Kalin, M.G. (1974) *The Utopian Flight From Unhappiness: Freud Against Marx on Social Progress*, Chicago: Nelson-Hall.

# PART II

Juliet Mitchell's work illustrates a central difficulty in the case I want to make. She can be read as claiming that a social structure – gender relations – is the product of the psychological processes involved in the oedipal stage, and at the same time as claiming that these same psychological processes are a result of social requirements. We can find the same difficulty in the work of a thinker I shall not be discussing at any length: Wilhelm Reich. Reich was a communist and undertook the first major attempt to combine Marxism and pychoanalysis. I respect some of his work immensely, especially what he has to say about sexual education and adolescence. Some is, I suspect, completely crazy. Be that as it may, his argument involves the assumption, on the one hand, that human beings can be free and control their fate if they are allowed free sexual development, and on the other, that they are at present the repressed victims of a repressive society. In other words, either people create society or they are created by it. I could, therefore, deal with Reich in Part I of this book or in Part II; it is a matter of emphasis whether the individual/human side comes to the fore or the social/structural side. In fact, the relationship between individual and society is more complex and cannot be understood by the simple juxtaposition of the two, although each way of juxtaposing them has something to offer. That is my excuse for some complicated arguments.

The writers considered in Part II often recognise the complexity of the relationship, but their emphasis is, I believe, on the side of society. They fall into three groups. The first is American, and has its roots in the development of 'ego-psychology' and less directly in the 'culture and personality' school of anthropologists of the 1930s, including figures such as Margaret Mead, Edward Sapir and Ruth Benedick. These writers focused on the idea of personality as bringing together all the human sciences – sociology, anthropology and psychology – and they drew a great deal from Freud. The emphasis was always on the way in which personality was a product of culture; consequently the instincts receded in importance. One major thinker who eventually takes up much the same position is Erich Fromm, who was also one of the original members of the Frankfurt School of Social Research, from which Marcuse came. I shall look only at two theorists from this group: Talcott Parsons, the most important sociologist amongst them, and Erik Erikson, the most important psychoanalyst to move towards social theory. As a coda, I shall look at Erikson's contribution to 'psycho-history' which opens up a new area which will become important in Part III.

The second group can be placed in the same tradition as Marcuse: the Frankfurt School and critical theory. Their concern is, however, less with drives and instincts than with the nature of the super-ego as the link between society and individual. I shall be looking at the work of two original members of the school, Theodor Adorno and Max Horkheimer, and a modern representative, Jürgen Habermas. I am also including here the work of Christopher Lasch, a modern American historian who takes up the same concerns.

The third group – really one major thinker – is the French psychoanalyst Jacques Lacan and some of his feminist interpreters. Lacan is not, on the face of it, sociologistic; he emphasises the irrationality and divided nature of the person and his followers would be the first to criticise the view that there is such a thing as 'society' to produce the person. Nevertheless, I shall argue that implicit in his work there is a similar reduction or undervaluation of the individual, and that he eventually locates irrationality not in the person but in the nature of language. Language in Lacan replaces society in the other thinkers, but in both cases it is the properties of super-individual entities that are important.

Throughout Part II, I shall be emphasising the side of these thinkers that gives priority to the social and to social structures. Although we can learn from them, the tendency is to underestimate the importance of instinctual drives, instinctual renunciation, internal conflict and the variety of ways that individuals have of resolving, expressing and living with these conflicts.

# 5

## LOSING THE INSTINCTS BUT GAINING MYTHOLOGY

TALCOTT PARSONS

I have chosen Parsons because of the clear way in which he absorbs the psychological into the social and illustrates the worst dangers of the approaches discussed in this part of my argument. For some twenty years after the Second World War, Parsons was the major English-language sociological theorist; he is the only theorist of such standing to have incorporated Freudian ideas into his work, yet the incorporation was at considerable cost.

Parsons' is an evolutionary theory in which history is seen as a development from the simple to the complex, through a process of differentiation of social institutions one from the other and increased specialisation. Simple societies can be seen as organised around one central institution, the kinship system; complex societies have many distinct institutions, and the kinship system has been reduced to the nuclear family, which has a clear-cut specialised task: that of the early socialisation of children to produce stable adult personalities. In modern society this involves presenting the child with two clear role models: the instrumental (the father/man) and the expressive (the mother/woman). These functions he regards as universal features of the family, existing in all societies but found in their purest and most specialised form in modern American society. What is important in this process of specialisation is that the different institutions maintain a proper functional balance with each other, each enabling the others to work more effectively. It is usual to draw on an analogy from biology here: the organs of the body depend for their existence on their mutually supportive functioning. Parsons also likens social organisation to a cybernetic system: those parts low on energy but high on information govern those high on energy but low on information, rather as the programmer in a washing machine governs the electric motor. Parsons sees society as a combination of such systems: each system is made up of a number (usually four) sub-systems, and in turn the whole provides a sub-system of some larger system.

Parsons looks at ego-development in terms of socialisation into the wider community: beginning with the mother–baby dyad, we move to the family structure as a whole, then the peer group and the education system, and so on. At each stage the ego becomes more clearly defined and differentiated and integrated into a system with others, and the modern family is able to specialise in taking the child through the early stages of socialisation and ego development more efficiently. In relation to the wider society, the family fulfils the vital function of 'pattern maintenance' – maintaining a stable set of social value choices. The oedipal stage is seen as the point at which the mother–baby dyad is broken, the instrumental father ensuring the child's separation from the emotional mother and the consequent development of the child's ego. The family remains the vital emotional centre of its members' lives, differentiated from the instrumental area of work and life in the outside world, and it is the prime area of women's responsibility. Parsons' way of describing this is in terms of the person's family position being determined by 'ascription', family members being loved because of what they are – father, mother, child – while in the outside world, status depends on achievement.

Parsons criticises Freud for ignoring the cognitive aspects of development, the more or less conscious social learning process, and concentrating on the individual rather than the interaction of social roles. In fact, what he does is concentrate on the cognitive and role-learning processes and describe them in Freudian language. He sociologises Freud more clearly than any other thinker dealt with in this book. This is clear in his association of Freud with G.H. Mead, who is solely concerned with the conscious processes of role learning, a matter of socialisation from the outside. When we learn a role, we internalise other people's expectations of what we should be and do, and act accordingly. In fact, we make other people's expectations our needs, so if we fail to meet them we feel dissatisfied. We begin by identifying with our mother; the father provides an escape from that identification and enables us to learn a more complex role. The school and peer group carry on the process. This is very close to Mead's conception of the growth of the self through to the internalisation of a 'generalised other', general social expectations. The end purpose is the production of men and women able to carry on in the same way as their parents, producing future generations of men who work and women who take charge of the emotional realm. As Mark Poster (1978) points out, Parsons translates the old adage, attributed to Freud, that 'anatomy is destiny' to 'the modern American family is destiny'.

In all this, the id is reduced to a simple supplier of energy for the personality system, in which the other sub-systems play the dominant role. The ego directs the personality, the super-ego integrates the personality into the wider social system and the ego-ideal integrates the personality into general cultural values. What Freud says about the conflict between different parts of the psyche, and between the psyche and its environment does not rest easily with such an approach. For Freud, the conflict was necessary, and there were more or less adequate ways of dealing with it; for Parsons, it seems that conflict which is not a stage in adjustment is a pathological occurrence. The most important adjustment is between individual and society.

Christopher Lasch illustrates this clearly. Even when Parsons does employ a more concrete notion of the unconscious, it serves simply to fit in with his theory of the functions of the nuclear family and its expressive role, and distorts what Freud had to say in an interesting way – in fact, it is a castration of Freud's argument. When Parsons discusses the unconscious processes of identification that take place during the oedipal stage, he sees them in terms of an unconscious identification with the mother, which enables him to maintain that the family fulfils only an expressive role, since that is the mother's role in the family. The father then intervenes to introduce the child to wider social roles. What he leaves out is the presence of the penis in Freud's equation and the consequent idea not that the little boy wants to be like the mother, but rather he wants to give her a baby; this introduces conflict, and the strong feelings of love and hate that each family member has to deal with. Lasch does not, typically, talk about the little girl, but it is no smooth ride for her either: she is forced into an identification with the mother, but one which involves her abandoning the mother as a love-object. Love and hate come into play here as well. The import of this is that when Parsons does take unconscious processes into account, he does so only to the extent that he can employ them to reinforce a process that he sees essentially in terms of conscious role learning. The expressive/instrumental aspect of parenting, essentially a cognitive process, takes the place of what in Freud was the primacy of the sexual and emotional links between parents and children, involving desire, conflict and repression.

Lasch is concerned to emphasise the way Parsons strips the family of its strong emotional content, and sees Parsons as reflecting the way the modern family has been stripped of its functions. He draws out the explicit parallel that Parsons makes between socialisation and psychotherapy. Neither parent nor therapist allows prolonged emotional dependency, but tolerates or encourages emotional expression, manipulates rewards and refrains from reciprocity (the mother must not be seduced by the child). The aim of psychotherapy and parenting in modern society is to minimise dependency; in the adult, reversion to childhood dependency is a threat to society; prolonged childhood dependency is a threat to the family. What Parsons does, according to Lasch, is to suggest that parents behave like professionals rather than like parents, and when it comes to sickness and stress in the family, to suggest that professionals are better at parenting than the parents themselves:

> The modern family provides indispensable modern services, according to Parsons, yet it performs them so badly, on his own account, that its efforts have to be supplemented by an army of healers who attempt to impair the emotional ravages inflicted, in the last analysis, by the family itself. Only a short step brings us to the conclusion that trained therapists ought to take charge of socialisation in the first place, in order to attack sickness at its source. (Lasch, 1977: 120)

The importance of this argument lies in what it shows about the tendency to use Freud simply as a theorist of the socialisation process. The instincts seem to disappear altogether, leaving us with a vision of people who are the product of social structures. In Parsons' work, this becomes a sort of therapeutic totalitarianism. The lesson for social theory seems to me to be that if socialisation is seen only in terms of what society does to individuals, who are conceived eventually as empty vessels to be filled, or as animals who can have their animality suppressed and replaced by the social, then we are left with puppets who fit into whatever version of society the theorist might want them to fit into.

On the other hand, there is a remarkable power in Parsons' distinction between the expressive and instrumental roles of mother and father and the way these correspond with wider social institutions, the world of work and the world of the home. We see it cropping up in radical and Marxist analyses of the family, and it is clearly influential in Chodorow's analysis of the socialisation of men and women, which is based on object-relations rather than instinct theory. This is an issue I shall be approaching later; for the moment I want to re-emphasise the distinction between levels of analysis on which this whole book is centred. The division between work and home, and the way that the different spheres have been allocated to men and women, are clearly indisputable and of crucial importance from social analysis. It does not follow that this automatically results from what are actually very complex and contradictory psychological processes in early childhood socialisation, nor that it is the cause of such processes. An over-sociological approach, like the over-psychological approach, loses all sense of multi-causality.

## ERIK ERIKSON AND THE STAGES OF DEVELOPMENT

### Ego-psychology and the self

If object-relations theory is 'British psychoanalysis', then 'ego-psychology' is American psychoanalysis. The leading figure in ego-psychology is Heinz Hartmann, a European analyst who emigrated to America as part of the mass exodus from Europe prior to the Second World War. Freud himself was part of this exodus, but he came to Britain rather than the United States, a central reason being his disagreements with American analysts on the question of lay analysis, the practice of psychoanalysis by those without medical qualifications. Freud did not believe medical training was necessary and lay analysts have been more generally acceptable in Europe. However, psycho-analysis in America rapidly became professionalised. American insti-tutes would only take on as trainees and members students who had already qualified in medicine. Psychoanalysis took on many of the trappings of the medical profession, including perhaps a too clear distinction between health and sickness.

Ego-psychology took up a general move in psychoanalytic concerns from the id, the unconscious drives and their objects, to the ego. The change is marked in Anna Freud's *The Ego and the Mechanisms of Defence*, in which she outlined the 'defence mechanisms', the means by which the ego deals both with the difficult parts of external reality and the instincts themselves. We all need these to survive in our everyday lives but when they are developed inadequately or in an over-rigid way, all sorts of problems can result. Hartmann himself, in his work on the ego, went so far as to suggest an independent ego-energy, putting the ego on a par with the id, and implying that adjustment to internal and, for our purpose, more important, external reality was a major force in the psyche.

It is common among more radical European (and American)

thinkers to come close to dismissing ego-psychology as an ideological product of American capitalism, concerned as it is with the ability of an individual to adjust to his or her environment and with an optimistic notion of personal growth, which can be clearly juxtaposed in cultural terms to the more pessimistic European concerns of conflict and death. Poster is damning in his indictment:

> Hartmann, Kris and Loewenstein, exiles from Nazi Germany, seemed bent on adapting psychoanalysis to the dominant American culture. Their notion of health through adjustment to society fits well into the ethos of liberal capitalism. They removed all the strange, threatening aspects of Freud's theory, such as the unconscious, sexuality and instinct theory. Ego psychologists remodelled Freud to the American ideal of individual autonomy through social adaptation. For support from sociology, Hartmann turned to Talcott Parsons, the leading social theorist of American middle-class values. (Poster, 1978: 64–5)

However, to concentrate on the ideological nature of ego-psychology, despite the fact that there is clearly some truth in the argument, leads to a loss of dimensions which are important and real and which this approach can help us understand. Erikson is a more subtle thinker than Parsons, who should only provide a backcloth for drawing out tendencies in Erikson's work which can clearly be placed within the development of ego-psychology. He prefers the term 'identity' to the more technical 'ego'; this is appropriate since he is talking not just about a particular element in the psychic structure but about a person's sense of self in all its aspects. He is concerned with how, and under what conditions, we arrive at our identity; and he sees it as something which occurs not only during early childhood, when the pre-conditions are laid out, but especially during adolescence. Thus the effect of the instincts, compared to Freud, becomes limited. The biological tends to be simple physical growth and its effects. In adolescence, the social is all-important. The formation of his own identity during adolescence seems to have been an important event for Erikson himself – a Nordic Jew in an anti-Semitic environment who spent much time wandering Europe in a familiarly romantic search for himself.

As Robert Coles (1970) points out, Erikson's notion of identity involves the passing of time: some sense of being able to integrate the past, the present and the future; and because of that, it is something in continual development, over a lifetime, taking on new dimensions and depths. The analyst, to work effectively, needs a sense of the direction of a person's life, in addition to our knowledge, of the id, ego and super-ego. Perhaps this, in a nutshell, is what I think is important about Erikson. I shall look first, therefore, at his conception of identity and the life-cycle.

## The eight stages

Erikson describes eight stages through which identity is achieved and developed from birth to death. The first stages follow Freud closely, but go much further than he did into the social surroundings of development, and translate what for Freud were primarily biological and psychological stages into primarily psychological and social stages. There are eight stages in all and each is conceived in terms of an opposition or conflict between basic features of the personality, one negative and the other positive, and the successful achievement of identity depends on the resolution of the conflict in a way that favours the positive over the negative quality. Perhaps each conflict is best considered as a continuum on which we all end somewhere, nearer one end or the other.

The first stage, equivalent to Freud's oral stage, is seen as the time when the baby develops either a basic trust or a basic distrust of his or her environment. Erikson describes this so well that it is worth quoting him in full:

> The first demonstration of social trust in the baby is the ease of his feeding, the depth of his sleep, the relaxation of his bowels, the experience of a mutual regulation of his increasingly receptive capacities with the maternal techniques of provision gradually helps him to balance the discomfort caused by the immaturity of homeostasis with which he was born. In his gradually increasing waking hours he finds that more and more adventures of the senses arouse a feeling of familiarity, of having coincided with a feeling of inner goodness. Forms of comfort and people associated with them, become as familiar as the gnawing discomfort of the bowels. The infant's first social achievement, then, is his willingness to let the mother out of sight without undue anxiety or rage, because she has become an inner certainty as well as a external predictability. (Erikson, 1977: 222)

This sense of trust involves the deployment of the basic defence mechanisms of splitting, introjection and projection, whereby the child is able to sort the good and satisfying experiences from the bad and threatening experiences, and if things go well, introject the former and project the latter, feeling itself to be good, to be sure of its own goodness even if the outside world is threatening. If this basic trust in the world is not achieved, then the likelihood is that the infant will develop a schizophrenic withdrawal; or if it is only precariously established, then the danger of such a withdrawal remains throughout life. The schizophrenic, for Erikson, is engaged in primitive attempts to distinguish between self and environment, between what goes on inside and what goes on outside, and achieve the sense of confidence and trust that was never developed in the original childhood experience. We all experience an early sense of loss, a loss of identity with the mother, of unity with the world, a 'fall from grace'. Thus trust must be strong enough to withstand that sense of loss.

Basic trust goes beyond the mother–child couple; it is a social process involving social expectations. The child must gain a sense of the social meaning and significance of his or her place in the world; for Erikson, it is not childhood frustration as such which produces a neurotic but meaningless frustration, frustration which is not presented with a social reason. What for Freud was inevitably a conflict between instinctual gratification and social restraint is for Erikson a conflict resolvable through socially learnt meaning. Beyond this, each of the positive qualities learnt during the childhood stages is supported and maintained through adult life by social institutions. Religious institutions maintain and allow expression to the sense of basic trust and place the individual in a guaranteed mutuality of relationships with others, allowing access to infantile desires and reinforcing the gains made as an infant.

The second stage Erikson characterises as one of the conflict between autonomy and shame. This is Freud's anal stage; muscular development allows the child to experiment with holding on and letting go – phrases which are not only appropriate for the act of shitting but are redolent with meaning for our conduct in the world and our relationships to other people. Holding on can be a matter of caring, or it can be restraining and destructive; letting go can be an unleashing of destructiveness, or a peaceful decision to let things pass. The initial experience of this ability to hoard or be profligate against others can threaten the sense of trust developed in the first stage. Parental reaction must ensure that the child does not feel that the achievement of basic trust will disappear: it must protect him or her against the uncontrolled unleashing of desires on the one hand and, against 'arbitrary experiences and early doubt on the other' (Erikson, 1977: p.226). The latter, referring to strict and punitive toilet-training, encourages the child to turn his or her desire to control inwards, producing somebody obsessed with inner order which is later projected in obsessive attempts to order the outside world. If the child feels ashamed, he or she wishes to be invisible, to hide the self, which is experienced as dirty and unacceptable. Too much shame can lead to a defiant desire to be dirty and unacceptable. With shame there is always, too, self-doubt. This stage, then, determines whether the child can grow and experience a freedom of self-expression and maintain and develop the sense of self achieved during the earliest stage; or whether he experiences a loss of self-control, a sense of dirtiness, and develops an obsessive internal control as a response. Again, for Erikson the parental response and the social meaning of self-control are more important than for Freud, and the social institution which maintains the progress of this stage and allows the remnants of the experience to be expressed is the system of law and order, which apportions the individual both possibilities and limitations, rights and duties: 'the sense of autonomy ... serves (and is served by) the preservation in economic and political life of a sense of justice' (Erikson, 1977: p.229).

The third stage is equivalent to Freud's genital stage and the oedipal conflict, but whereas for Freud this is seen in terms of sexual conflict, for Erikson it is the period when the child develops initiative or a sense of guilt. Initiative is bound up with the development of physical powers as well as the development of genital sexuality. It is the period when the child becomes divided within itself between the desire to do things spontaneously and the internalised parental prohibitions, which are initially punitive and over-strict, and if allowed to stay so will produce in later life a crippling sense of guilt which will inhibit initiative. The function of the parents is to provide the child with a situation in which to form and realise *realistic* ambitions without strangling the source of ambition altogether. His comments about the institutional equivalent at this stage are more vague than previously: 'Social institutions offer children of this age an *economic ethos*, in the form of ideal adults recognisable by their uniforms and their functions, and fascinating enough to replace the heroics of picture book and fairy tale' (Erikson, 1977: 232).

From now on, the child who has successfully negotiated these early stages moves forward to adult life and the social responsibilities and privileges that go with it. He or she, at the end of the oedipal conflict, gives up the desire to remain in the family for ever, and for Erikson this is less the sacrifice of a vital desire that continues to affect our life and feelings than a realisation that the desire itself is futile, that it is better to move forward and outward into the world, to develop and exploit autonomy and initiative. The fourth stage Freud called latency; the powerful sexual drives of early childhood are put into abeyance and the child sets about learning the skills necessary to fulfil his or her role in the wider society. This stage occurs in all societies, but the actual skills, methods of teaching and teaching personnel vary. In our society, education is carried out in a complex and highly developed institution separate from the family. In others it is carried out in the family itself. In both cases the child learns what Erikson calls 'industry': the ability to develop and have confidence in skills, to set realistic aims and achieve them, whether in reading or writing, learning an industrial skill or working on an academic ability. These skills are needed by the society as well as increasing the confidence of the child. The conflict, or the alternative outcome at this stage is a sense of inferiority, of having inadequate skills, of being unable to learn or feeling incompetent when compared with one's peers.

If the desires are in abeyance during the latency stage, everything erupts again during puberty and adolescence. Erikson does not deal with this in terms of the vicissitudes of unconscious desires, but in terms of the physical impact of maturation. The adolescent changes very quickly *physically:* the body grows and becomes awkward as we do not have time to adjust to a different size before it changes again. It is as if we switch overnight from driving a Mini to driving a Rolls Royce without realising it, and we take corners too tightly and try to park where there is no room; and this goes on happening. In addition, there is the immense impact of coming to sexual maturity, the development of adult organs, breasts, pubic hair, the start of menstruation, the ability to ejaculate real rather than imaginary sperm capable of producing real rather than imaginary babies; and the apparent sudden availability of members of the opposite sex also interested in exploring these new capabilities. The sense of integration and stability that the child has developed during the early years is threatened by these sudden changes, and experienced as role confusion. The successful negotiation of adolescence leaves the new adult with a firmer and clearer identity; failure leaves him or her in a state of role confusion. Falling in love, peer-identification, ideological idealism, all are ways in which the adolescent tries to hold on to and develop a sense of identity. The most important source of confusion and achievement generally has to do with occupation, which provides the adolescent with his or her place in the wider society. Throughout this period everything is questioned and reintegrated:

> The integration now taking place in the form of ego identity is, as pointed out, more than the sum of the childhood identifications. It is the accrued

experience of the ego's ability to integrate all identifications with the vicissitudes of the libido with the aptitudes developed out of endowment, and with the opportunities offered in social roles. The sense of ego identity, then, is the accrued confidence in the inner sameness and continuity of one's meaning for others, as evidenced in the tangible promise of a career. (Erikson, 1977: 235)

This quotation not only summarises Erikson's view of this stage, but captures the central difference between his approach and Freud's: he starts with the libido but ends by giving central importance to the career, to society.

If ego-identity is achieved, then the new adult can risk him- or herself in new and intimate relationships, can distinguish between situations where love and support are appropriate and those where feelings of competitiveness or even of hostility are appropriate. The other side of the equation at this stage is isolation, the inability to form a satisfactory relationship with another adult. Erikson concentrates on the heterosexual relationship that produces children: for him, this is the real mark of maturity and of social and individual health:

While psychoanalysis has on occasion gone too far in its emphasis on genitality as a universal cure for society, and has thus provided a new addiction and a new commodity for many who wished to so interpret its teachings, it has not always indicated all the goals that genitality should and must imply. In order to be of lasting special significance, the Utopia of genitality should include:

1. mutuality of organs
2. with a loved partner
3. of the other sex
4. with whom one is able and willing to share a mutual trust
5. and with whom one is able and willing to regulate the cycles of:
   a. work
   b. procreation
   c. recreation

It is apparent that such Utopian accomplishment on a large scale cannot be an individual or, indeed a therapeutic task. Nor is it a purely sexual matter by any means. It is integral to a culture's style of sexual selection, cooperation and competition. (Ibid. 1977: p.239)

I shall return to this quotation, and what will be to the modern sociologist its self-evident difficulties, later.

The next stage is generativity against stagnation. An intimate relationship with another person of the opposite sex enables a new productivity, essentially in relation to the species: it is the central period of adulthood when we produce and raise the next generation and employ our skills and abilities in the world of work, contributing to the society as a whole. If we can survive through this period and carry on the ability to integrate our experiences in terms of our own life-history and life-cycle, and understand that this particular life-cycle, which we have in common with every other human being, is also specific in its relation to a particular social environment; if, in other words, we can continue to accept our life and what goes on in it, even when we have no control over it, we reach the final stage of ego-integrity, when we can see our place in life and prepare ourselves to accept death. The alternative at this stage is despair, the feeling of meaninglessness and pointlessness.

### The over-emphasis of the social

I have profoundly ambivalent feelings about Erikson's work. Unlike Parsons, he clearly maintains a sense of internal conflict but it is attenuated. We are left with the impression that life can and indeed should be a constant progress towards the final goal of integrity. We *could* conceive of his eight stages as a development which not only moves through stages of conflict but carries all the earlier conflicts through each stage and in a more marked form than he allows. He simply does not discuss this possibility. Although inner conflict and turmoil are allowed a presence, they seem momentary, they can be resolved at each stage and they are not rooted inevitably in our make-up as animals living together; rather, they are necessitated by our smooth integration into society, and they are resolved by that integration. I am also suspicious about what he has to say about integrity and the acceptance of death. His conception of integrity seems to miss the experience which most of us have of real internal conflict, real inadequacies and real damage, which can become a painful part of our wholeness. I can think of one example from my own practice: a man in his fifties who has managed to mourn his wasted years, but feels pleased with his children and wife, and faces the future knowing that he will probably continue to suffer panic attacks and depressions that threaten to be crippling, but that he can still manage them sufficiently well to start thinking again about possible career ambitions. This seems to me to involve an integrity that includes damage and conflict and pain and depression, as much as the sense of peace that Erikson implies. It is interesting to compare Erikson to Winnicott, whom I shall discuss in Part III. For Winnicott, depression is an indication, if not the beginning, of what he calls integration, a state not dissimilar from what Erikson means by integrity.

There certainly may be societies in which the old accept death as appropriate, and occasions in our society when people can choose to die – whether it be in war or during the course of a terminal illness. But what I really question is the magnanimity with which he implies people may face the loss of their faculties and their physical decline towards death. This might be a function of my own age: death and real ageing are still some way away and it is difficult to project oneself forward. Furthermore, my own experience of old people dying has been one of seeing death fought bitterly and futilely. But I do wonder whether one might not be able to maintain a notion of integrity which none the less emphasises the reality of the loss of physical powers, the loss of friends, the loss of a future, and the fight against death, despair and fear. These might also be part of human wholeness.

I suspect Erikson underestimates the power of internal conflict partly because he seems to adopt the functionalist conception of society as a set of interlocking and mutually reinforcing parts, rather than as a structure which itself (apart from the individual psychology) might be internally and necessarily contradictory. Society smooths out the internal conflicts. His approach works best with simple, comparatively undifferentiated societies. In his reconstruction of Sioux culture (1977: pp.102–49), for example, he is able to make interesting and persuasive links between child-rearing methods (breast-feeding, toilet-training, etc.), adult personality structures, the economic organisation of the tribe, its family patterns and customs and the nature of its culture. When he talks about Hitler, by contrast, he seems to have little or nothing to say about the real social conflicts that split German society during the first half of this century: they are nothing more than circumstances.

It is perhaps because of this implicit functionalism that the most frequent criticism made of his theory of the life-cycle is that it is culture-specific – more than that, that it is specific to the careers of white, middle-class males in the United States after the Second World War. It can be said in his defence that at least in the early stages – up to and including the child's education – he is talking about universal features of growing up. The same might be said of his discussion of adolescence, but in some societies adolescence consists of a short period approaching initiation rites and the depth and importance of the identity issue is nothing like it is in modern Western society where adolescence is an extended state. The physically mature and able youth is kept dependent on the family at least to the end of full-time education, and for the privileged among us this extends into the twenties. It is, in fact, quite conceivable that a new family has been created before the proper break has been made from the family of origin. Clearly adolescence – the space between childhood and fully-fledged adulthood – is a more painful and important process in some cultures than in others. Generativity too is variable. For women, for example, it might have two stages, one concerned with raising children, the other with work in the wider society; and for men Erikson assumes the presence of fulfilling work and it is arguable that even in conditions of full employment, such fulfilling work has been available only to a minority.

Even more difficult is Erikson's conception of mature or, as he prefers it, Utopian genitality. Here the difference from Freud is clear: gone altogether is the understanding of the variety of human sexuality and the complicated and varying combinations of object-choice, together with the idea of a basic bisexuality. All doubt is eliminated and we all ought to be heterosexual. The main problem with such a position is that it does not correspond to what we know empirically of human sexuality, the proportion of homosexuals in the population and the homosexual feelings and activities of the rest of us. In other words, the normality of bisexuality, at least in desire, is lost. It is worth noting that with the exclusion of physical procreation, a homosexual relationship can meet all of Erikson's other criteria of maturity. Here we find the ideological bias of Parsons' work. If we try to see the individual as a product of society, we end by accepting what that society thinks of as 'normal' as right. It does not follow.

## THE SENSE OF A LIFE

Despite this, Erikson's notion of integrity and the sense of life as a whole is important, therapeutically and theoretically. The sort of integration that a person can achieve, a person's ability to see and perhaps understand personal experience in terms of their life as a whole, as it has been in the past and as it might be in the future is important: the sense of a life being a whole and an acceptance of pain and conflict, even if sometimes it is difficult to see the meaning of the pain or conflict. It is important, too, for the therapist to try to gain a sense of the patient's life as a whole, and to do this it is important to have some sense of the requirements of the social structure and of the opportunities and obstacles it presents. So often the therapist too easily dismisses everything outside of the unconscious and phantasies. At the very least, Erikson enables a way into this.

What is clear from his work, but not from Parsons', is that the form of social institution, the family, the school, and so on, can inhibit growth and accentuate conflict. In other words, unlike Parsons, he provides the basis for a critical approach. On the other hand, he does not develop that approach and lacks the sociological tools to do so. Further, despite the criticisms of cultural bias, he does argue that a person who has achieved 'ego-integrity' will be a different sort of person from culture to culture, but will share and be able to recognise ego-integrity in those from other cultures:

> Each individual, to become a mature adult, must to a sufficient degree develop all the ego qualities mentioned, so that a wise Indian, a true gentleman, and a mature peasant share and recognise in one another the final stage of integrity. But each cultural entity, to develop the particular style of integrity suggested by its historical place, utilises a particular combination of these conflicts, along with specific provocations and prohibitions of infantile sexuality. (*Ibid.* 1977: 242)

This statement, or rather this way of looking at the process across cultures, seems to meet the criticisms, since provision can be made not only for what is required in a specific culture but also for differences between different parts of the same culture. It leaves us somewhere near the point I reached at the end of my discussion of the oedipal stage: that there are certain universals to human development but many ways in which those universals are realised.

Overall, then, my point is that although Erikson adds a social dimension to development that is missing in Freud's work, he loses the importance of what Freud does say. The instincts tend to merge into physical growth and its implications, the significance of internal conflict and instinctual renunciation is reduced, and a social wholeness is assumed, as against Freud's emphasis on the contradictions of civilisation. His contribution to psycho-history develops the positive side of his work and his conception of identity.

CODA: THE IMPORTANCE OF MYTH

*Psycho-history*

'Psycho-history' is simply the bringing of psychoanalytic forms of understanding to the study of history. Attempts to bring disciplines

together tend to have a stormy history for all sorts of reasons, and when
one of those disciplines is psychoanalysis, the history is likely to be
even stormier. I do not want to go into the development of psycho-
history or the debates surrounding it – Peter Gay (1985) has offered a
recent account, sympathetic to the approach, which is well worth
reading. I am doubtful of the value of psycho-history as history for
reasons that will emerge shortly, but it does have something important
to tell us: first, about subjectivity, the way in which people live in
society; and secondly, about the role of the social scientist him- or
herself. It introduces something new and important to my argument.
Erikson presents some of the most stimulating aspects of the approach,
the sociological concerns of his writing sometimes overcoming the
inhibitions of his functionalist presuppositions.

## Levels of identity

When Erikson discusses identity and identity crises, he argues that
these are all situated at three levels: 'the somatic order', by which he
means the physical adaptation of the body to its environment (where
Freud would have concentrated on the unconscious and its conflicts);
'the personal order', the ability to adjust inner and outer reality; and
the 'social order', which he sees as the result of the combination of
individuals acting together. We can find in this model the same
problem that I discussed earlier. In the first place, his concentration on
the physical structure of the body rather than on the symbolisation of
the body in the unconscious is much clearer, and this leads, despite the
denials and qualifications that he adds, to an over-emphasis on the
biological, especially when he talks about differences between men and
women. He suggests that the physical differences lead to a different
conception of space and of inner space. Starting with the child's use of
toys, he directed attention to their spatial arrangement, noting that
different configurations and themes recurred 'strikingly often'. The
boys emphasised free motion, order and height; the girls closure,
ornateness and often portrayed people (usually men) entering the
enclosure. The phallic and vaginal imagery is clear and I would not
dispute that it is meaningful. However, one can dispute the meaning
that Erikson attaches to it – a direct association with genital differences. We know, for example, that a little girl has a clitoris – it is not
apparent that Erikson knows this, and certainly apparent that, if he
does, he does not regard it as important. It is also true that little boys
can conceive of penetration, and can in fact be penetrated anally.

Again this is missing in their play. One could argue that their play representations do *not* reflect their biological make-up or possibilities, which is and are bisexual: play, therefore, is part of learning a fundamental social role, which is heterosexual. I have a strong suspicion that play representations, like any empirical evidence, can be interpreted in different ways, and that an observer who was looking for it might find evidence of an attempt to integrate different aspects of sexuality into a dominant pattern. If one accepts the theory of bisexuality, not to mention polymorphous perversity, then the process of integration within the individual and the conflicts that this entails are likely to be a significant and changing factor throughout life. The somatic order, then, is more complex and contradictory than Erikson allows for, and the borderline between the somatic and the psychic is, as Freud was well aware, a much more difficult and blurred area than it is for Erikson.

In the case of the middle order, the personality, the difficulty is that, by and large, integration is seen as going on at the conscious level and as involving a resolution rather than a coping with internal conflicts. However, the concept of identity does allow us to talk about what is and is not creative in a life, of what people make out of the conditions, including their physical structure, into which they are born. He modifies his functionalism when talking about the relations between the orders to allow for the creativity which conflict can produce:

> Much of man's creative tension as well as his debilitating conflict will be seen to originate in their incomplete adjustment to each other. For these orders seem to wholly support each other in Utopian schemes; while man seeks forever the restorative means to correct, at intervals, the accrued dangers to health, sanity or social order. (Erikson, 1975: 48)

Whereas Erikson seems to see the opportunity to create as deriving in part, if not wholly, from various disjunctions between and within the different orders, I would argue that each of the orders is necessarily contradictory and the possibility for creation is a normal condition for social life. However, unlike Parsons, for example, he offers a space for talking about the irrational as the source of creativity, even if at the expense of under-emphasising the permanence of the destructive and conflicting aspects of life. This is something that is hardly ever touched upon in conventional sociological work, at least at a theoretical level, although it is often remarked upon. It tends to be a residual category, like G.H. Mead's 'I' (1934). For Erikson, human creativity is intelligible in terms of the raw materials out of which human beings make

themselves and the psycho-dynamics of the process of making themselves.

### Difficulties and contributions of psycho-history

I want now to come back to some problems of the method of
psycho-history. Beginning with Freud, the psychoanalyst delving into
history has built intricate and grandiose interpretations on flimsy
evidence. In his study of Leonardo, Freud built much upon a
mistranslated word, and, as Peter Gay points out, made much of the
appearance of Saint Anne in Leonardo's painting of the Virgin with
mother and child, doing 'less than justice to the artistic convention of
blooming Saint Annes available in Leonardo's time' (Gay, 1985: 182).
Similarly, Erikson's study of Luther lays great emphasis on episodes
that might have no historical reality. The problem of evidence which
can be dealt with in therapy where the internal world of the patient is
the main focus, cannot be dealt with in history, where the internal
world of the subject is not available. This leaves psycho-history as a
rather shaky form of history.

Paul Roazen (1976), discussing Erikson's work, accuses him of
being a myth-maker. Many conventional historians would agree. This
is precisely what I think he has to contribute. Erikson is concerned
with mythology, the way in which great men – and he does seem to be
concerned with men – become great or, more accurately, effective
leaders. This often, according to Erikson, seems to be a matter of their
ability to create a myth. For example, in his study of Hitler, the way in
which a 'legend' of the dictator's childhood developed and satisfied
widespread needs is central. Erikson directs attention to the historical
moment, the needs and problems shared in common by a particular
group of people at a particular time. Although social structure is very
much a background matter, he does make links between structure and
personality via family structure and the role of the father, as we shall
see in the next chapter, a common focus of psychoanalytic social
analysis:

> The other Western nations had their democratic revolutions. They, as Max
> Weber demonstrated, by gradually taking over the privileges of their
> aristocratic classes, had thereby identified with aristocratic ideals . . .
> This . . . was fused with revolutionary ideals and created the concept of
> 'free man' – a concept which assumes inalienable rights, indispensable
> self-denial, and unceasing revolutionary watchfulness . . . The German
> identity never quite incorporated such imagery to the extent necessary to

influence the unconscious modes of education. The average German
father's dominance and harshness was not blended with the tenderness and
dignity which comes from participating in an integrating cause. Rather, the
average father, either habitually or at decisive moments, came to represent
the habits and ethics of the German top-sergeant and petty official who . . .
would never be more but was in constant danger of becoming something
less; and who had sold the birthright of a free man for an official title or a
life pension. (Erikson, 1977: 300–1)

The links that Erikson then makes move through the internal and
external adolescent conflicts that occur in such situations. Hitler's own
real childhood and youth, and the way in which Hitler was able to map
these conflicts on to national and international politics, creating in the
process his own myth. We can see here, although I am reluctant to talk
about 'greatness' in Hitler's case, the way in which Erikson conceives
of greatness: the ego-strength to transform neuroses from crippling
individual inhibitions into a solution or attempted solutions for all. In
his study of Luther, he talks about the ability to move from individual
to universal patienthood.

Thus we create myths of and for ourselves. We build up stories
about ourselves and part of the material we use for that is our
identification not only with real people, but with phantasies gained
from fiction and politics and history. We internalise the figures from
our cultural surroundings and construct a history for ourselves which
often goes beyond the facts of our existence. Perhaps the simplest
example of this is adolescent identification with a pop-star, or some
such figure. I can remember being torn between Trotsky, Lord Byron,
Jack Kerouac and Mick Jagger, which provided the ground for some
very erratic and appropriately self-indulgent behaviour, but also for a
way of looking at the world which, although largely modified, has
endured and proved useful: a way of making sense when perhaps the
truth or reality is unreachable or too painful, and perhaps a means to
change the world. My adolescent myth, for example, enabled me to
start a sex-life. Myth can help us through from day to day without
sense collapsing; and the study of the way others have made their
myths might be in part history but is also in part art, through which we can
gain and grow as we might from reading a novel or the Bible or poetry.

Identity, then, is in part myth, constructed out of the social,
psychological and somatic levels of our life; this approach offers a way
into the issue of creativity. The issue goes beyond this, however, for
when we study the myths of others, we are creating myths for
ourselves. Much psycho-historical work can be seen less as history

than as part of a collective attempt to understand ourselves and make something new of our problems. Erikson's comments here point to a vital contribution of psychoanalysis.

## The social analyst as psychoanalyst

To begin with, he is concerned with the fact that historians – and sociologists, one might add – work with an implicit psychology of some sort, even if they never talk about it. It is necessary and unavoidable if we are saying anything about human life. It is only a short step from here to thinking about other things that the social scientist brings to his or her subject-matter. In sociology this has frequently been discussed in terms of values and value-freedom. The very fact of being a sociologist involves a commitment to a range of values: the importance of the discipline, the power of rational (or other) forms of explanation, the values of academic work: scholarship, disinterest, and so on. Some people have been able to recognise that there is something personal in the choice of what we study, whether it be political concerns or some aspect of personality. It is also recognised, but not often explored, that we do make psychological and philosophical assumptions in our work. Psychoanalysis brings an extra dimension to all of this: we bring our own internal conflicts, with all the feelings that they involve, and project them on to what we study.

In psychoanalytic practice this is known as counter-transference. Generally, the term is used to cover any or all of three different but interelated phenomena. The first and most prominent in the literature is the therapist's unconscious response to the client's transference. It is a difficult task for the therapist to distinguish between his or her own feelings and those which respond directly to and say something about the patient. It might be easier to understand by comparing counter-transference inside and outside of the analytic situation. In teaching, as in therapy, it is common for the student (or patient) to experience a dependent need for the teacher/therapist. In the teaching situation, it is fairly easy to see two reactions. The teacher can experience the need as confirming that she or he is worthwhile and wanted, liked, and respected: the student will be given everything that is asked for: information, help, tolerance, even indulgence. The student will find it difficult to do anything on his or her own account and will feel a sense of gratitude and honour which will confirm and meet the teacher's need. Alternatively, the teacher might feel afraid of the need, afraid of being drawn into the student's life, and will keep him or her at arm's length, sometimes with barely concealed hostility. The student is likely to respond by feeling even more inadequate. In both cases the teacher will be conscious of this either in the warm feelings of 'being a good teacher' or angry feelings at 'these bloody students', but will not be conscious of his or her own needs, desires and fears about being needed and the way in which they respond to the student's feelings. Similar reactions might occur in the therapeutic situation. The therapist who is aware that he or she has become a therapist perhaps in part through the desire to be needed, or perhaps even to avoid the occurrence of being needed in the real world (the 'therapeutic attitude' can be a wonderful defence), should be able to watch these reactions and understand what they say about the patient's unconscious feelings. It is more difficult for the teacher who is unlikely to have had any training in understanding emotional life.

The second meaning of counter-transference is the direct opposite of transference. In the latter the patient brings unresolved conflicts and very intense feelings to the analytic situation, where they are focused on the analyst. In counter-transference the analyst brings his or her unresolved conflicts and focuses them on a patient. It might be, for example, that my reaction to a particular woman in late middle age reproduces my reaction to my mother, and that quite unconsciously in my interpretations I reproduce my feelings about my mother and the way in which she behaves. Again, teachers frequently do this: treating their students as if they were themselves at an earlier stage of development, identifying with some, reacting against others. Part of the function of a training analysis is to reduce this level of counter-transference. The third level is the broadest: it includes everything in the analyst's personality that might affect the treatment. The tendency of analysts is to remain as anonymous as possible, not only in terms of not talking about him- or herself but also in dress and decoration.

Now all these levels are at work in the social scientist, whether historian or sociologist. In the case of the latter they can be as direct as my earlier example: the empirical sociologist does come face to face with the people he or she is studying, and that is a transference situation for all participants. But often it is the raw material, not people but data or ideas, that play a role equivalent to that of the patient. The way we see this inanimate matter can be as much a result of projection as our perceptions of other people. Elsewhere, I have tried to show how certain unconscious phantasies and desires, usually narcissistic, can be expressed and 'acted out' in theoretical writing, affecting the way the social world is conceived and portrayed. I suggested that the counter-balance to this is to keep an 'openness' to the world, a realisation that no approach is thoroughly confirmed by evidence, that there are always likely to be instances which do not fit the theory; that it is unlikely that we shall ever understand everything; that the world is, in fact, quite a complex place with many interacting causal processes, and perhaps, too, some processes that cannot be conceived in terms of cause at all. It might be that this too is a product of counter-transference, a use of the defence of confusion. It is all so difficult that I cannot say anything conclusive at all, thereby avoiding committing myself to the possibility of being shown to be wrong.

The 'antidote' to counter-transference is not an obsessive concern with one's own motives, but rather watchfulness, and as far as possible an openness and an awareness of the meaning of what one is doing or seeing. In the case of this book, for example, it follows a pattern of my inner world and of my ideas in the area of social theory. The move is from an omnipotent and obsessive concern with totalising theory to a sense of the fragmentation of the theory to a sense of being able to achieve some balance between fragments: this last concern basically is what the book is about. In my personal development, the nature of my inner world, there is the parallel move from a need to be in charge of everything through the chaos of the collapse of that need to what, at the moment, feels a greater sense of balance.

It is this sort of issue that Erikson draws attention to: not so much the irrationality of the social life we are studying but the irrationality of the student: 'psychological discovery is accompanied by some irrational involvement of the observer, and that it cannot be communicated to another without a certain irrational involvement of both' (Erikson, 1974: 36).

Perhaps paradoxically, given Erikson's involvement with ego-psychology and his tendency to underestimate the role of the unconscious and instinct theory, he does draw attention to the irrationality of the observer in a way that no theorist considered so far has done. It is this, and his embracing of his own experience through his psycho-historical work, that lays him open to Paul Roazen's charge that he is as much a mythologist as an historian. He raises the possibility that we are all as much mythologists as whatever else we are. This, however, does not prevent us from being other things – sociologists, historians, etc. – as well, any more than the fact that a psychoanalyst as a human being prevents him or her from being a psychoanalyst. And if myths are as useful as I have claimed, we are not only right to be, in some of our work, myth-makers; we ought to set about being good myth-makers.

# 6

## FATHERS AND THE RATIONAL SOCIETY

The theorists I shall be dealing with in this chapter are all concerned, explicitly or implicitly, with the idea of a rational society as a possibility and as a standard against which present society may be measured and criticised – hence the label 'critical theory'. By direct relationship, descent or theoretical concerns, they come from the same stable as Marcuse: the Frankfurt School of Social Research, founded in the late 1920s. Their employment of psychoanalysis is different from that of Marcuse. I shall begin by discussing the work of Habermas, a contemporary writer, since it seems to me that we can find there the clearest concept of the organisation of a rational society. I shall then return to Marcuse's contemporaries, Adorno and Horkheimer, and conclude with a discussion of the work of Lasch, a modern American writer whose ideas fit fairly neatly into this approach.

I have presented psychoanalysis as dealing with the irrational aspects of human life, yet one often finds Freud referred to as a rationalist: the aim of treatment is to release the patient from the force of his or her unconscious and enable the conscious control of actions: 'Where id was, there ego shall be.' In this respect, the analyst represents the often still small voice of reason, pointing out to the patient, at well-chosen moments, what is happening, what he or she is doing, helping to interpret his or her unconscious back to the patient. The difficulty with this becomes clear if one thinks about the use of reason in everyday life: most people are open to persuasion, and occasionally the power of reason asserts itself, but often apparent rational conversion depends upon non-rational conditions. If it were simply a matter of rational argument, there would be no prejudice, no wilful ignorance, no angry or violent political debate, and a large part of psychiatric treatment would be a matter of explanation and persuasion rather than drugs, electric shocks and operations. There would not necessarily be universal consensus either. There would be calm discussion and weighing of the arguments. We would simply have to be told the truth to act on it. Yet most people have direct experience of knowing something about themselves or about the world, but of being unable to act on it, accept it or change their behaviour.

Freud was aware that rational argument is not enough, despite the fact that he often spoke of treatment in this way. In the course of his work, he developed an idea which took account of all the non-rational conditions for a treatment to be successful: transference. The patient brings to the analytic situation a range of feelings about past relations, usually the most important being from relationships with parents. These feelings are then projected on to the analyst. We all do this in our lives as a matter of course. The mysterious business of falling in love usually involves the transference of very intense past feelings on to a new object, and indeed many people describe their feelings for their psychoanalyst in terms of love. In the outside world, people respond to these feelings and we have a remarkable knack of choosing to fall in love with people who will react, at least to begin with, in the way we desire. In the consulting room, the analyst remains anonymous, apparently detached, often silent. The transference of feelings, instead of being absorbed and hidden in the relationship, is drawn out and becomes the focus of the analytic work, and the treatment proceeds through working with the transference feelings. The victory of the rational depends upon and is made possible by the irrationality of the patient's reactions and the 'therapeutic alliance' between the analyst and the already mature, rational part of the patient's ego. The point of this argument is that the victory of the rational is not simply a rational victory, that it deploys the irrational in a particularly effective way.

## HABERMAS AND RATIONALITY

Habermas is a present-day representative of the Frankfurt School; I am looking at him first because the tendencies I am criticising are set out most clearly in his work. His concern is with the human ability to act rationally, to make choices, relate means to ends and control behaviour, and with the social conditions that make this possible. We are prohibited from rational action by a range of external, social and internal psychological conditions in which we have to operate. We can look at history as a movement towards, or as an attempt to achieve, a rational society. Such a society presupposes conditions of social and economic equality, and also equality in terms of access to knowledge and means of thinking, and of access to opportunities of participation in collective rational debate. It requires that people become able to recognise their wants and needs, express them in a way that can be understood, and be able to understand others. If these conditions do not exist, then we are dealing with a situation of 'distorted communication'. It is a conception of rationality that presupposes autonomous individuals, able to co-operate with each other. In this respect, psychoanalysis is of interest to Habermas in two ways.

### Repression and evolution

In the first place, Freud's insights into social organisation provide a way of understanding social development and criticising current forms of society. Like Marcuse and Mitchell, Habermas points out that the general processes dealt with by Freud may have different historical and social manifestations. In particular, the level of instinctual renunciation and repression may vary from society to society. However, as production increases, as we become more and more able to remedy scarcity, more gratification and less repression becomes possible. This does not happen automatically, nor does he see it as leading to a polymorphously perverse Utopia. Social institutions pass on an inherited repression which we each adopt and make our own as we become members of these institutions. As we do so, usually unconsciously, we adopt as well the control mechanisms which appear in individuals as neuroses and in social organisations as distorted communication. Indeed, it seems to me that one way of looking at a neurosis is as a distorted communication with oneself: when I light yet another cigarette or grab another handful of biscuits, I am telling myself in an inefficient and distorted way that I am anxious and in need of comfort.

As with most Marxists who turn to Freud, Habermas is interested in developing a theory of ideology that does more than relate ideas to simple economic interest or position in the class structure. In this respect, ideology can be understood as distorted communication stemming from unnecessary repression of instinctual gratification. Although this will vary from society to society and from class to class in the same society, it is not directly dependent upon economic structure.

Like Marcuse, Habermas uses the idea of the identity of ontogeny and phylogeny, but in a more modest way. In some ways very much like Parsons he develops an evolutionary theory. He is an inveterate classifier, and his most common classification is into three, in this case three evolutionary stages. The central principle of evolution is the movement from the specific and the situationally limited to the universal. Freud's account of individual development through the oedipal stage into maturity can be seen in these terms: the infant begins in a symbiotic state of unity with the mother, moves to individuation through the oedipal stage, submitting to the power of the father, and as he or she reaches maturity, develops an autonomous moral system which frees the self from parental power. There are several aspects of social development where a similar evolution can be found: the evolution of world-views, general ways of conceiving and understanding the world, from the primitive animistic-magical conception to the modern rational universal conception; the formation of social identity from the basis of the natural through social role to the rational capacity for constructing identity from the raw material of a number of roles; and the evolution of law and morality from a system based on the immediate consequences of an action through a normative system based on social role to a system based on universal principles. Habermas's schemes are much more complex than the crude outline I have given here, and are full of reservations. All I am trying to do here is give a general idea of what he is up to. In his employment of Freud's ideas, he is truer to the original than Parsons, but the drift is towards the resolution of conflict via social development, rather than the persistence of conflict as a necessary condition of life. Again, the framework is far too general to make sense of individual ways of coping with the same situation.

### *Psychoanalysis as an emancipatory science*

In the second place, and more importantly, psychoanalysis is an example of what Habermas calls an 'emancipatory science', a science that enables the release of humans from irrational and unknown forces. Here, there is yet another threefold classification. Human beings are seen as motivated by three cognitive 'interests' or reasons for seeking knowledge: a practical interest in the mastery of nature, the overcoming of scarcity, which leads to the development of the empirical-analytic sciences (roughly, what we call the natural sciences); an interest in communication, the ability to understand one another and co-operate in human enterprises, which leads to the interpretive or hermeneutic sciences (the social or human sciences); and finally an emancipatory interest, a concern to overcome the distorted communication which inhibits the development of free rational action, and this leads to the critical sciences. What marks off psychoanalysis, and the critical sciences in general, from the others is that while the first two groups involve a gap between knowledge and action, the critical sciences are a matter of self-reflection, bringing knowledge and action together. The act of knowing oneself, of discovering something new about oneself, is at the same time a change in oneself.

Habermas distinguishes between (inevitably) three levels of psychoanalytic theory, all of which are at work in the treatment. The first and most general comprises the basic concepts of the discipline, and this would, I imagine, include the structural conception of the psyche and instinct theory itself. At the second level, there are general theories of development, and at the third, the reconstruction of individual life-histories. The therapeutic treatment closes a gap between the patient's understanding of his or her history and his or her behaviour: the successfully treated patient will understand his or her actions in the same terms that explain them. Thus, for example, I might, prior to treatment, understand my passivity in terms of moral obligation and righteousness; for those around me I shall be a pain in the neck, a martyr. After treatment I might recognise my passivity as stemming from a previously unconscious and unrealistic fear and need, and my behaviour will change and my understanding will be, within limits, compatible with that of enlightened observers. The successfully treated patient no longer needs actions explained: he or she understands them. The proof of psychoanalysis lies in practice, but it involves the construction of causal explanations, employs dialogue and depth interpretation, and can be tested indirectly by looking at the accuracy of the reconstructed life-histories.

Throughout Habermas's account, the emphasis is on self-*knowledge*, for which the irrational experience of the transference is only a background. From my earlier account of Freud's conception of therapeutic treatment, it is clear that this is not sufficient. One can know oneself without undergoing any change in behaviour, or any consistent personality change at all. It is possible to collect self-knowledge *ad infinitum* without any significant change taking place.

In his distinction between the levels of psychoanalytic theory, there is an implicit recognition that as well as social and institutional variations in repression, there can also be individual variations. However, Habermas's interest in the structure of psychoanalytic theory as a critical science seems to carry elements of a rationalist Utopia. Here again, I want to make the same reservations about utopianism. It seems to me a necessary part of social theory, if theory is to point any way forward, to go beyond simple description and analysis.

I think that Habermas goes beyond the mark of a reasonable utopianism. He talks about psychoanalysis as if it were able to eliminate the irrational, as if working through the transference and counter-transference eliminated it. Some analysts might agree with him, but it is debatable and perhaps too little debated. For example, the difficulty in leaving an analyst can be immense, and analysts themselves have coped with it by becoming analysts – a full identification with the replacement parent (Malcolm, 1980). If we are to take Freud seriously, then it amounts to saying that any human bond raises problems of instinctual gratification, and carries echoes of earlier relationships, sometimes more, sometimes less intense. We do not, *nor can we*, become entirely rational beings; what we can do is limit the damage that our irrationality might cause and maximise the benefit.

By and large, Habermas focuses on the aspects of psychoanalysis that are most amenable to a rationalist interpretation. This always leads to difficulties. The life-history presented by a patient, for example, is and must be in part phantasy. This is something Freud himself discovered in his abandonment of his seduction theory. His first thoughts were that neuroses were the result of an act of infantile seduction, something we would now call child abuse, often but not necessarily incestuous. Such events were so often reported that he became suspicious and the suspicion led away from the seduction theory to his understanding of childhood sexuality, the oedipal complex and the rest of it. He came to understand the reports of incest as often involving childhood phantasies remembered as real events. This makes the reconstruction of a life-history problematic as scientific evidence but more importantly focuses attention on the patient's inner world; this world is not rational nor can it become so. Treatment in this respect is not a matter of getting rid of the irrational, but enabling the patient to recognise the difference between and the interrelation of reality and phantasy. This way of looking at it means that we can extend the scope of the rational without eliminating the irrational.

We need to take a further step before we can see the real difficulty: the irrational, our unconscious phantasy life – what later I shall consider in terms of our madness, our psychotic and depressive parts – are important constituents of our personality, the source of creativity, a fuel that can feed our rational selves. As Winnicott says: 'We are poor indeed if we are only sane' (1975: p.150). Even if we maintain the classic model of treating neuroses that Habermas uses, it is necessary to modify his argument. As Macklin (1976) points out, we can only talk about relative human freedom, ranging from the psychotic, who seems to be governed by very primitive unconscious processes through the neurotic, to what we might call a 'normal' range where we have more but not complete rational control over ourselves. To repeat: the irrational and its attendant conflicts cannot be eliminated: and I shall argue later, even if it can be tamed, this is not necessarily a good thing.

## THE FAMILY AND SOCIETY

Marcuse's contemporaries, Adorno and Horkheimer, look at the family structure as a mediation between the individual and society and centre on the role of the father. I shall concentrate on *The Authoritarian Personality*, with which Adorno's name is usually associated. The book was the result of the work of a number of scholars and part of a wider project involving many more. In the background, there is the familiar question: what is necessary, in addition to Marxist economic theory, to understand social development? Marxism is clearly not sufficient by itself. For German exiles during and after the Second World War, the crucial question was not only how Hitler came to power against the force of the German Communist Party, but also how he came to power with the support of many ex-socialists and communists. Practically everything about orthodox Marxist theory would deny such a possibility. The turn to psychoanalysis was to provide an explanation of what in many ways had been unthinkable.

Described by one modern critic as 'one of the most far-reaching studies ever conducted in social psychology', *The Authoritarian Personality* is a peculiar animal. An immense empirical work, it is associated with a source notorious for the abstraction and density of its theory. Typically, Adorno said that he did not regard the study as testing the underlying theory; rather, the theory was employed simply to generate questions and the studies should be judged in their own terms. This is fair enough, but it is the theory that I am most interested in here, rather than the empirical details of the study. Frankfurt School theory is always difficult. At its best it is difficult because of the level of abstraction, the complex theoretical arguments and the delicate relationship that Adorno in particular tries to maintain between style and content. Their philosophical work is interesting and often inspiring. I find their sociological work difficult for a different reason: its confusion and over-generalisation. They tend to move from the most abstract categories of thought to concrete social analysis with nothing in between, and not surprisingly, their philosophy has been more influential than their sociology. My guess is that they were bored by difficult empirical detail, the sentiment behind Adorno's statement, in a different context, that 'economics is no fun' – one has to make oneself an economist to understand it.

## The authoritarian personality

The sociological theory behind *The Authoritarian Personality* is, in its crudest form, that authoritarian personality structures are produced by authoritarian families, and in particular authoritarian fathers. The authoritarian personality itself involves a rigid adherence to conventional middle-class values; a tendency to a strong hostility towards people who do not conform; an uncritical submission to moral authorities; hostility to the imagination; a tendency to see things in rigid terms and hold mystical ideas about fate; an exaggerated concern with power and being tough; cynicism; and a tendency to believe that there are lots of dangerous and especially sexual things going on 'out there'. It is easy to see how this can be linked to childhood experience and the formation of the ego and super-ego on the one hand, and to social and political positions on the other. The rigid super-ego is the dominant part of the personality, holding down everything that might threaten it, and pushing – 'projecting' – on to other people many of these internally dangerous feelings. If a strong leader emerges who attacks a nonconformist or minority group, then the authoritarian personality must feel immense relief. It is no longer his duty to fight the evil around him single-handed; he can do so with others and under the protection of someone who is strong, authoritative and morally right. Another Hitler would obviously appeal to such a person, but in a less dramatic way, so would a Mrs Thatcher or President Reagan.

## The social determinants of the authoritarian personality

The most straightforward statement comes not from Adorno but from another member of the school, Max Horkheimer, who sees the bourgeois family as the source of authoritarianism; it exists to break the spirit of the child and substitute a compulsive obedience. *The Authoritarian Personality* goes into rather more detail about the process. The authoritarian personality structure is one way of resolving the oedipal conflict appropriate to a particular type of family background. The child is forced into behaving in a socially acceptable way; sexual love for the mother is tabooed and so is the reverse side of ambivalence.

The child is not allowed to hate his or her parents either. The enforcement of socially acceptable behaviour creates conditions which emphasise hatred. The father is strict, cold and often arbitrary in punishment. Whereas Horkheimer seemed to see this family type as near-universal in modern society, Adorno seemed to see it primarily as a feature of lower middle-class life, a result of the pressure on this stratum from both above and below, from a powerful industrial ruling class and a powerful organised working class. The decline in petty-bourgeois property relations, due to growth of large-scale industry, was matched by a decline in actual status, but no decline in the status aspired to. The adult male response in this situation is to see conformity (wrongly) as the way to status achievement and to see anything that threatens this conformity, including normal childlike behaviour, as a threat.

Socially, membership of this class involves a great deal of insecurity. We can go beyond this to the argument that the position of the father is systematically undermined in modern society. In the family, the father is a representative of society itself, he is expected to be firm, moral and consistent. In the outside world, he is stripped of his power in proportion to the growth of corporate power, stripped of the ability to make rational and moral choices in proportion to the growth of bureaucracy and the dominance of modern technology. We are left with the form of fatherhood – power and strength – without its content – morality and rationality. Discipline, therefore, becomes arbitrary and love difficult. Beyond this, the separation of home and work which comes with the growth of industry means that the father is absent from his children much of the day, so the son, in the process of growing up, does not have a whole person with whom to identify; he is left instead with a rather frightening stranger.

The child's reaction to this situation is to feel at least strong ambivalence, if not positive hatred. One of the defence mechanisms discussed by psychoanalysis is 'reaction-formation': Adorno argues that the child turns his ambivalence and hatred into love, the reverse of the dominant feeling. He feels love, but does not allow himself to feel or acknowledge hatred. One thing discovered by *The Authoritarian Personality* was that those with such a personality idealised their parents and were uncritical of their family. In fact, in clinical practice one of the surest signs of reaction-formation is an over-idealisation of a parent or spouse, and an uncritical acceptance of any situation. Interestingly – a point I shall elaborate later – the reality of the situation is that children with such backgrounds actually *feel* little strong attachment to their parents either way. The child is left with an over-strict and rigid super-ego, and is in a vital sense unintegrated: he has not been able to organise a range of positive and negative feelings into his personality.

### PSYCHOANALYSIS AS A BUILDING-BLOCK

In many ways, this is a powerful theory; however, it is too general and too exclusive. This is so in various ways. On the level of concrete social analysis, although in principle it offers a way of looking at the differences in family structure which result from class or other sources, the thrust of the whole approach is that there is a much more general tendency to authoritarianism in modern society. However, there is little attempt to look at the universality of the tendency or at ways in which it might be manifested differently at different social levels. In the writings of Horkheimer, it seems the assumption is that authoritarianism is built into the bourgeois family form *per se*. Even though it is in principle possible to employ the theory to look at different family structures, we are still left with the problem of understanding individual variations within the same social class.

Although it would be unfair to claim that Frankfurt theorists ignore the instincts, their role as a source of conflict, danger or liberation is secondary to the power of society: the authoritarian personality is a product of a particular type of society, as is the type of conflict involved in the personality. The implication is that the solution lies in the development of autonomous, rational people, which in turn would result from social change. The rational ideal is similar to Habermas's and to be achieved through the establishment of a different form of super-ego. The tendency is to use psychoanalysis as a building-block in the theory of socialisation; the intention is to explain a particular social phenomenon, and much that is important in psychoanalysis is overlooked. Again, this does not mean that the approach is useless. One way of making the link between the individual and society is through what goes on in the family, through the early processes of socialisation. The relationship between father and child is important for the development of the super-ego and again we find the link between state and the individual super-ego – the less-developed the latter, the stronger the former. The problem is that the socialisation process is only one half of what is going on, and the other half, the drive to instinctual gratification, persists. Generally, the sociologistic theories presuppose that this drive is overcome or tamed, that rationality or conformity or submissiveness triumphs.

## CHRISTOPHER LASCH AND NARCISSISM

I am considering Lasch here because he develops the themes of the Frankfurt School in what I believe to be an interesting and fruitful way, despite his over-generalisations and vast cultural surveys. He is important because while he maintains the sociological focus of Adorno and Horkheimer, and while I think this sociological focus eventually triumphs, he also maintains a notion of unconscious drives and necessary internal conflict. The result is that he produces what is arguably one of the most interesting and provocative exercises in social criticism in recent years.

It is convenient to start with his comments on *The Authoritarian Personality*. His basic argument is that the Frankfurt School's analysis of the authoritarian personality came at a point when that personality was ceasing to be useful to capitalism. In fact the history of the family in modern capitalist society is one of the decline of authoritarian rule by the father and a gradual restriction of the family's role, not only in the more obvious way such as the separation of work from the home and the development of state education systems, but also through the growth of the social services and what he refers to as the 'therapy-oriented' society. The recurring theme of such a society is that child-rearing is too serious a task to be left to parents, even in the earliest stages, that parents at least need to be trained and in some cases, perhaps, ought not to be allowed to raise children. The same social processes that I referred to in the discussion of Adorno have undermined not only the role of the father but also the role of the family as a whole. The over-strict, authoritarian super-ego identified by Adorno is a stage in the development which undermines rather than depends on the family:

> The bourgeois family, Horkheimer wrote in 1936, had the 'indispensable function of producing specific, authority-oriented types of character'. For this reason, totalitarian regimes stressed the sanctity of the family in their propaganda, and tried to shore it up by relieving it of some of its educational functions. In fact, the dependence of fascism on the family is purely rhetorical and sentimental . . . fascism rules not through conscience or guilt but through terror, psychological manipulation and a primitive loyalty to the blood brotherhood . . .
>
> The gradual erosion of authoritarianism and the authoritarian family,

which went on throughout the liberal phase of bourgeois society, has had an unexpected outcome: the re-establishment of a political despotism in a form based not on the family but on its dissolution. Instead of liberating the individual from external coercion, the decay of family life subjects him to new forms of domination, while at the same time weakening his ability to resist them.' (Lasch, 1977: 91)

Lasch's solution sometimes seems close to suggesting a return to the old-fashioned, strong, patriarchal, bourgeois father as the protector of freedom, but I am not sure that this necessarily follows from his argument. The idea that seems to lie behind his work, without being properly formulated in any one place, promises something new to the discussion. It is not the liberation of polymorphous perversity that we find in Marcuse, nor the sexual liberation of Reich. Indeed, he sees such tendencies as the product of a profound malaise in modern society. Nor is it the androgynous or bisexual individual that is perhaps implied by Mitchell – this too is a sign of the malaise (indeed, for me, one of the difficult things about Lasch is his apparent hostility to feminism). It does involve the free rational actor of the Frankfurt School, with an emphasis on morality, on a strength of personality which can resist outside pressures. The promise of a new contribution lies in the significant emphasis he gives to the ability to experience and cope with strong emotions, feelings of love and hatred, and to cope with the ambivalence that characterises human emotions, to make firm and lasting commitments to other human beings. The family is for Lasch the place where such a character structure can emerge. The family is not the simple mediation of the power of the wider society but can provide a bastion against that power.

For Lasch, the crucial point to emerge from *The Authoritarian Family*, but not noted by the authors, is implied by the finding that the authoritarian personality actually *experiences* no strong positive or negative parental ties. Horkheimer realised later that 'What they seem to suffer from is probably not too strong and sound a family but rather a lack of family' (Lasch, 1977: 92). Lasch cites more recent studies of 'schizogenic' families by Bateson and others, including R.D. Laing, to support his contention that it is the illusion of intimacy, the need the family feels to keep up a conventional front, rather than real (and very messy) intimacy that is the cause of difficulties. Concern with authoritarianism (Adorno), or with the isolation and claustrophobic structure of the nuclear family (Mitchell), hides the absence of real intimacy and its consequences for character structure. Real intimacy is seen as terrifying and to be avoided. At the same time, the decline of the family leaves primitive feelings close to the surface. The result is that the dominant personality structure of our age is not authoritarian but narcissistic.

## *The narcissistic personality*

Unlike the other thinkers considered so far, Lasch insists upon the importance of clinical evidence from psychoanalysis: since every society reproduces itself in the individual, we can discover the culture through the individual:

> Psychoanalysis best clarifies the connection between society and the individual, culture and personality, precisely when it confines itself to careful examination of individuals. It tells us most about society when it is least determined to do so. Freud's extrapolation of psychoanalytic principles into anthropology, history and biography can be safely ignored by the student of society, but his clinical investigations constitute a storehouse of indispensable ideas, once it is understood that the unconscious mind represents the modification of nature by culture, the imposition of civilisation on instinct. (Lasch, 1980: 77)

Modern psychoanalysis shows that attention has moved from Freud's concern with the id, and with the repression and sublimation of instincts through the oedipal period, to the self–not Erikson's steadily blossoming self, but the anxious, unhappy self. It could be argued that this is a development internal to psychoanalysis, that it is simply what psychoanalysts have become interested in. Lasch thinks it is more than this: he points to evidence that the people who have presented themselves for treatment over the last thirty to forty years are no longer the sort of patients that Freud saw, the obsessional and hysterical neurotics; rather they are people who are experiencing a generalised unhappiness, an obscure sense of discontent; they are frequently successful in the outside world, rather than inhibited and failing, and they have no clearly definable symptoms.

Lasch takes the description of 'pathological narcissism' as representing a 'heightened version of normality'. The narcissist tends to develop a careful protective shallowness, and has difficulty with intimate and deep relationships because they threaten to resurrect the immense, seemingly uncontrollable rage originally directed towards his or her parents. For that reason, the narcissist cannot mourn, since mourning involves rage against the lost object. Mourning, as we shall see when I discuss object-relations theory in more detail, enables the development of a more complex and rich inner-object world, and consequently the narcissist has to cope with an impoverished internal world, populated primarily by harsh, punitive parental figures or idealised, loving, parental figures. He or she tends to be sexually active rather than repressed, but promiscuous, using sexual contact to avoid intimate emotional contact and unable to treat sex as a form of play. As the good and bad figures in their inner world fight it out, they experience intense fluctuations in self-esteem. They tend to assume that they have a right to have their needs met, but also experience their needs as dangerous and deploy primitive defences against them. They conform through fear of punishment rather than the workings of conscience. The bad internal parental figures are often experienced by the narcissist as possible physical illness (the fear of any serious or fatal disease that cannot be easily identified serves this purpose: witness the example of people worried about AIDS who have not had sexual intercourse of any sort for a decade or more) and he or she is prone to hypochondria. There is an attraction to therapy which provides the narcissist with a series of insights which need have no effect on his or her behaviour. The modern cultural phenomenon of concern with health – the anti-smoking campaign, emphasis on exercise, health foods, etc. – and the popularity of 'easy answer' therapies can be seen as narcissistic symptoms.

As a patient the narcissist is a candidate for eternal analysis. Lasch quotes the analyst Herbert Rosenfeld to the effect that the narcissist 'often uses his intellectual insight to agree verbally with the analyst and recapitulates in his own words what has been analysed in previous sessions.' Lasch continues: 'He uses intellect in the service of evasion rather than self-discovery resorting to some of the same strategies of obfuscation that appear in the confessional writing of recent decades' (1980: 86). We can see here the problem with Habermas's idea that self-knowledge necessarily involves change.

Since the narcissist is unable to mourn, his or her inner world remains empty of a store of good experiences that can be drawn upon in bad or difficult times. There is no good past to make easier the process of ageing and approaching death. Both terrify the narcissist, who tries to maintain an illusion of eternal life.

### The culture of narcissism

In the wider culture, rather than in its pathological forms, narcissism involves a concern with appearances over everything else. Lasch develops an argument, just discussed in the work of David Reisman in the 1950s, that distinguished between the 'inner-directed' and the 'outer-directed' personality. The former is the personality centred on an internal moral code and operating with a sense of right and wrong and a conscience. The latter is concerned with success in the eyes of others. One aspect that Lasch identifies in the narcissistic personality is that while there is an inability to form close relationships, there is a desire for parasitic relationships based on more or less intense admiration, feeding the all-powerful good self-images; such relationships cannot stand disillusion – in other words, they cannot withstand the arrival of reality. 'Appearances' amount to success, the avoidance of punishment, of being found out, above all, to *survival* in a world which is experienced as constantly hostile and threatening – and which, given the dominance of amoral self-seeking, often is really hostile and threatening. Morality is regarded with suspicion, distaste or even hostility; loyalty to people or to organisations is subordinated to the desire to use both for self-seeking purposes. There is a pessimism about the future, and no sense of an ability to risk anything by investing in the future, either in material form or in one's children. Parents tend to adopt an approach to their children that is both indulgent and abstentionist, at least as far as discipline and moral teaching is concerned. The aim of living becomes the immediate satisfaction of the internalised omnipotent good images.

## The psychological origins of narcissism

Lasch's argument is that narcissistic, borderline patients, people with 'personality disorders', are in fact the result of social changes; they represent the chronically unsatisfactory character best suited to survival in modern society. The social problem is now no longer the over-repression or too rigid repression of the instinctual drives, resulting from an over-strong father, but the failure of people to reach the state of repressing infantile drives; rather the drives are (quoting from Joel Kovel):

> stimulated and perverted and given neither an adequate object upon which to satisfy [themselves] nor coherent forms of control . . . The entire complex, played out in a setting of alienation rather than direct control, loses the classical form of symptom – and the classical therapeutic opportunity of simply restoring an impulse to consciousness. (Lasch, 1980: 90)

Lasch at this point draws on object-relations theory rather than instinct theory to elaborate his thesis, taking the basis of his argument in Freud and developing it through Klein and relying for his description of the modern narcissistic personality on Otto Kernberg, one of the two most innovative modern American psychoanalysts. Narcissism originates in the newborn infant's sense of being the centre of the world, satisfying its own needs through some magical extension of itself. When the baby is hungry and cries and is fed, he or she has no idea that what happens is that the mother hears the cry, responds with a mixture of anxiety and anger and exhaustion, getting out of bed, preparing herself or the bottle and delivering the food. For the baby, there is the crying and there is the food, and the one has produced the other. When as grown-ups we react to a difficult situation by throwing a tantrum, or engaging in extreme emotional behaviour, begging and pleading, we are reverting to that primitive feeling that if we cry or scream or feel long enough, we will get what we need.

As the baby develops, both psychologically and physically, he or she becomes aware of the separation, aware of its dependence on the outside world, and in particular on its mother. There is a loss, a loss of omnipotence, of a sense of identity with the loved object, and a rage against the loss, compounded by a rage against those who fail to satisfy the infant's demands immediately. 'Growing up' is, among other things, a long and painful process of accepting that others will not meet one's needs immediately. One way of responding to this, which we all do to some extent, is to create a phantasy parent who is ideal and all-powerful and who is merged with the child's own ego. The occasional feeling which most of us have that we can do everything, that the world is a good place made especially for us, and that there is no threat or danger worth worrying about, draws on the identification with a phantasised, all-powerful parent. Klein's contribution to this was to conceive of the child as reacting to a world of good and bad, and as having considerable difficulty in reconciling them; the most frequent and comforting way of coping with the world is to project the bad experiences outside and introject the good experiences. Phantasy images of the parents, particularly the mother, are equally split: there is the all-powerful, fierce, arbitrary and punitive parent, and the all-powerful, loving parent who responds immediately to and satisfies all needs. The narcissist grows up but at a fundamental level remains at this stage. In Part III, I shall be looking in more detail at the Kleinian theory that Lasch takes up. For the moment, I want to return to Lasch's analysis of the social-structural dynamics behind the dominance of narcissism, since his argument is that, in fact, this character-structure is best suited to deal with modern society.

## The social origins of narcissism

As a general overview, Lasch is describing a process by which the dominant ethic of industrialisation, the Protestant work ethic, has been consistently undermined by the development of capitalism. This takes up a theme already present in the work of Marcuse and elsewhere: the necessity for less repression in advanced industrial society. The lowering of repression, as it were, involves the 'return of the repressed', the emergence of polymorphous desires and a cultural regression to the stages of early infancy, with anything but the Utopian results wanted by Marcuse. The crucial social process is what Lasch calls the 'socialisation of reproduction', the taking over by the state in various forms the work previously, and usually, according to him, better fulfilled by the family. Most important is the absence of the father, who no longer has anything to teach his children, particularly his sons. The speed of technological and the resulting cultural change means that paternal skills become outmoded during the father's own life, well before his son could employ them; and the parents' way of life appears outdated and often irrelevant by the time children reach their teenage years. In such conditions, there is no possibility of the development of a firm and rational super-ego, and an ego strong enough to withstand the powerful emotions involved in intimacy. The shallowness of children's feelings for their parents provides the basis for a lifetime of shallowness, the best way to survive in modern society.

There is much in Lasch which I think enables a development of the argument I began in the discussion of Juliet Mitchell's work. To draw this out, I want to defend Lasch against some of his feminist and radical critics.

## Lasch and feminism

Lasch is clearly hostile to much, if not all, of modern feminism, which he sees as returning to pre-oedipal narcissism in its concerns and prescriptions. He also sees himself as of the left, although much of what he says concerns the individual and individual responsibility. The feminist and left reaction is summed up in a discussion in Barrett and McIntosh's *Anti-Social Family*. There is a maze of issues, and I shall concentrate on those I think most central. I ought to say at the start that I disagree with much of what Lasch has to say about feminism, and that I am content to think of him in that respect as simply losing a sense of perspective in his polemics. It is an annoying habit but does have the advantage of stimulating thought. In fact, I would argue that perhaps modern feminist theory has much to say about the productive handling of pre-oedipal material that he cannot seem to approach.

His tendency to over-generalisation is, in fact, one of the issues I want to explore. In terms of empirical correctness, it leaves him open to all sorts of criticism. Barrett and McIntosh point out that he does not, and by implication could not, substantiate a claim he makes about the emotional content of the pre-capitalist family; more importantly, he sets up as an ideal a patriarchal bourgeois family which, if it existed at all, had only a very limited social and historical existence and perhaps was not that ideal at all. It seems to me that we can accept this criticism, but what matters is that he offers us a way of thinking about how families *should* work if they are to produce responsible adults. I shall explore this in greater detail shortly.

Barrett and McIntosh make much of Lasch's implication that we need a return to the bourgeois family (disparaging a suggestion that he makes about the need to explore other communal forms of child-rearing), his apparent sympathy for religion and his attack on the authoritarian nature of the welfare state – their arguments resonating with the dominant socialist concerns of this century. They point out that, for example (quoting Eli Zaretsky), the welfare state has not only been a source of increasing social control in the capitalist state, but has also been a victory of working-class struggle, improving working conditions generally. This is true, but it does not follow that because it has been the result of working-class struggle it is necessarily anything other than what Lasch says it is. The important questions are about who controls the welfare state, its immense bureaucratic and pro-fessionally-based organisation and its connections to the people it is supposed to serve. It would be possible to go as far as to say that if working-class families were being stripped of their abilities to raise their children properly, it makes sense for them to struggle for the introduction of agencies that would appear to do it better; this does not mean that it is a desirable thing.

I think that what emerges at the centre of all this, however, are the issues of authority and suffering and morality. Lasch is saying that suffering is part of being human; his critics take that as being in favour of suffering. He is saying that there is a place for authority, and is concerned with the psychological preconditions for the rational exer-cise and control of authority; he seems to be taken as justifying any sort of irrational authority that has existed in history. He is concerned, too, with looking at the role of morality in containing and perhaps sublimating our instinctual and essentially selfish drives, and the battles that must be pursued if this is to be achieved. Religion, he implies, at least recognises that such a struggle must exist. If such a struggle exists, then there is a place for individual responsibility and morality. Barrett and McIntosh seem to read him as supporting the most irrational forms of religious tyranny. In this sense, the left's reaction can itself be seen as a narcissistic symptom, a denial of suffering and struggle and the need for compromise if any real improvement is to take place. In practice, it seems to me that the modern left cannot actually speak to the suffering with which psycho-analysis is concerned, the frustration of our strongest feelings, our need for love, our inner struggle with what we can recognise at some level as our destructiveness, and the feelings of our connection with other human beings which some people understand through religion. The left offers social diagnoses and social cures, with most of which I usually agree; and there is no doubt that a better society would eliminate much unnecessary suffering. However, we would remain inadequate, weak, destructive and greedy as well as all the other good things that we are, and we would still have to die; in other words, we would remain unhappy much of the time, subjected to conflicts and misery. If psychoanalysis is interesting to sociology because it can take us to the irrational which everybody knows exists but which sociolo-gists generally do not talk about, it is important for socialists because it takes us to the suffering that we would like to blame on things outside of us; that is what makes Lasch's work so difficult for the left.

## Patriarchy

Critics seem to assume that Lasch is in favour of patriarchy, the rule of men. This is understandable. There is an implication that what we need is a return to a particular type of male dominance in the family. However, there is a different way of taking what he has to say. This involves drawing the distinction I suggested earlier between patriarchy in the sense of a male-dominated society and patriarchy referring to the role of the father during the oedipal stage. It is conceivable that the father's role during the oedipal stage need not be reproduced as part of a social system. The role of the father in the family provides the means by which people gain the ability both to accept legitimate authority, and the ability to be critical of and challenge authority. In other words, it is the means by which we become able to participate in a free society. The fact that this ability originates in the father's power does not mean that it has to be continued in the form of male power in society at large. All that continues is the ability to recognise and criticise authority. Lasch argues that the violence that seems to pervade family life and is aimed mainly against women and children and the social oppression of women, is a result not of patriarchy, but of the breakdown of patriarchy, just as social unrest does not result *per se* from the existence of authority relations in society but from the breakdown of authority relations. Speculating on Lasch's behalf, perhaps this could be seen as pointing to a society in which there are different spheres of authority but no hierarchy, so that patriarchy, as it is conceived in psychoanalytic theory, can exist within a situation of general sexual equality, as a relation confined to fathers and children. In an interview, arguing against Weber and some feminist writers, Lasch claims that Protestantism presents a version of authority that has distinct feminine aspects and is, in fact, inimical to the development of capitalism. This version of authority, he seems to think, is perhaps closer to what he desires. Political and industrial authority, on the other hand, he argues, does not stem from rational authority, of the sort implicit in Protestantism, but rather from the charismatic authority appropriate to military and monastic life.

These remarks, together with my comments on penis envy, are in part speculation: that we can use Freud's work to develop a conception of maturity that does not involve male dominance. They are partly based on a sense of what clinical practice aims at: a recognition of unpleasant feelings and an ability to tolerate them rather than turn them into actions. If male dominance in society is related to the oedipal stage, then it is as a pathological continuation of what really belongs to childhood.

### *The disappearance of the instincts*

I now want to embark on the opposite argument: that we cannot eliminate the irrational from our lives or from our society. This is the argument that places Lasch in the same context as the other thinkers in this chapter and this part of the book. In Lasch's case it is a softer form of the criticism, for he recognises Freud's crucial insight into instinctual conflict and maintains an important place for the passions of love and hate. However, the implication seems to be that once we learn to handle these in the family and other institutions, the social becomes the main determinant, and indeed it is society that makes it possible or impossible to do this in the first place. He also works at a level of generality that makes it difficult to be anything but sociologistic. His implication is that there is a solution, and it is a social one. Yet what emerges from the clinical evidence of psychoanalysis is the immense complexity of the individual psyche, as well as the shared common human features. This is not just a matter of the difficult mixture of masculine and feminine in each of us, but also of the various dimensions of neurosis and psychosis in each of us. There is not just conflict between civilisation and instincts; there is a conflict within each of us. With Lasch, as with Adorno, the individual is formed by society, and individual unhappinesses are eventually a product of society. Yet if within each of us there remains a specific version of that general conflict, the forms of our unhappiness, the resolutions that we attempt, will not be formed by society, neither will they be the direct product of instinctual satisfaction, but they will result from the specific dimensions and nature of the conflict and our creative ability to deal with it. In a paradoxical way, the fact that we are subject to an inner conflict which gives very specific meanings to the wider conflict sets us free of the things that drive us and oppress us.

There are perhaps a number of different ways in which pre-oedipal material can be dealt with: Lasch's concern with the father leaves him, as I said earlier, implying that we must return to a better form of the past. I have suggested that an alternative might involve conceiving of a patriarchy that dissolves itself in maturity: a father who does not impose rigid instinctual repression and the generation of the sort of neuroses that Freud had to treat. It might also be within the schema that perhaps pre-oedipal desires may remain into mature life and find different forms of sublimation. In fact, of course, like everything else from infancy and childhood, these things continue into adult life in modified, sublimated forms which need not reproduce the features of the childhood experience, just as I argued earlier that the experience of penis envy might remain, for both sexes, transformed into socially useful desires. Beyond even this, perhaps, these primitive infantile feelings, from whatever period of development, need to reassert themselves for new transformations to take place – it is necessary for the irrational to break out in new ways and at different times. Before developing this argument further, however, we need a rather fuller understanding of what goes on during this pre-oedipal period. Object-relations theory does supply this fuller understanding and I suspect that is why Lasch eventually turns to it.

# 7

## THE UNCONSCIOUS AND LANGUAGE

If British psychoanalysis is object-relations theory, and American psychoanalysis has been dominated by ego-psychology, then modern French psychoanalysis has been dominated by one figure: Jacques Lacan.

On the face of it, Lacan belongs to Part I; he has stood more than anything else for a return to the original work of Freud, the fundamental importance of the unconscious and its irrationality and the inadequacy of the traditional rationalist conception of the human being. I shall argue, however, that his return to Freud leads to a paradoxical inversion of his original stated intention. We end with a psychoanalytic theory which essentially conceives of people as the product of their social environment, that environment being conceived of in terms of language and discourse.

It is tempting, but not really appropriate, to go into the philosophical background of Lacan's work in some detail. The most important influence has been structuralist and post-structuralist philosophy, to which he is a major contributor. It has been taken up, paradoxically again, in the light of his adherence to the orthodox Freudian conception of the oedipal complex and the significance of the phallus, by modern feminist theory. His work was an influence on Juliet Mitchell. By way of an introduction, I shall pick out some central ideas from structural linguistics since Lacan models his conception of the psyche on language. Psychoanalysis has long been known as 'the talking cure', and while this manages to be true and not true at the same time, the nature of language is something which faces every practising analyst in both theory and practice.

### STRUCTURAL LINGUISTICS

Structural linguistics originated in the work of Ferdinand de Saussure;

there are plenty of good accounts available and here I am only going to discuss a few ideas central to Lacan's work.

## Speech and language

Saussure distinguished between speech and language. Speech is what we say, and everything we say is unique in some way. It cannot, therefore, be the object of scientific knowledge, which deals with things that are common to different situations. The language is an underlying structure, consisting of 'signs' and rules which govern the combination of sounds. By using this battery of signs and rules, we can produce our statements. There are several implications to this: the first is that time or history is a surface phenomenon; the underlying structure of a language does change, but very slowly. More rapid changes in speech can be accounted for by the rules that exist, unchanging, on the underlying level. The second is a change in how we think of the speaker. Traditional rationalist conceptions view the person, the ego or the self as a 'subject', an originator of action. *I* decide what to say and when to say it. From Saussure we gain a conception of the 'subject' as something or somebody who only exists in the framework of the language, whose utterances and thoughts are the product of the language to which they are 'subjected'. It was for a while fashionable to talk of people 'being spoken', rather than of people speaking. In psychoanalysis, the unconscious can be seen as the underlying structure, of which our conscious thoughts and actions are the product. Rather like the language, the unconscious for Freud is timeless, and it is not governed by logic.

## The sign

In describing the language, the concept of a sign is the constant and most important theme in Saussure's work. A sign is seen as a combination of a 'signifier' and a 'signified'. The former, the signifier, is the material element, if we are speaking it is the sound (not the meaning) or if we are writing it is the marks on the paper; the signified is the idea to which the sounds become attached. A language is a structure of signs and rules that governs their combination with each other. Note that the signified is the idea and not the thing that the sign refers to. In common sense we often tend to think of words as somehow inextricably attached to things: we cannot think of a table without seeing the object in front of us. With some thought, however, it becomes clear that, at least on those occasions when we do not have a table in front of us, the word carries the idea of the table rather than a thing in itself. We cannot eat our lunch off the concept of a table. There is no *necessary* connection between a word and a thing: we could call tables tulips and tulips tables and nothing would change in the world; gardens and living rooms remain the same. Another way of saying this is that signs are 'conventional'. A matter of agreement. We agree that on the road a red traffic light means 'stop' and green 'go': it could as well be the other way round, and the same is true of linguistic signs. The meaning of each sign is further defined by its relation to other signs: red, amber and green form a system in which each colour takes its meaning from the others. In another system, say on a snooker table, the colour red has another meaning. Lacan's way of making this point is with a drawing of two identical doors, but one has a man drawn on it, the other a woman. The difference of a few lines in the drawing gives a different meaning to each door.

Lacan emphasises the signifier – it is change in the signifier that produces a change in the signified. The end-result is a conception of the world as governed or determined by language, by signifiers. Lacan, in common with many literary critics influenced by structuralism and post-structuralism, emphasises the importance of two familiar figures of speech: metonymy and metaphor. Metonymy involves using a part to represent a whole: we might say a factory has 500 hands when we mean 500 workers. Metaphor is describing one thing in terms of another, for example, to describe life as a journey. I am not clear about this interpretation of Saussure, but I find the idea of metaphor most useful: we do not have access to something we call reality, only to the sign, or rather, for Lacan, the signifiers: language is a metaphor for reality. We live in a world of metaphors, constantly being referred from one to the other.

## PSYCHOANALYTIC THEORY AND DREAMING

One essential part of Freud's work is his analysis of dreams – 'the royal road to the unconscious'. I am introducing it here because the linguistic ideas I have been discussing can act as a metaphor for the workings of the psyche and this is best seen in Freud's analysis of dreams. For Lacan, the unconscious is governed by metaphor and metonymy.

In sleep the protective defences we erect in our waking lives are relaxed and unconscious thoughts come closer to the surface. Some defences remain, and therefore dreams are not the direct expression of unconscious ideas; rather, they are disguised in a process that Freud refers to as dream-work. There are a number of aspects to dream-work. The first is the process of symbolisation: we do not dream ideas, we dream pictures and sometimes words. An idea has to be symbolised, represented somehow. Freud gives numerous examples in *The Interpretation of Dreams*. A favourite from my own dreaming involved a swimming pool into which a colleague (Ken Plummer) dived to take out the plug. There was a variety of associations here, but one important aspect was the representation of the idea of a plumber, of somebody whose job it is to deal with things like plugs, being symbolised in the person of a man called Plummer. Another dream reported to me involved the dreamer laying a table with knives and forks that had no handles: she was afraid that she could not handle a particular situation.

The two central aspects of dream-work Freud called 'condensation' and 'displacement', directly comparable to metonymy and metaphor. Condensation is the process of combining several, perhaps many, unconscious ideas into one dream symbol. During the British election in 1983, I dreamt that I was assassinating Michael Foot, then leader of the Labour Party. Foot in that context not only stood for a politics that was, consciously, making me angry, but also represented in myself something old and rather threatening, a loss of power, an inability to use power or to gain power – a range of feelings and ideas about power, and beyond that he was also a father figure. Displacement involves moving away from a symbol that is too close to the original idea to one that is safely removed from it. I remember at one point it seemed safer for me to dream about a cat than about sex (it was some time before I realised that the connection was 'pussy'); or to dream about my wife in boots rather than some particular ruthlessness in myself. Displacement is the dream equivalent to metaphor, condensation to metonymy.

Finally, there is the process that Freud called 'secondary revision'. This is a sort of logical gloss we give to our dream images to form them into something like a story, rather than an irrational combination of symbols. All of these processes serve to hide the original unconscious idea. In waking life, the rational is usually dominant, but the psychoanalyst listens to the patient's talk as if it were metaphor or metonymy, Thus, when a patient talks to me at length about changes in the social security system and his worries about what will happen when he leaves college, I wonder if he is also saying something about his fear that I shall not give him enough to survive the forthcoming holiday. Similar processes to dreaming are going on here but they are much more carefully hidden.

For Lacan it is not that the unconscious works *like* language. It depends upon language and is actually constituted by language, by the child's entry into language. Before language there is no unconscious; hence psychoanalysis is the talking cure. Language literally creates our world for us. Whereas, perhaps, traditional idealism can be typified as maintaining that the world is a product of thought, for Lacan and post-structuralism generally the world and thought are a product of language. This is where the conventional nature of signs, and the lack of any necessary connection between signs and things is relevant: the things in our world are what they are because that is what we decide to call them. It seems to me that there is a truth in this but not the whole truth. When we learn a new subject, or become converted to a new set of beliefs, the world does change: for a Freudian, a man squeezing his blackheads is probably never again just a man squeezing his blackheads (although a cigar is sometimes just a cigar, because the master said so). I have argued elsewhere (Craib, 1984) that it does not follow that there is not a knowable, independent external world out there, full of things to which language refers despite – in fact, because of – its conventional nature. Because we decide that a table is a table, it does not follow that the object in front of me cannot be known and understood. The concept of a dog does not bark, but it does refer to certain hairy creatures who do. Lacan drops this reference to a real external world.

The child's entry into language is, then, for Lacan, the point at which the unconscious appears and the child becomes part of the human world proper. This involves what Freud would call the renunciation of instincts, Lacan the replacement of desire by 'demand', in which the word replaces the desired thing in the infant's psyche, becoming a substitute for a reality that can never be reached. He makes much of Freud's report of a game played by his nephew making objects appear and disappear and at the same time producing the German sounds *fort* and *da* – there it goes and here it is. I imagine that most people who have had regular contact with a young child will have played or witnessed such a game. Freud analysed it on a number of levels. Only one is important for Lacan: it is an instinctual renunciation, where the child gives up its desire for the constant presence of the object (mother) and replaces it with a word that s/he can keep all the time.

The entry into language carries with it a division, both within the child and between the child and the outside world and other people. Here the radical difference between Lacan and ego-psychology appears. The split within the child is between what for Freud is the ego and the id, for Lacan the part of ourselves that we experience as the speaking subject whom we present for others, and the true self, which remains unconscious. From Lacan's point of view, ego-psychology supports and strengthens a fundamental alienation from self, and works solely with the self-for-others; the true purpose of psychoanalysis is to work with the true self. Lacan is notoriously difficult to understand and he does not help matters by referring to this true self as the 'Other', always with a capital O.

There is a further split within the child in which what conventional psychoanalysis calls the 'ideal ego' develops. We have already come across the ideal ego in our discussion of Freud's work on group psychology. What Lacan offers is a sort of gloss on the idea, which at one level I find a useful analogy to capture a process, and on the other, a very inadequate summary of a complex and difficult process. The analogy involves the idea of the child looking into a mirror, and Lacan identifies what he calls a 'mirror-phase'. This actually precedes language acquisition, beginning at six to eight months, and is the time when a child learns to recognise its reflection in a mirror, to sort out the difference between the reflection and the reality, and the difference between his or her own image and that of other people. The important thing about it is that as the child recognises the image, s/he gains for the first time a sense of the totality of its body, and as it watches the reflection sees itself apparently in control of itself. Previously, it has experienced itself as a host of conflicting desires and unconnected or uncontrollable parts not properly distinguished from the world. Lacan puns on the French 'omelette' or 'hommelette', the little man who is also a scrambled bundle of desires.

This recognition begins a fundamental alienation, the phantasy attempt to identify with the image and be perfectly together and in control of oneself. Lacan talks of three realms or areas of existence. There is the 'Real' to which, in the last analysis, we do not have access as we never perceive it except through language; there is the 'Imaginary', which has to do with our phantasised identification with the perfect mirror-image, the ideal ego; and the 'Symbolic', the realm of maturity, which we enter into an appropriate language, surrendering the impossible desires that take us into the imaginary. To explain this surrender, Lacan relies, as did Freud, on the oedipal conflict, but he gives it a particular lingusitic twist. The father for Lacan is a symbolic figure, the representative of social rules; Lacan talks not about the real father but about 'The name of the father' and there is another French pun here between name, *nomme* and no, *non*. It is the father who as symbolic figure intervenes between the child and its mother. The child is forced to replace his desire for the mother by a symbol. For Lacan, even more than for Freud, the little boy's history is the essential model.


### LACAN'S CONTRADICTION

The central problem in Lacan's work, as I see it, is a confusing one to get across. What I want to argue is that while Lacan explicitly argues for a return to the original Freud and the central importance of the unconscious, against ego-psychology and its emphasis on social adjustment, in fact he constructs a theory which conceives of the individual as a social product at the most fundamental level and this is taken a step further by his followers.

Now there is in fact a sort of residual category which Lacan leaves to the individual, that of desire, but it is the desire for the impossible: for identity with the world and with the mother; this is the pre-social individual. The social individual, of whom the unconscious is one part, is entirely a product not of society as such but of the social artefact of language. It is language, or discourse, which constitutes the individual. The names we can give to desire are likewise the product of our language – the unsocial must always and by definition remain unknown and recognised only obliquely. Everything else is social, and everything social is linguistic, a product of language. Or perhaps, more accurately, everything else is linguistic, and the linguistic is social. Psychoanalysis is the talking cure. There are two reasons to dispute this, one is empirical, at least in the sense of clinical experience, the other theoretical, a problem with Lacan's argument.

The theoretical objection has to do with the concept of desire and the theory of the mirror stage and the general linguistic conception of reality. The problem with desire is that it is unnameable: once we have moved into naming desire, we are in language and the desire has been 'alienated'. Yet the learning of language and the mirror stage itself presupposes some very specific and nameable qualities. The ability to learn a language presupposes at least certain physical attributes (for example, vocal chords) but beyond that the way a child learns language presupposes certain possibly innate abilities to think and to talk, to string words together in a certain order. It is true that emotional problems can interfere with or even prohibit the realisation of these abilities, but the ability itself is arguably not learnt: it is part of the speaking subject. Similarly, the ability to recognise oneself in a mirror presupposes certain abilities of a subject to recognise which precede language: indeed, the expression or recognition of self in language, by use of the various personal pronouns, tends not to develop until several years later. My point is that it is possible to conceive of certain properties that we have as subjects before we become, in Lacan's sense, subjects. We do not have to confine ourselves to a concept as wide as 'desire' to describe what is there before language. We shall see in Part III that we can deduce a great deal of the infant's pre-linguistic life from the psychoanalysis of children, and that from the beginning, the infant is in some sense a subject.

All this implies the existence of a knowable world outside of language, which we can know by means of language. Lacan's position seems to me to deny this. It takes us back to Christopher Lasch and the concept of narcissism. It leaves us able to talk, endlessly; it involves a resignation from knowledge of the world and therefore the possibility of any *effective* relationship to the world. Now given that Lacan has been taken up by feminists of various persuasions who are interested in changing the world, this is clearly not quite a fair or accurate point; it seems to me, however, that is it fair to say that the nature of the theory prevents the development of any effective politics.

The empirical objection has to do with the experience of analysis. It works through words, it is true. The patient talks, the analyst comments, but it must be more than this. I was struck recently by a comment at the end of a paper in *The British Journal of Psychotherapy*. The article discusses the relationship between psychoanalysis, the theatre and the cinema, and ends with a comment about a particular film:

> Thus *The Purple Rose of Cairo* seems to represent the cinematic exploration of Roland Barthes' concept of a narrative text. Perhaps the evidence is that the author, Woody Allen, is the analytic patient of our times *par excellence* and his filmic text is one in which the loss of narrative, understood as an immediate and spontaneous production, is no longer fraught with an anxiety which has the flavour of castration anxiety but integrated into the text as knowledge and insight. (Antinucci-Mark, 1986: 29)

The film is not relevant to my point nor is Barthes' concept. What is important is that the loss of narrative is accepted. I shall try to explain how this is implicated in Lacan's work, and then what is wrong with it. For Lacan, eventually, what is important is our place in language and our acceptance of language instead of the unreachable external reality. Once we accept this it seems to me that it does not matter which language or languages we are placed in: what becomes important is our ability to play with words – precisely the activity that Woody Allen is engaged in. In that sense any narrative, any conception we might have of a life and its course, is as good as any other, or none at all. Perhaps the latter is most desirable: to play with narratives without feeling threatened. Now think about what Christopher Lasch has to say about the narcissistic personality: someone who is capable of endless analysis with a great deal of intellectual insight, which is used as a defence against any real change. Such a person would indeed be happy playing with different narratives; any conception of morality, the ability to make rational choices and commit oneself through action has disappeared.

The alternative conception of psychoanalytic treatment is that under the words there are not desires in the Lacanian sense, but strong feelings, desire in an everyday sense, which are frightening, often destructive, and for which language can act as a control, a mediation. The treatment is in part an emotional as well as a linguistic learning, and it is in the control or lack of control, of feelings, in the ability to take responsibility for oneself and arrive at decisions that a successful outcome is measured. It seems to me that the experience of psychoanalysis is as much an emotional one as an intellectual one, and often effective even if it is not understood. I am not trying to say that the implications of Lacan's work are wrong, and the ability to be able to play with narratives without feeling threatened is an important one, but it can also be an impenetrable defence against emotional, real learning.

## LACAN AND SEXUALITY

At first sight, Lacan is the least likely psychoanalyst to recommend himself to feminists: the centre of his work is the oedipal stage, the castration complex and the role of the father. However, those feminists who take up Lacan do so because, they argue, he turns sexual identity into a problem, rather than offering a solution. 'Normal' sexuality is seen by Lacan as a 'construction', an ordering of desire by language, not a result of the biological possession of a penis. It is the symbol of the penis, the phallus, that is important. The penis usually is a rather flabby piece of flesh; its symbol, the phallus, is a powerful tool that can appear anywhere and everywhere.

The crucial point for feminists seems to be reached through language and its relation to desire. Desire is originally the desire for a complete identification with the mother. Language provides us with an opposition: male/female, man/woman. The little boy during the oedipal stage and then on through adolescence translates his desire for the mother into a 'demand' (the result of an adjustment to and acceptance of – linguistic – reality) for a woman. As Jacqueline Rose states:

> Sexuality belongs in this area of instability played out in the register of demand and desire, each sex coming to stand, mythically and exclusively, for that which could satisfy and complete the other. It is when the categories 'male' and 'female' are seen to represent an absolute and complementary division that they fall prey to a mystification in which the difficulty of sexuality instantly disappears. (Mitchell and Rose, 1982: 33)

The way out of this confusion, the mixing of 'desire' and 'demand' is a 'deconstruction' of what we mean by masculine and feminine, to show that they are social, not absolute or 'natural' qualities.

I want now to take a quote from a book written by Stephen Heath from a largely Lacanian perspective, and look at it in some detail:

> What we need above all to grasp and retain is this: there is no natural sex or sexuality (the only thing that might conceivably be called natural is the reproduction of the species but that too is to run the risk of abstracting from culture and ending up by essentialising – exactly naturalising – some particular social organisation and representation of reproduction: reproduction might be natural, mothers and fathers never are). There is no natural sex or sexuality; sexuality is not some absolute and eternal entity at the beginning of an underlying human being – it simply does not exist. Or rather its only existence is as specific construction, specific definition of the sexual. (Heath, 1982: 145)

It seems to me that this quotation, typical at least of many followers of Lacan, but perhaps less of the man himself, reveals a number of things. First, it shows the tendency to reduce everything to the social. It tends to pose issues in either/or terms: either sexuality is natural, or it is socially constructed; either we posit the existence of something natural and are 'essentialist', or we do not and are not. Neither of these juxtapositions is necessary or valid. In the first place, there is no *a priori* reason why sexuality should not be natural *and* in some sense constructed: it is not, after all, a result of social definition or linguistics that I have a flabby piece of flesh hanging between my legs, any more than my possession of a liver or lungs, or the absence of wings sprouting from my shoulders. The bodily features and functions are there as given: I have a penis, it is the organ through which I urinate, it can become erect if I am sexually excited, I can use it to achieve a physical union with a woman (or a man or sheep or whatever), and the seed I produce in such a union can fertilise the first of these and produce another human being. However hard we try, no discourse will turn that piece of flesh into something else – a bottle opener, perhaps, or a fountain pen. I also experience, like every other human being, a sexual drive and sexual frustration. What society, or discourse, settles is whether I am attracted to sheep or women, what exactly I do with them, whether or not I experience my desire as controllable, uncontrollable, my frustration as good, bad or indifferent. We can say, at the same time that sexuality is natural, it is just part of being human and that the myriad ways in which sexuality is expressed is in some sense a 'construction', it is the result of some sort of social channelling.

Further, to acknowledge the existence of something 'natural' is not to be 'essentialist' in any meaningful sense of the term. Essentialism, as far as I understand it, involves a sort of reduction: everything that happens is seen as the result of, or as caused by, some essential factor. Everything I argued in the previous paragraph indicates that the positing of a natural sexuality does not involve essentialism. It is at the same time true that calling something 'natural' often serves an ideological function; some people try to justify capitalism by talking about the 'natural instinct' to make a profit, or to justify male dominance as 'natural', or argue that it is 'natural' that once men are sexually aroused they need to find a release. We need to be careful to distinguish such an 'ideological' use of the term from an attempt to identify what is given to us as part of our physical existence. I suspect the borderline will always be blurred but it does not follow that we cannot know or come close to knowing what exists independently of our social life and our language, even though we can only do so from the context of our social life and by means of language.

My next point is that the argument presented by Heath is just too easy. In a recent discussion with somebody holding a similar position, we came to the conclusion that the crucial difference between us was that I assumed that the psychoanalytic theory I was using actually referred to an external world, whereas she took psychoanalytic theory as pointing to the power of language, of discourse to define the outside world. I had presented my version of psychoanalysis as part of a rather pessimistic political argument; her claim was that her position enabled a more optimistic political standpoint. This is true: the point is which is more realistic and the question of realism, or appropriateness, is begged by the Lacanian position. The implication is that we can transform the world by changing the way in which people think. It is true that if everybody thought that men and women were equal, that different ethnic groups had a right to their own ways of life and deserved respect, the world would be a better place; but however hard I might try to look at the world differently, I shall not be able to give birth and that is an awkward fact; and I suspect much the same is true of human destructiveness and duplicity.

Finally, it seems to me that the narcissistic content of the quotation is apparent: the either/or of the argument is paralleled by the internal object world of the narcissist, which fluctuates between the wild self-confidence and omnipotence of the perfect parent and the despair of the evil parent; the argument contains insight (into the social construction of sexuality) but no knowledge of sexuality, a fear of recognising an independent reality that might restrict our actions.

In this sort of argument, the notion of drive is interpreted away from its biological implications: the argument runs that for Freud, drives can be sublimated, therefore the object of a drive is indifferent to the drive itself. What is important is the way in which the drive is attached to its object, and this is the result of psychological and social (linguistic) processes. I have indicated before that as an argument against the biological determinism attributed to Freud, this is effective and acceptable, but it does not take us away from the fact that we are also animals, biological creatures with, usually, different genitalia and different roles in the reproduction process, and that somehow or other this is likely to have an effect on the sort of people we are. Another way of putting this is that, for Lacan, anatomy is not a cause of the differences between men and women, rather the social differences between men and women are imposed on anatomy. I am not a man because I have a penis; rather closer to the truth is I have a penis because I am a man. It is the fact that I am 'constituted' as a man which makes my possession of a penis significant. Any meaning the genitalia might have is put there socially. The way this happens is through the phallus, the symbolic father, which intervenes between the mother and child to break the identity. The phallus offers both a sense of identity and, since it is symbolic, the recognition that there can be no safe or secure or permanent identity. This is as true for women as it is for men. Femininity is a sort of charade as is masculinity, an attempt to *be* something definite, reminiscent of the definiteness desired in identification with the mother. Sexuality is haunted by the desire for identity at the same time that it renounces identity. The biological basis disappears.

I am aware that what I am saying here in some ways contradicts my arguments against Erik Erikson in Chapter 5. There I argued that Erikson placed too much emphasis on biological difference, and no attention to biological and, more important, psychological bisexuality. I think both sides of my argument are compatible. We are animals; men and women are biologically different in some ways and this has its effect on other areas of our existence. We are also biologically similar in some ways and our biological make-up can be given different social meanings, our instincts can be channelled in different ways.

Having said all this, I think there are useful things we can take from Lacan's work. His conception of the self as divided against itself, the product of a conflict of and contradictions between different parts or discourses is important. Rather as a word takes its meaning from its relation to other words in the same sentence, the 'I' takes its meaning from whatever it is related to. This can be taken a step further to talking about the subject as essentially divided from itself and as a product of those divisions.

Feminist interpreters of Lacan argue that 'woman' is constituted for and by men as an absolute identity, as something over and against which a man can find his own (impossible) identity. In this sense, Lacan argues, strikingly, that 'The woman does not exist'; she is a product of desire, the imaginary, like the imaginary ideal ego discovered in the mirror. Language defines her as in some way outside or excluded. Many Lacanian feminists have looked at this in terms of women actually being excluded from language itself and have attempted to explore what that might mean in terms of the development of a feminine language, a different way of speaking. Others see it in terms of women being defined against men, as 'not men', in which situation women become the object of male fantasies. This cannot be changed by attempting to look for the specifically feminine, as something that really exists but has been hidden by phallic language; that only takes us back to the undifferentiated relation between mother and child, to pure identity. Women, and men, are a product of language, and neither exist before language, where we can only find nameless desire. The problem is that desire, rather than demand, permeates this linguistic product. The solution is the deconstruction of the terms 'man' and 'woman' – the position I have just criticised.

I am, however, intrigued by an idea of a 'feminine' language, even though it is right, I think, to argue that those writers who have tried to develop the idea presuppose a sort of pre-oedipal unity between women. I also suspect that women seek the same sort of identity in their love of men. There is a phenomenological truth in this search for an identity with another. By this I mean it corresponds with part of an experience that we usually call falling in love: the sense of urgency, of need, for the beloved and for physical union can all be seen through the light of this insight; and the failure, not of love, but of the achievement of that full and complete identity, the impossibility of that identity, the experience of internal divisions, is something which many of us have to go through and learn again and again. We cannot lose ourselves in another person. The idea of the 'decentring' of the subject, the way we are divided against ourselves, necessarily and unavoidably, is again true to our experience. It might be that falling in love with another, whatever the sex of the people involved, and the disillusionment that follows, is a normal part of being human. I suspect that Lacan recognises this, but I am not sure his interpreters do. This is the realm of the irrational, which is always there. The argument about deconstruction might have its place in the realm of the rational, as part of a rhetoric against sexual inequality, but it implies that the irrational itself can disappear.

Lacan himself is a theorist of the irrational, but he leaves himself open to being absorbed into sociologistic arguments and in the linguistic foundations of his work, encourages such an absorption. At the same time, it enables him to point to the pervasiveness of metaphor.

# REFERENCES AND FURTHER READING

## INTRODUCTION

Although I do not discuss Reich at any length, those interested in his work might look at:

Rycroft, C. (1971) *Reich*, London: Fontana.

I have found the most interesting of Reich's works to be:

Reich, W. (1957) *The Sexual Revolution*, London: Vision Press.

For a modern discussion, see:

Chasseguet-Smirgel, J. and Grunberger, B. (1986) *Freud or Reich? Psychoanalysis or Illusion*, London: Free Association Books.

Kovel, J. (1986) 'Why Freud or Reich?' *Free Associations* 4: pp.80–99.

For a discussion of and further references to the work of the 'culture-personality' school, see:

Lasch, C. (1977) *Haven in a Heartless World: The Family Besieged*, New York: Basic Books, Chapter 4.

A fairly simple culturally-determinist position, with its origins in the Frankfurt School, is:

Fromm, E, (1941) *Escape From Freedom*, New York: Farrer and Rinehart.

For a critique of culture-based approaches, including that of Fromm, see:

Marcuse, H. (1969) *Eros and Civilisation*, London: Sphere Books, Epilogue.

## CHAPTER 5 LOSING THE INSTINCTS BUT GAINING MYTHOLOGY

For an account of Parsons' general social theory, see:

Craib, I. (1984) *Modern Social Theory: From Parsons to Habermas*, Brighton: Wheatsheaf.

Parsons' own discussions of Freud can be found in:
Parsons T. (1949) 'Psychoanalysis and social structure', in *Essays in Sociological Theory*, New York: The Free Press.
  (1964) 'The father symbol: an appraisal in the light of psychoanalytic and sociological theory'; and 'Social structure and the development of personality: Freud's contribution to the integration of psychology and sociology'; both in *Social Structure and Personality*, New York: The Free Press.
  (1973) 'The superego and the theory of the social system', in Roazen, P. (ed.), *Sigmund Freud*, Englewood Cliffs, NJ: Prentice Hall.

For critical discussions of Parsons, see:
Bocock, R. (1976) *Freud and Modern Society*, Walton-on-Thames, Surrey: Nelson.
Lasch, C. (1977) *Haven in a Heartless World*, New York: Basic Books.
Poster, M. (1978) *Critical Theory of the Family*, London: Pluto Press.

Poster also offers a critical discussion of ego-psychology, where further references may be found. In the text, I mention:
Freud, A. (1936) *The Ego and the Mechanisms of Defence*, London: Hogarth Press.
See also:
Hartmann, H. (1939) *Ego Psychology and the Problem of Adaptation*, London: Hogarth Press.

Erik Erikson's work:
Erikson, E. (1958) *Young Man Luther*, New York: Norton.
  (1968) *Identity, Youth and Crisis*, New York: Norton.
  (1969) *Ghandhi's Truth*, New York: Norton.
  (1974) *Insight and Responsibility*, New York: Norton.
  (1975) *Life History and the Historical Moment*, New York: Norton.
  (1977) *Childhood and Society*, London: Triad/Paladin.

Useful commentaries on Erikson:
Coles, R. (1970) *Erik H. Erikson: The Growth of his Work*, Boston: Souvenir Press.
Kovel, J. (1988) 'Erik Erikson's psychohistory', in *The Radical Spirit*, London: Free Association Books.
Nkotre, J. (1984) *Outliving the Self: Generativity and the Interpretation of Lives*, Baltimore: Johns Hopkins University Press.
Roazen, P. (1976) *Erik H. Erikson: The Power and Limits of a Vision*, New York: The Free Press.
See also:
Mead, G.H. (1934) *Mind, Self and Society*, Chicago: University Press.

For discussions of psycho-history, see:
Gay, P. (1985) *Freud for Historians*, New York: Oxford University Press.
Loewenberg, P. (1985) *Decoding the Past: The Psychohistorical Approach*, Berkeley and Los Angeles: University of California Press.

In the text, I mention a paper of my own:
Craib, I. (1987) 'The psychodynamics of theory', *Free Associations*, 10, pp.32–56.

## CHAPTER 6 FATHERS AND THE RATIONAL SOCIETY

Crucial texts from the Frankfurt School:
Adorno, T. et al. (1950) *The Authoritarian Personality*, New York: Harper.
Habermas, J. (1971) *Knowledge and Human Interests*, London: Heinemann.

The most useful secondary texts I have found are:
Held, D. (1980) *Introduction to Critical Theory: Horkheimer to Habermas*, London: Hutchinson.
Keat, R. (1981) *The Politics of Social Theory: Habermas, Freud and the Critique of Marxism*, Oxford: Basil Blackwell.
McCarthy, T. (1978) *The Critical Theory of Jürgen Habermas*, London: Macmillan.
Poster, M. (1978) *Critical Theory of the Family*, London: Pluto Press.
Pusy, M. (1987) *Jürgen Habermas*, London: Tavistock.
Thompson, J.B. and Held, D. (eds.) (1982) *Habermas: Critical Debates*, London: Macmillan.

In the text, I also referred to:
Macklin, R. (1976) 'A psychoanalytic model for human freedom and rationality', *Psychoanalytic Quarterly*, 45, pp.430–54.
Malcolm, J. (1980) *Psychoanalysis: The Impossible Profession*, London: Pan Books.
Winnicott, D.W. (1975) *Through Paediatrics to Psychoanalysis*, London: Hogarth Press.

Works by Christopher Lasch:
Lasch, C. (1977) *Haven in a Heartless World: The Family Besieged*, New York: Basic Books.
   (1980) *The Culture of Narcissism: American Life in an Age of Diminishing Expectations*, London: Sphere Books.
   (1981) 'The Freudian left and cultural revolution', in *New Left Review* 129, pp.23–34.
   (1984a) 'Family and authority', in Richards, B. (ed.) *Capitalism and Infancy: Essays on Psychoanalysis and Politics*, London: Free Association Books.

(1984b) *The Minimal Self: Psychic Survival in Troubled Times*, London: Picador.

For critical discussion, see:
Barrett, M. and McIntosh, M. (1982) *The Anti-Social Family*, London: Verso.

Works on narcissism from which Lasch draws:
Kernberg, O. (1975) *Borderline Conditions and Pathological Narcissism*, New York: Jason Aronson.
Kovel, J. (1988) 'Narcissism and the family', in *The Radical Spirit*, London: Free Association Books.


CHAPTER 7 THE UNCONSCIOUS AND LANGUAGE

For a background to structuralism and structural linguistics, I usually recommend Jameson's *The Prison House of Language*, although many others are available. The following is a very limited selection:
Culler, J. (1976) *Saussure*, London: Fontana.
Hawkes, T. (1977) *Structuralism and Semiotics*, London: Methuen.
Jameson, F. (1977) *The Prison House of Language*, Princeton, NJ: Princeton University Press.
Lodge, D. (1981) *Working with Structuralism*, London: Routledge and Kegan Paul.

Of Lacan's own works, I found *The Language of the Self* most useful; others recommend *Four Fundamental Concepts*. The essay on the mirror phase is in *Ecrits*; I have listed only his most central work:
Lacan, J. (1968) *The Language of the Self: The Function of Language in Psychoanalysis*, Baltimore: Johns Hopkins University Press.
(1977) *Ecrits*, London: Tavistock.
(1979) *Four Fundamental Concepts of Psychoanalysis*, Harmondsworth: Penguin Books.

Freud on dreams:
Freud, S. (1976) 'The interpretation of dreams', *Collected Works*, Vol. 4, Harmondsworth: Penguin Books.

Useful secondary works on Lacan: I find the Bird paper very useful, and there is a good discussion in Sayers:
Bird, J. (1982) 'Jacques Lacan – the French Freud?' *Radical Philosophy* 30, pp.7–14.
Lemaire, A. (1977) *Jacques Lacan*, London: Routledge and Kegan Paul.
Muller, J.P. and Richards, J.P. (1982) *Lacan and Language: A Reader's Guide to Ecrits*, New York: International Universities Press.

Sayers, J. (1986) *Sexual Contradictions: Psychology, Psychoanalysis and Feminism*, London: Tavistock.
Schneiderman, S. (1983) *Jacques Lacan: The Death of an Intellectual Hero*, Cambridge, Mass: Harvard University Press.

Sayers also offers an extremely good account of feminist interpretations, and further references can be found in her work. In the text, I discuss:
Gallop, J. (1985) *Feminism and Psychoanalysis: The Daughter's Seduction*, Ithaca, New York: Cornell University Press.
Heath, S. (1982) *The Sexual Fix*, London: Macmillan.
Mitchell, J. and Rose, J. (1982) *Feminine Sexuality: Jacques Lacan and the Ecole Freudienne*, London: Macmillan.

Antinucci-Mark, G. (1986) 'Some thoughts on the similarities between psychotherapy and theatre scenarios', *British Journal of Psychotherapy*, 3, pp.14–19.

# PART III

When I discussed attempts to build a theory of society on the basis of the need for the repression and sublimation of instincts, I argued that these approaches, whether conservative or radical in political terms, produced an oversimplified picture of social structures; they could only succeed at the cost of ignoring what we might call properly social processes and structures that do not have their origin in the unconscious or even, in any direct way, in conscious activity. Economic activity, for example, involves human beings in relationships over which they have little control or awareness and which cannot be understood through the workings of the psyche. Marcuse's Utopia depends, in effect, upon the disappearance of such restraints on human behaviour, in a sense the disappearance of society.

This orthodox approach does, however, point to a necessary conflict between human desires and an outer reality, a conflict which is internalised as part of the human psyche. The difficulty of the approaches dealt with in Part II, which employ psychoanalysis as an adjunct to or part of a wider sociological analysis, is that they underemphasise or even lose this awareness of human conflict. In the case of Parsons and Lacan, or perhaps more accurately Lacan's followers, there is a tendency to produce conceptions of the individual as simply a social product and to present what we can call an 'ideological conception' of the individual. Parsons' conception of the individual can be seen as a product of mid-twentieth-century capitalism; Lacan's as appropriate to a narcissistic culture. In the case of the Frankfurt School and Lasch, there is a tendency to assume that the internal conflict can be ironed out into more or less rational behaviour – it is as if they employ psychoanalysis to emphasise not the permanence of irrationality but its possible removal.

Perhaps the most contradictory part of my argument has been around this issue of rationality and irrationality. One reason I suggested for taking psychoanalysis seriously is its concern with the irrational, the mad parts of our make-up. The under-emphasis of these is precisely the problem with the thinkers discussed in Part II. At the same time, I have argued, particularly in connection with feminist interpretations of Freud, that irrationalities of childhood, of the oedipal stage, do not have to result in their reproduction as a form of social organisation, i.e., patriarchy. It is possible to conceive of the oedipal stage being worked through within the context of a rational, comparatively free society in which there are no systematically structured inequalities between the sexes. This was part of my argument against Mitchell's attempt to derive a social theory of patriarchy from the theory of the oedipal stage. I backed it up by drawing on some themes from Lasch.

In terms of social analysis, one way of summing up my argument is that psychological structures and processes have an effect on the external, social world and at the same time are conditioned by that world. This is true but simplistic, so simplistic that I imagine it would be acceptable to any of the writers I have discussed. I argued in the Introduction that the psychological and social are qualitatively different phenomena, and this must be kept in mind to go beyond the truism. What we can draw from Parts I and II is that the connections have to do with the role of the father in the family, particularly in relation to young children, the role of the state and the nature of the super-ego. But I have also argued that in the case of psychic structures and processes, internal conflict means that there is an area of freedom. We do not take in what is outside of us and simply reinforce its external existence in our actions; rather we take it in and it enters into and is transformed by our internal conflicts and comes out as something else, that in turn is transformed through social processes and conflicts.

This brings us back to the importance of irrationality. Here it is a matter of paradox rather than contradiction. It is simply that we are rational and irrational beings at the same time. The conflict and co-operation between the two, which clinical evidence seems to show is clearly an individual matter, is the area of creativity. None of the approaches considered so far (with the exception of Erikson) has been able to get close to this, and I have frequently made the point that they provide over-general explanations that they simply cannot account for the real individual differences in the ways people live.

The promise of object-relations theory is that it offers a way of thinking about these problems. By and large, it is unattached to any but the most naive social theory; it concerns itself almost entirely with the structure of the inner world and the immediate family conditions in which that world is formed. In this sense, it is a theory of the psyche that can be employed to think about the limits of sociological analysis and explanation. I have pointed the way to these concerns by drawing on Freud's analysis of group behaviour, Erikson's concern with historical figures, Lasch's emphasis on the importance of strong emotions and Lacan's notion of the internal divided subject.

I want to introduce object-relations theory by concentrating in some detail on the work of Melanie Klein and D. W. Winnicott. I think it is fair to say that the school is famous for its clinical work, but not for its ability to produce systematic theory and, on the whole, I suspect this is a good thing. All the theorists I have discussed so far have been systematic in the sense that they have been concerned with a more or less complete understanding/explanation of particular phenomena. They have dealt explicitly or, in the case of Lacan, implicitly with causal relationships and have tried to conceptualise underlying structures and causal mechanisms, whether they be psychic, social or linguistic. Klein comes close to this but on balance remains descriptive, mapping the baby and the child's experience from the evidence of her clinical work and by and large not engaging in the sort of meta-psychology that Freud allowed himself. In the course of the mapping she produces concepts – the paranoid-schizoid position, for example, and the depressive position – which are not explained in terms of an instinct seeking satisfaction but which can be seen as providing a formal model of the internal psychic world we all possess; it has these and those components, organised broadly in this or that way. The actual content of the components and the process of movement from one form of organisation to the other can only be charted for each individual, not laid down in advance in quite the same way as, say, in Freud's theory of psycho-sexual stages of development. In other words, she offers us precisely what I have argued has been missing from the other theorists: a way of grasping the depth and difference of each individual psyche, together with their similarities.

By way of an example involving material I have already touched on, we all internalise parental figures who make up part of our inner object world. It will become clear when I discuss Klein that we split these figures: we have a good internal mother and father and a bad internal mother and father. This much is common; what is to some extent always different for each of us are the internal relations that exist between these figures – it is what we can do with our internal object world that is important, not only in terms of its organisation but in the way we project it back on to the world and use it to create new situations and repeat old ones. The concepts I shall be dealing with in Part III are concepts relating to the organisation of our internal object world, and beyond that to our sense of self and our relationships to others in the broadest sense. It focuses much more upon the psyche, the individual and the personal, and, apart from the following through of some social policy implications, there has been little attempt to connect this approach with social theory.

Before moving further, I shall recap my comments about why object-relations theory is so named. The distinction is already in Freud: the sexual aim is, roughly, what you want to do, and the object is whom you want to do it to. Object-relations theory gives priority to the second, whereas Freud gave priority to the first. Some people find the term 'object' distasteful on the grounds that it reduces other people to objects. In a limited sense this is right: the other, real person in the world to whom I relate is, as well as being an acting subject in his or her own right, also an object of my desire, and psychoanalytic theory is concerned with the desiring person, who does, at a primitive level, reduce others to objects. But the 'object' as a real person is only of secondary importance for most object-relations theorists. What they concentrate on are the 'internal objects', not people at all but those 'images' or 'figures' of others we internalise and make part of our own personalities. Here, in a more intelligible way than in Lacan, we find the idea of the subject divided against itself, over and above the divisions already posited by Freud. I am not just one person: I have inside me a mother figure, a father figure, figures of siblings, teachers, friends, lovers, psychotherapists, and so on. There is some sense in which I can become one or the other of these in different situations. An important point is that as we internalise or introject these figures, we change them, make them something other than what they are in the outside world. Beyond this, with the most primitive figure, the mother, our first relation is literally to an object, 'the breast', rather than the person as a whole.

The crucial difference between object-relations theory and Freud, however, is that for Freud object-choice did not become relevant until several months after birth, so whatever happened to the instincts was not connected to an object. Klein insisted that clinical evidence from the analysis of very young children showed that there was no mental life which did not involve object-relations, even from the very earliest moment. What happens to the instincts must always be considered in the context of object-relations. As we shall see, this leads to a very different set of clinical and theoretical emphases. As no social theory emerges automatically, as it does from Freud, it is more a matter of speculation and probing. I shall thus resist the temptation to engage in a full account of object-relations theory bringing together the work of writers such as Fairbairn, Balint, Bowlby and Laing, and the modern American theorists of the self, Kohut and Kohnberg, and concentrate instead on the two most prominent founding figures.

# 8

## MELANIE KLEIN: THE BALANCE OF LOVE AND HATE

Melanie Klein, a second-generation analyst, came to Britain earlier than Freud, and her ideas received a sympathetic hearing from the British Psychoanalytic Society. They brought her into conflict with more orthodox Freudians, and, over the issue of child analysis in particular, with Anna Freud and her followers. The 1930s and 1940s were times of intense, often bitter and difficult, debate around Klein's ideas. It would be easy, and perhaps even interesting, to start by asking the question: was Klein a Freudian? But I do not think it would be very useful. Although ideas, theories and schools of thought often develop through bitter arguments, expulsions (real or metaphorical) and division, the history of ideas is rather different. Perhaps, people being people, the divisions and arguments are necessary, but ideas develop with continuities and discontinuities. It seems to me that clinical experience suggests that there are many aspects to truth and no one psychoanalytic theory or method of practice says everything. Perhaps the best way to think about Klein's ideas is as following one of several paths which can be taken from Freud, all of which lead somewhere. My justification for choosing Klein is that her work contributes to the problems I am looking at here.

Klein's main achievement is to take us into the consciousness of the baby. In terms of technique, Klein worked with very young children and her undisputed advance was to use play and the interpretation of play as a method. She was able to work with children much younger than many analysts thought possible; for the more orthodox Freudians, the child's ego was not strong enough to cope with analysis until a much later age. However, the movement back to the baby as the starting point was already there in Freud's work. He did have things to say about the earliest months, even if he did not concentrate on them, and the crucial difference is Klein's claim that object-relations are central from birth. This led to a revision of the psycho-sexual stages –

she argued, for example, that signs of the oedipal conflict were to be found at a very early stage. This is fairly easy to grasp if one takes Freud, as I argued earlier, as describing not so much stages as levels of organisation that are present all the time, in various degrees of development, with one or the other becoming the most important at any particular time.

Perhaps the most startling, intriguing and difficult development of Freud's work lies in what Klein had to say about instinct theory. She started where Freud left off in *Beyond the Pleasure Principle*. There he suggested the existence of a life and a death instinct. Both had the same aim, stasis, the eventual release of all tension, but different modes of achieving it: the death instinct is destructive, turned against either the self or projected outwards against others. Klein seems to take the existence of these instincts literally: and one way of charac-terising her work is as dealing with the conflict between the two as it continues over a lifetime. It is a controversial position, especially as far as the death instinct is concerned; and many object-relations theorists shift the focus of attention elsewhere and implicitly or explicitly deny its existence. It is indeed something difficult to justify in theoretical terms, although it often seems to me self-evident in experiential terms. As I said in the Introduction, I think it would be pointless to try to argue that we are dealing with something that is genetically patterned. I also think it does not work to argue, as later object-relations theorists do, that the death instinct is not innate but the product of particular environmental frustrations, although this certainly plays a part. In my limited clinical and normal everyday experience, the death instinct is universal and perhaps the main question is the degree to which it is turned against oneself or others. It might, I suppose, be regarded as a product of normal environmental frustration, but all in all, I find myself content to think that, somehow or other, we are destructive to some degree and that our destructiveness, when it is directed towards appropriate targets, can perhaps be harnessed in the service of life, but the conflict is there in our nature. I am aware that this is not a satisfactory position but it is not a satisfactory world.

Klein's work describes the means by which the infant, then the child, then the adult deals with the internal conflict of good and bad, that conflict being fought out among and by means of its 'inner objects', the internalised or introjected others, and by means of usually but not always unconscious phantasy. Klein describes the infant as working through two 'positions', rather than stages, in its progress towards maturation: the paranoid-schizoid position and the depressive position. In this progress a series of defence mechanisms are used which I see as particularly important in grasping the relationship between the individual and society. This infantile experience and our ways of coping with it are significant for what happens in later life. Before looking at these positions, however, I want to look at two other central ideas in Klein's work: phantasy and envy.

## PHANTASY

When I discussed the unconscious in the Introduction, I commented that an objection to Freud's conception was that it left the impression that the psyche somehow contained acting parts, a little person labelled id, or ego or super-ego; and I added that sometimes it is useful to think of the psyche like this. Hanna Segal, the foremost living interpreter of Klein's work, suggests that the notion of phantasy helps to make this a little clearer. For example, when we talk about the super-ego, it is a phantasised introjection of a parental figure. Phantasy is seen as ever present in everybody. It is the 'psychical representative' of the instincts about which Freud talks. At the beginning of life, there is no distinction between the phantasy and reality:

> an infant going to sleep, contentedly making sucking noises and movements with his mouth or sucking his own fingers, phantasises that he is actually sucking or incorporating the breast and goes to sleep with the phantasy of having the milk-giving breast actually inside himself. Similarly, a hungry, raging infant, screaming and kicking, phantasises that he is actually attacking the breast, tearing and destroying it, and experiences his own screams which tear him and hurt him as the torn breast attacking him in his own inside. Therefore, not only does he experience a want, but his hunger-pain and his own screams may be felt as a persecutory attack on his inside. (Segal, 1964:13)

Phantasies are unconscious, but may often be brought to consciousness, and one way of looking at the development of the child, and of the adult, is as an ongoing process of testing phantasy against reality. In the case of infants, the way in which reality 'responds' (usually in the shape of the mother) to the infant's phantasy can have important effects on modifying or confirming the phantasy.

The quotation is fairly typical of Kleinian interpretations and people often find them difficult to understand at first, although, interestingly, children can often relate to them immediately. Perhaps the idea of phantasy is easier if we can think about adult contexts where it governs our reactions to real situations and often becomes involved in what we take to be reality. One example I frequently come across in therapy groups is a phantasy that to attack or even criticise somebody verbally is equivalent to a violent, destructive, physical attack – criticism or anger is felt, not expressed, or perhaps immediately suppressed, or perhaps not felt at all. If it is expressed, then people often find it difficult to deal with, but are able to learn that it is not as destructive or damaging as it is in phantasy. Some psychoses take the identification of phantasy and reality to the extreme: the man, for example, who thinks he is Jesus Christ and tries to act accordingly.

Unconscious phantasy can be distinguished from conscious fantasy, although in some of their functions they are not dissimilar. Just as our conscious fantasies, in daydreaming, for example, might try to avoid or get over an unpleasant external or internal reality – I might, for example, imagine my lover here in her absence, or go over what I should have said to somebody who has just belittled me – so unconscious phantasies can be a defence against the recognition of an unpleasant external or internal reality. For the purposes of my argument here, it is important in that external, social events and processes are always experienced in relation to unconscious phantasies, and the interesting possibilities lie in the way that these phantasies can reinterpret and effect the meaning of an external, social reality, whether it be in the family, work or politics.

## ENVY

For Klein envy is the clearest everyday manifestation of the death instinct. She regards it as part of our genetic make-up. Some people are simply more envious than others. It is normal to follow Klein and define envy in distinction to greed and jealousy, with which it is often merged in everyday thought and speech. The crucial distinction is that envy is entirely destructive while greed and jealousy have some connection to love. If I am greedy, I want to take in the whole of the object because it seems so good to me, regardless of the consequences, which might well be destructive. If I eat all the cherries in the bowl, then nobody else will be able to have any, and there won't be any more because these are the last of the season. If I occupy all my lover's time, then she won't have any for her children or friends, who will suffer. But in both cases, I am after something that is good and the destructiveness is incidental, not the aim of my actions. In the case of jealousy, there is something I perceive as full of goodness and somebody else has it. I want it. Again, if my jealousy is destructive, if, for example, I feel jealous of the love and attention my child receives from my wife, and I react by arguing, getting angry and sulking, and making life miserable for everyone, the destructiveness is a by-product of my jealousy, my desire for a love I am not getting.

Envy does not aim at taking in or possessing the loved object, but, to begin with, at being as good as the loved object. When this fails, the goodness seems unbearable, and must be destroyed, spoilt. Envy is pervasive in a 'gentle' form in our everyday lives. If, for example, there is a competition for a senior post and it goes to my colleague, I could be jealous: 'She/he doesn't deserve it, I do more work, am a better teacher than him/her.' In fact my reaction is envious: 'Who wants to be a senior lecturer anyway, it just involves more administrative responsibility, there's less time for research and writing, and people change and become unpleasant when they get promoted.' This reaction can of course be presented as a virtue: I am not really ambitious, just interested in doing a good job, I have a different scale of values, etc. The everyday manifestation of envy is the spoiling comment which tries to reduce achievement, success, etc: 'It's all right for him'; 'But she started with all the advantages'; 'I could do that if I had their money.' Much rumour and gossip is destructive in the envious sense, emphasising or even creating a bad side to somebody to devalue the good side.

In the infant, envy involves phantasised attacks on the breast or the mother; again, bodily metaphors are employed in the formation of the phantasy. I commented after the earlier quotation from Segal that her description might sound odd to many people, because in adult life we tend to separate bodily metaphors from the reality to which they refer. In the infant, phantasy and reality can be experienced as identical. When it experiences envious, destructive feelings these are phantasised in terms of 'spitting, urinating, defaecating, passing of wind, and by projective, penetrating looking (the evil eye)' (Segal, 1964:41). We are used to hearing or speaking about people pissing or shitting on somebody else, but we do not allow ourselves to become aware of the primitive force of the feeling behind it; in our phantasies this is what we are really doing or having done to us. In Kleinian interpretations, it is the phantasy that is important, and the putting into words of the feeling as if it were a real desire (which it is, unconsciously) strikes us as frightening or bizarre.

As a defence against envious feelings, we often idealise something or somebody; but because of the strength of the envy that idealisation is often brittle, and likely to be transformed into its opposite, an envious hatred. It seems from my experience that such idealisation and its reversal is a comparatively common experience for teachers, at least in higher education. The teacher possesses what the student desires: knowledge, skills, recognition, adulthood. The student is being kept dependent long after he or she has the physical and mental ability to be an independent and responsible adult. All students will experience some envy in this situation; some will experience a great deal. Teachers will often find themselves idealised. It is, of course, impossible for anybody to live up to such idealisation, and there is likely to be a sudden reversal, and instead of admiration, an envious rage erupts. In my experience, this often happens around the examination period.

The conception of the life and death instincts, envy as a manifestation of the death instinct, and the central importance of phantasy together make up the setting to enable us to understand what Klein had to say about the psychic 'positions' through which the infant matures. The problem of the growing infant is to cope with good and bad experiences, the feelings which push him or her forward into life and growth, and the desire to destroy. These feelings are expressed in phantasies which at one level are experienced as absolutely real, the body and its functions providing the most primitive material for the child's phantasy life.

### THE PARANOID-SCHIZOID POSITION

According to Klein, the baby has the ability at birth to experience anxiety at the internal conflict between the life and death instincts, and at the impact of the external world of reality. Hence it possesses an elementary, weak and unorganised ego. The maturing process can be seen as a process of strengthening and organising the ego against anxiety, experienced as the threat of annihilation. In this process the baby (and the child and the adult) deploy what are known as 'defence mechanisms'. These are best seen as mental operations to reduce anxiety and produce some sense of security and safety. In everyday life, the comment that somebody is being defensive is usually meant as a criticism; the implication is that they have something to defend, usually something unpleasant; at the very least, there is an implicit juxtaposition to openness which is regarded as desirable. In fact, we are all defensive and we have to be: it is our defences against pain, against our own destructiveness and the refusal of the world to gratify our desires, as well as the more positive threats that it presents, that enable us to go through life and, in whatever way, 'make something of ourselves'. The problems occur when our defence mechanisms are inappropriate, exaggerated or too rigid.

The most primitive defence mechanisms that Klein talks about are projection, introjection and splitting. Remember that the baby is attempting to cope not only with good experiences, of satisfaction, comfort and growth, but bad experiences, both internal, its own destructiveness, and external, since no parenting is perfect. The first way of dealing with this is to split the world into 'good' and 'bad'. Klein talks, in fact, not of the infant splitting the world but splitting the breast. We can take this literally and metaphorically – literally in the case of talking about babies who are breast-fed, and metaphorically, as referring to the life-source. The point is that the baby does not yet have any perception or conception of the mother as a whole, separate person. It does have an immediate experience of something good and something bad. Projection refers to the psychic operation of putting something outside of oneself, into someone or something else: introjection to the operation of taking something in, making it part of oneself. They are stronger concepts than internalisation and externalisation, which are usually used in connection with ideas; they refer to parts of ourselves. Generally, the baby projects its bad feelings on to some outside object and introjects its good feelings, the feelings that come from the satisfaction of its most primitive needs. Sometimes the process will be reversed: the good will be projected outside into the external world in order to protect it from what are felt to be overwhelming internal destructive feelings. In both cases there will tend to be a process of idealisation. 'Perfect' babies who sleep without difficulty and never scream have perhaps split their world rather too well.

Splitting accounts for the 'schizoid' part of the label. Projection of the bad into the outside world leaves the child experiencing a paranoid anxiety of external attack – the fear is that the bad feelings will come back and destroy it from the outside. Of course, not all the baby's destructive feelings can be projected in this way, and the residue can be converted into aggressive feelings aimed at attacking the already projected threat. In extreme circumstances, the projected threat can be further split, a process of psychic fragmenting, the bad breast being, in the baby's phantasy, broken down into little bits; the paranoia then takes the form of feeling under attack from many sources, from all directions.

Klein also talks here of a defence she calls 'projective identification'. I certainly find this difficult to understand, and in my experience, it tends to be hotly contested among therapists and analysts. Hanna Segal defines it in the following way: 'parts of the self and internal objects are split off and projected into the external object, which then becomes possessed by, controlled and identified with the projected parts (Segal, 1964: 27).

The forms of illness that we label psychotic are, for Klein, a matter of fixation at and/or regression to the paranoid-schizoid position. These tend to be the most intractable forms of mental illness, usually involving a more or less complete loss of touch with an outside reality. These can be juxtaposed to neuroses, a less disabling set of problems. The difference is summed up in the phrase 'neurotics build castles in the air, psychotics live in them'. (I shall pass over the final clause about psychoanalysts collecting the rent.) Freud generally considered psychoses outside the range of problems that could be treated by psychoanalysis, although Kleinians will treat them. Problems at this stage arise if anxiety is especially acute, for internal or external reasons. It might simply be that, for purely genetic reasons, the infant has a particularly strong death instinct; the external reasons would include a particularly difficult environment or parental neglect or abuse. What happens is that the bad objects are fragmented, split into many pieces, each one of which is found to be particularly threatening. The good object cannot be introjected, and especially if envy is strong, it too is fragmented. This falling or breaking apart of the ego is the final defence. It sounds odd to call it a defence – most of us talk about falling apart as if it were the final catastrophe, and we all have an intuition of the possibility. In fact, it enables survival in the absolute minimum sense. Again, most of us have an intuition of the experience of what Bion called, appropriately as usual, 'bizarre objects' (1964), everyday things that suddenly and for no apparent reason seem threatening. An experience I have occasionally on the street or on a train or bus is that people suddenly seem ugly and dangerous, as if all beauty, and indeed all possibility of beauty, has disappeared from the world. As ever, Hanna Segal presents a very precise clinical example:

> For instance, a border-line schizoid patient said 'I can't get in touch with you. Here is my head on the pillow and there are you in your armchair. But in between the top of my head and you there is nothing but horrible bloody mish-mash.' On further analysis, we understood that this 'bloody mish-mash' was associated with his experience of feeding from a breast where a breast abscess was forming. The 'mish-mash' was perceived by him as bitten-up, pussy particles of the breast, containing the patient's own urine, faeces and broken-off bits of his teeth. He could preserve something of his

'head', standing for his sanity, and a remote analyst in the armchair, but there was no relation between him and myself. The real relationship between his mouth and the breast was happening in the 'third area', in the 'mish-mash' split off from both the analyst-mother and the patient-infant. (1964: 57)

Given, however, that envy is manageable and that by and large the good experiences of the infant outweigh the bad, the defence mechanisms employed here are healthy in the sense that they enable growth and continue throughout life to enable the individual to hold on to psychic survival. We all split, project and introject, and on occasions it is necessary to do so. Even projective identification forms the basis for empathy. If there is a predominance of good experiences, then the ego continues to introject and identify with an ideal object, the bad experiences become less threatening and the split between good and bad narrows. It becomes possible for the infant to move forward by integrating the good and the bad: this takes us to the depressive position.

### THE DEPRESSIVE POSITION, REPARATION AND THE IMPORTANCE OF MOURNING

In what we might call healthy development, the baby begins to feel that his or her good feelings outweigh the bad and will have less need to project the latter, be less haunted by paranoid fears. The process of integrating both good and bad feelings into the increasingly strengthened ego leads to the depressive position. It involves not only a reduced need to split and project and an increased integration of good and bad objects, but also a move from perceiving a part-object to perceiving a whole object, to recognising the mother as a whole and separate person. In many cases this leads to a clear and easily perceived change in the baby's behaviour. The baby can recognise that both self and mother are responsible for both good and bad experiences. Anxiety moves from fear of destruction to the fear that the newly accepted bad feelings will come to outweigh the good feelings and he or she will destroy through hatred the person who is also loved. This is a powerful feeling, and it must be remembered that the person the baby loves is also the person upon whom the baby still depends for its existence. The feeling of hating the mother and possibly destroying her is no mild intellectual speculation on the baby's part, but has all the urgency that in adult life we experience in our most acute moments.

What the baby learns at this stage, if all goes well, is something we all have to continue doing for the rest of our lives: coping with ambivalent feelings, the closeness of love and hate. There is a sense of loss involved in all this, which troubles us throughout life: the loss of the ideal object, now integrated with the bad object in the ego. As the baby becomes aware of its own destructiveness, it becomes anxious lest it destroy the mother on whom it depends. In phantasy the mother is destroyed. The child's phantasy is not only that he or she has destroyed the real external mother but also that the internal good object has been destroyed. This leads to guilt, and a possible regression to paranoid defences in order to avoid it.

If good and bad objects are integrated, the super-ego itself develops beyond the primitive punitive stage and becomes a source of guilt and love. As the infant has less need to project, so it is able to get a better grasp on external reality. Repression replaces projection as a primary defence and the infant learns to symbolise and therefore rescue and preserve what has been lost and destroyed. Segal's development of a Kleinian analysis of the origins of the symbol and the appearance of language actually echoes that of Lacan. For Lacan language emerges as a replacement for the oedipal desire for the mother, a desire which is surrendered under threat. For Segal too, the symbol replaces an object which is given up, and what is given up or lost is the mother. However, it is not the mother as the object of oedipal desire, but the mother as a phantasised ideal object and the baby's apprehension of itself as the ideal object. One might say it is the baby's omnipotence that is surrendered, not because of a social intervention (the father's 'no') but because of a natural process of psychic and physical growth, combined with a reasonably satisfying environment. The process is that of sublimation; the instinct is inhibited and displaced on to a symbol. It is important, however, to realise that while, for Lacan, this is *the* crucial moment at which we can find something approximate to the foundation of civilisation, for Klein it is a crucial moment, which takes its place in the much wider context of the child's psychic growth and relationship to its environment. For Klein, what makes a baby human is less the acquisition of language than the existence of object-relations which are there from birth, and which render the acquisition of language possible.

In this process, the parallel to mourning is particularly important. The loss of the ideal object and the phantasised loss of the real object are the first experiences of loss on which all future experiences are based, and it is worth spending some time looking at the mourning process in connection with the depressive feeling because, in some senses, it can be taken as a model for the life-process as a whole. Our life can be seen as a series of losses, from those I have just been discussing, through loss of infancy, childhood, adolescence, youth and, as we get older, various physical powers. This goes alongside the loss of friends, lovers, parents, whether or not through death; and the loss experienced when we change school, move house, change job, and the losses that occur through social and environmental change, from the loss of free time on the arrival of a new baby to loss of a pleasant woodland walk when a new housing estate is built. All involve, to a greater or lesser intensity, mourning.

Klein develops Freud's conception of mourning in an interesting way. For Freud, mourning involved a withdrawal of psychic energy from the outside world, where it had been invested in a lost object, a sort of internal refocusing of the energy, involving an unwillingness to relinquish the loved object, and then a directing out of the energy again into new relationships. For Freud, the pathological form of mourning was melancholia: the internalisation of the lost object, as it were, trapping the energy inside the psyche and preventing a return to new relationships in the outside world. Klein, developing the work of Karl Abraham, argued, on the basis of clinical evidence, that even in normal mourning there was an internalisation of the lost object. The difference is that the successful mourner internalises the loved one in a loving way, adds him or her to the internal stock of 'good objects'. The melancholic, on the other hand, cannot do this because of the level of hostility he or she has towards the lost object. Again, the model implied is of the conflict and balance between the life and death instincts, between good and bad internal objects. If we think about this in a common-sense way, not necessarily in connection with death but with other forms of loss, then we can see the sense behind it. As I said earlier, growing up is an ongoing loss, of infancy and the comforts we received, of childhood and its excitements and pleasures, of adolescence and its freedom and often socially sanctioned irresponsibility. All of these are good things, appropriate to the relevant stage in the life-cycle. It is also true that a successful childhood and adolescence enable a successful adult to develop. The better, the more loving the childhood, the easier it is to move forwards into adulthood, since the loving memories are established and carried forward. There is also a saying about love affairs: the affairs that have the easiest end are the good ones; the difficult, the painful and fraught affairs are the most difficult to end. At first glance, at least to those of us who experience real separation difficulties, this might appear paradoxical: the best relationships must be the most difficult to leave, but separation anxiety itself has to do with difficulty in establishing good, loving internal objects which can be relied on and drawn upon during difficult times.

The ability to mourn depends eventually on our infantile ability to experience the anxiety of separation from the mother and the successful introjection of a good object which can be kept with us when the mother is absent. If the loss in later life is one of our closest relations or friends, then we are likely to re-experience that early fear of complete abandonment and helplessness, as if it was not only the external, real person who has been lost but also as if the good internal-object world is under threat of destruction or has actually been destroyed. The first reactions will be to defend against this, often by denying to ourselves in the immediate reaction that the loss has occurred; the recently bereaved often talk of a feeling of numbness, of disbelief; some people can continue to deny the loss for a long time, keeping the possessions and room of the dead person in place as if nothing has happened, perhaps even laying a place at table. The most gruelling literary example I have found is near the beginning of Olivia Manning's *Levant Trilogy*, where a mother sees her child killed by a shell and carries him indoors, saying he has fainted and trying to revive him by feeding him through a gaping hole in his cheek. Once this initial denial is overcome, the defences can include anger, holding an external person to blame for the loss, and over-idealising the person who has been lost. Eventually, if all goes well, the real work of mourning, feeling the loss, the sadness and tears, the pining, begins.

The connection between mourning and the depressive position should by now be reasonably clear. Both involve the development of a good inner object world which is sufficiently strong to withstand both internal and external threats. Just as we defend ourselves against those threats in the first stages of mourning the lost loved one, so we defend ourselves against the newly internalised bad objects in the depressive position. These defences in one way or another try to remove the bad objects. I have already referred to the possibility of regressing to the previous position and re-projecting them, and several of the earlier defences are used again. Klein calls these defences the manic defences. In later life, we can be caught in a manic-depressive cycle, the term usually being used to refer to a movement between acute depression, an inability to function anywhere near adequately in the external world, and a state of hyper-excitement, wild ambitions and hyperactivity. The normal development of manic defences – and they are a normal part of everybody's repertoire – does not involve these extremes, and they are geared to the avoidance of depression and guilt, the avoidance of feelings of dependence and ambivalence towards the person we depend on, and against the recognition of an internal object world at all involving what Segal calls a denial of psychic reality itself, the blaming of external circumstances: 'The relation to objects is characterised by a triad of feelings – control, triumph and contempt. These feelings are directly related to, and defensive against feelings of valuing the object and depending on it, and fear of loss and guilt' (1964: 83).

The connection of these defences with envy is fairly clear: they are attempts to spoil the valued object. I imagine that everybody must have an experience of these three; at the end of a love affair or a friendship, for example, all three come into play. People often end a relationship as a form of pre-emptive strike, feeling that if they do not end it first and keep the situation under their control, the other person will end it and they will be swamped by loss and pain. The feeling of triumph is one of having defeated the other person, perhaps by making a new and 'better' relationship, perhaps simply by drawing on one's ability to survive without showing signs of pain. Contempt in this context is close to envy: a spoiling of the object: 'How on earth could I have fallen in love with her? She's a wreck, crazy, not worth spending the time of day with.' All of these feelings draw on infantile omnipotence, the phantasy of being in control of the world and of oneself, of being invulnerable to danger.

The most important and effective of the defences against depression, however, is reparation. In phantasy, and in practical activity, the child (and the adult) can take steps to 'repair' the lost or destroyed object, restore it to its former state. There is a difference between reparation and guilt, although it is one that I personally find difficult to conceptualise. I suspect that is because I – and perhaps, generally, people – experience guilt largely in connection with defence mechanisms that attempt to deny it. I automatically think of guilt as a feeling to be avoided, a feeling that leads me to a general defensiveness and a temper that is all too ready to be lost in a torrent of self-justification. It is a feeling I want to wipe out by wiping out the act that created it. I want forgiveness in such a way that the original misdeed somehow disappears. For the Kleinian, guilt is a feeling to be borne and must be recognised. Perhaps reparation can be seen in this context as the ability to make amends while recognising the original misdeed. It is based on the infantile experience of being able to lose and recover the lost object, of being able to recreate the mother in the head when the real one is out of the room. As we become more sure of our power to recreate or restore the lost object, through continued phantasised experiences of destruction and recreation, so our own destructiveness becomes less of a threat, more bearable. Reparation is based on the experience of pain and guilt, and in that sense it can barely be regarded as a defence, although it can certainly reduce the likelihood of despair. Basically, reparation enables the growth of the ego. Something like this happens during the mourning process as the lost external object is restored as a good internal object.

There is, however, a manic form of reparation which aims at restoral without the experience of pain and guilt. What is cared for must therefore be a distant object, not of great significance and it must be an inferior object. Segal adds to this, eventually, a contemptible object. It seems to me that there is a great deal of manic reparation going on in the form of good works and causes. There are always any number of social victims to be helped and the helping enables the helper to feel good, and often be effective in practical terms, without having to acknowledge not only pain and guilt but also his or her own limitations and destructiveness. Manic reparation has to keep its object dependent, since if it were to achieve real independence, it would be open to destructive attacks from the helper. One can see this process at work in some friendships. There is a type of person who will be very helpful and kind to someone in trouble, someone who feels dependent and needs help, but who will not be able to maintain the relationship as the troubled person overcomes their troubles. There might even be attempts to keep that person in a dependent state.

## CONCLUSION

What I have presented here is the core of Klein's work. I want now to look at the work of one major object-relations theorist, D. W. Winnicott, before moving on to the central question of this book, the implications of this sort of work for sociology.

# 9

## D.W. WINNICOTT: SPACE AND MORALITY

I want to argue that the object-relations tradition opens up new possibilities for the sociological deployment of psychoanalysis and enables us to identify in a very clear way the limits of sociological explanation. By way of an introduction to Winnicott, I shall give a preview of my argument based on my own history.

If there is one clear message from object-relations theory, it has to do not with theoretical but with clinical creativity. Almost without fail, the theoretical insights are developed from clinical work, and there is little attempt at systematisation. Winnicott begins one of his papers by saying that his method is not to read first but to develop ideas on the basis of evidence and then look around to see if anybody else has had them. Good clinical practice leaves the patient free to find his or her own compromises and solutions within a broad range of behaviour that we might call 'mature' or 'integrated'. The theoretical equivalent is not to produce a theory of this creativity, except in its broadest outline, but rather to identify the space in which it takes place. I have selected Winnicott not only because of his objective importance as a psychoanalyst, but also because I think his approach to patients can be translated into an approach to theory.

Those of us who are social theorists, or intellectuals generally, are constantly trying to invade people's space and bind them there, frequently by denying the existence of that space. A sociological 'invasion' of Winnicott would argue that he was the product of a privileged and temporarily optimistic social class which led him to idealise childhood in a theory that assumed and reinforced male dominance, and that worked as an ideology for liberal capitalism. I find myself in the position of somebody who would once have agreed with these criticisms, but shall now dispute them. The crucial experience for me was fathering a child, and rediscovering my own childhood, with its joys and its agonies, through that of my son. In terms of my internal object world, this seems to have involved a realignment and strengthening of the good objects against the bad and an increasing confidence in my ability to make reparation. When I speak about the invasive potentiality of theory, one of the things I mean would be the attempt by theory to deal with this significant personal change in terms of situational constraints and ideological changes. It is more than a cognitive process, and more than a result of situational factors, which have in fact been adverse, and would have led to a prediction of personal change opposite to the one that took place. The good thing about object-relations theory is precisely that it offers an understanding of such changes, in either direction, while leaving me the responsibility for what change takes place. Winnicott's attitude is summed up in the following quotation: 'Children *are* a burden and if they bring joy it is because two people have decided to take that kind of burden; in fact, have agreed to call it not a burden but a baby' (1964: 131).

I think it is fair to say that Winnicott is *the* major theorist of the British school. By all accounts he was a remarkable man. Davis and Wallbridge (1983) begin their account of him by saying that perhaps his most important quality was his belief that life was worth living. In cultural terms, this is perhaps an unpopular view these days, but certainly for this reader it glows throughout his work. He was a paediatrician with regular and everyday contact with young children and trained as an analyst in the 1920s. His training and general way of thinking led him to see psychoanalysis as offering explanations of dysfunctions that medicine itself could not provide and of uniting in its theory body and mind. In this sense he was very much in the tradition of Freud himself, but he went beyond a concern with our sexual drives and what happens to them, to our general experience of our body, the way we feel our physical relationship to the outside world. His clinical experience of babies in his paediatric work led him back from the oedipal stage to the very earliest stages after birth, and even before birth. In this sense he was concerned with the same experiences as Klein. Unlike Freud his concern was with something we call the 'self' – the total experiencing person – which includes the id, ego and super-ego, and rather more besides. Unlike Erikson, his concern was with the internal rather than external integration of the self. Unlike Klein, he could not accept the theory of the death instinct and instead worked with an idea of there being, given the right conditions, a natural growth and flourishing in the personality. This led him to talk more than Klein about environmental factors in growth and child-

rearing practice; aggressiveness and destructiveness were seen as the
result of environmental frustrations. Growth is seen in terms of
integration, but his concept of integration covered rather more than
the integration of good and bad objects. Finally, the key to development was the move from the infant's dependence on the mother to a
relative independence in adulthood. This leads to a different conception of the unconscious, one that I discussed in the Introduction as
involving the repression or avoidance of feelings of helpless dependency. Guntrip (1964) argues that the development from Klein to
thinkers such as Winnicott is an overcoming of a defence. To see
ourselves as, if only in part, fierce destructive beings is a form of
self-aggrandisement, a defence against the recognition of a real
helplessness that characterises the earliest experiences of every human
being.

If Klein is the theorist of the death instinct, then perhaps Winnicott
might be called the theorist of the life instinct. I do not think there is a
contradiction between these positions, and again we are dealing not
with mutually exclusive but with different truths. There are elements
in Winnicott's work, not explicit but implicit in his conception of
human nature, that can allow for the inclusion of the death instinct.
Davis and Wallbridge (1983) sum up his theory in terms of an
aesthetic sense, a balance, a proportionality, a sense of everything
needing its place. From this point of view the exclusion of an opposite,
a death instinct as opposed to a life instinct, seems to me to leave a
lopsidedness, a blind spot, and that it would not destroy his vision to
include a natural destructiveness as well as a natural growth; in fact, it
would balance it, and one might argue against Guntrip that an
emphasis on helplessness as opposed to destructiveness is in turn a
defence against the latter, and that integration, in both Winnicott's and
Klein's sense, involves a recognition of both.

I shall begin my discussion of Winnicott by looking at his conception
of the growth enabling environment. I shall then turn to the central
features of his theory of development. In the first section, I shall
discuss aspects of social life that have not yet been touched on in this
book. This will give a good idea of Winnicott's originality and his
significance for sociology.

## THE GOOD-ENOUGH ENVIRONMENT

Mothering is perhaps a difficult issue given the concerns of modern
feminism. Winnicott's term, which I deliberately modified for the title

of this section, is 'good-enough mothering'. For Winnicott, the environment is important from before birth and at that stage the environment *is* the mother, her very body itself. In the child's history, a whole range of factors is important, including the baby's conception and what it means to both parents, although to begin with this has to be refracted through the mother. What happens through the pregnancy is important not only in physical terms but also in psychic terms. Most important for Winnicott is that the mother develops during the final stages of pregnancy and the early stages of the newborn infant's life what he calls a 'primary maternal preoccupation'. Certainly as a man, I find I can only think of this state as 'strange', although I have witnessed it and been involved in it as an adult, and I imagine I have some distant, inarticulate memory of participating in such a state. It is very close to an illness, a withdrawn state in which there is an identification with the about-to-be and newborn baby which enables the mother to know what the baby desires and needs and to respond appropriately. It is as if the baby becomes the good object of the mother's internal world, or perhaps the good object becomes the baby. It is, I suppose, a form of schizoid projection in the Kleinian sense, but it cannot be regarded as a defence nor as an illness, because it is appropriate to pregnancy as a normal occurrence. Women who do not experience this state, which lasts for some months after birth, then find they have to make it up later; Winnicott describes them as acting like therapists rather than parents. Alternatively, the identification can become a pathological preoccupation, replacing other previous preoccupations. The important thing is that the mother can be preoccupied without becoming ill.

One way in which we can regard the mother is as an external ego which the infant gradually internalises. The importance of the preoccupation is that it lays the basis for future internalisation and provides the infant with an identity, through identification, from which it can then separate, developing its own identity. It is, to use a phrase usually given a material meaning, a good start in life.

It is easy to see why this should create problems for modern sociological and feminist theory. The emphasis in both is on the social and cultural production of relationships. Nancy Chodorow, for example, argues that biological mothers are not necessarily the best or only people who can take responsibility for children; it is simply that our society organises things that way and tries to justify this on the grounds that it is 'natural'. Winnicott can easily be seen as supporting and reinforcing this social definition, especially when he offers a conception of the father's role as protecting and providing for the mother within her preoccupation, reproducing in his theory the very conventional sexual division of labour that characterises capitalism. His view is opposed by a critique of the mother's social role, which sees it as forcing her into difficult personal contradictions, as having to choose between her baby and career, of forcing her to subordinate herself to the child and often forcing her into a subordinate and exploited social position.

My own view is that the debate tends to take on an either/or quality and what is needed first is a sense of balance and the reality of what Winnicott is talking about. For he does allow that people other than the biological mother, and not necessarily women, can take on the mothering role; the message is not that only biological mothers can raise their children, but that it is usually better if this is the case. This is a minor reservation rather than a reply to the critics. Then, there is a tendency to assume that the preoccupation is eternal. When Winnicott writes about primary maternal preoccupation, when there is a real and total identification between mother and child, he is talking about a period of months before and after birth. What he then goes on to say is that the mother's return to her own interests and life is important for the development of the child. It is the comparative brevity of the period which is important.

Returning to the biological issue, it seems impossible to deny that the fact that a woman carries a child as part of her own body is significant for both the woman and the child, although that significance can vary from individual to individual. It is simply a description of reality to say that the biological mother/child relationship is important.

My final point repeats my argument about the oedipal stage. It is possible to acknowledge the biological differences, and the importance of the mother/child relation, without implying that the social positions of men and women automatically and naturally follow from this importance. It is our society that chooses to make the fact of child-bearing central to a woman's career prospects and social position in such a way that she becomes exploited and subordinated. There is no reason why the relationship between mother and baby that I have just described, nor the aspects of it that I am going to describe, should entail subordination or exploitation. The mother, in her preoccupation, is carrying out a vital social function which our society chooses to devalue, and it is quite possible to imagine systems of maternity and paternity leave and collective child-care which would leave the space for the natural development of the mother/child relationship without damage to either. What would be required would be a degree of flexibility in working arrangements and career patterns for both parents which would entail something like a social revolution but this is not to say it is an impossibility.

Returning to Winnicott's conception of mothering, we should, I think, be clear that one thing we cannot avoid is accepting that having children entails some sacrifice as well as a great deal of pleasure. As Winnicott says, we decide to call the burden a baby. That conflict between self-interest and the child's interest is present for both mothers and fathers, although it can be and usually is exaggerated by forms of social organisation into real stress, especially for the mother. Given, however, that the conflict remains, what is the role of the mother during infancy? The first stages of the infant's complete dependence he again talks about in relation to the mother's physical care. Words such as 'holding' and 'handling' have physical and psychic meanings – we use them in adult relationships where no physical contact is implied. Proper holding and handling, carried out without tuition by the good-enough mother, enable the infant to gain a sense of itself as a unity bounded by its own body. A patient of mine subject to recurring and acute panic attacks frequently associated the feeling with a memory of his head being allowed to drop back off his mother's lap during nappy changing. Failure of 'holding' in a psychic sense can produce a feeling of panic and of falling apart. One of the beneficial aspects of psychoanalytic treatment is the 'holding' and 'handling' provided by the psychoanalytic situation, its regularity, predictability and fixed pattern, and the willingness of the analyst to hold the patients' feelings without letting go. Holding produces a sense of continuity, of boundaries.[1]

The development continues in the intricate terms of often implicit communication between mother and child, during which the mother presents the world to the developing child little by little, allowing it to develop and change in response. What Winnicott emphasises all the time is the fact that the child must be allowed the space to react creatively to its environment, and that real humanity on the part of the child involves more than his or her response to a stimulus. Steadily and in much the same way as was outlined in Klein's account of development, the child sets off on the path to relative independence, the mother requiring less and less to meet that child's every need, and being able to devote more and more time to herself. The child, certainly by the age of two, according to Winnicott, should be able to tolerate the mother's absence. What Winnicott meant by the 'good-enough mother' was what most mothers do most of the time, and of course, most of us grow up to be normally capable, normally happy and unhappy adults. He likened the baby to a lodger who would for a period control the household, but it is important to remember that it is only for a period. The problem is perhaps the sort of social arrangements that are possible to cope with it, without damaging the mother's adult life. It is clear that an increased involvement with the father is important and I shall be returning to this when I look at feminist theory which uses the object-relations approach.

Winnicott's view of the father was that he should be essentially different in role from the mother, although he recognised wide variations in the maternal component of men. During the period of primary maternal preoccupation, and until the child begins to gain some independence, the role of the father is as protector; after that his role is to provide the child with an experience of difference (from the mother) and uniqueness, which the mother cannot do through her identification with her child. He also acts as a means by which new and different aspects of the wider world are introduced to the child. One of the advantages of having two parents is that it enables the child to love and hate at the same time. It can be seen that Winnicott adopted the dominant cultural view of the father, and how far this is a psychological necessity is I think open to question in a way that his view of the mother is not. Nancy Chodorow points out that, generally, male psychoanalysts working in this area tend to ignore the mother's external interests and Winnicott's comments that the father can provide a valuable mother-substitute does provide scope for an alternative view.

Next I shall consider the development from the child's point of view.

THE DEVELOPMENT OF THE PERSON

Turning to the internal development of the baby, I shall outline not the process as a whole but certain crucial aspects that Winnicott identified in the course of his career.

*Unintegration*

I always find this a more interesting idea than integration, partly because of its gentle juxtaposition to the feeling of disintegration discussed earlier. I do not think that it is necessary to oppose integration to one or other of its partners, rather they simply deal with different aspects of experience. For Winnicott the child moves towards integration through the continuity of its care, which is both physical and psychological, but it does not have a sufficiently developed ego to maintain a sense of integration all the time. Lack of integration – unintegration – in spatial terms involves the baby's inability to distinguish him- or herself from the environment. It is difficult to conceive of this in adult experience, but I sometimes suspect that I get close to it when I come home late, exhausted, and slump in front of the television unable to turn it off or over, or even sometimes on. Temporal unintegration is the experience the baby has, according to Winnicott, of being a different self when it is well-fed and contented and when it is screaming for food. Winnicott argues that unintegration is involved with the ability to relax, which in infancy depends upon the presence and safety of the environment supplied by the mother; the ability to relax in adult life develops from this, as does the ability to be alone (as opposed to loneliness). Here the theme of space emerges; the baby must be allowed the space to feel unintegrated without feeling threatened.

I think there is an important point to be made here in connection with Christopher Lasch's theme of cultural narcissism. Unintegration, to be safe, implies integration, initially on the part of the mother, and then on the part of the child. It could be argued that modern industrial society, with its proliferation and fragmentation of roles, encourages unintegration without the surrounding comfort of an integrated self. We experience ourselves as different people in different situations, and indeed there are two central schools of social thought which see temporal non-integration as reality. Symbolic interactionism argues that continuity of the self is by and large situational rather than internal: if we experience ourselves as integrated it is only because of a stable position in an external role structure; and we have already seen how post-structuralist theory deconstructs the unity of the subject. Again, it seems to me that in modern society the ability to be alone is a comparatively rare achievement, certainly in terms of cultural emphases on the role of friends and family, 'togetherness', 'sharing', etc.

### Infantile omnipotence and transitional phenomena

For Winnicott, infantile omnipotence is a crucial experience, basically the experience of creating the world out of one's own need. It has no conception of the mother as a whole person; it is hungry and it screams; a breast or bottle arrives as if from nowhere in its mouth, it feeds and it is content. Adults can revert to this in extreme and perhaps not so extreme moments, and I suspect most of us would call it throwing a tantrum – the need is experienced as so powerful that its loud and violent expression must bring its satisfaction. The satisfaction is probably, according to Winnicott, phantasised in the first place and the conjunction between phantasy and reality, brought about by the mother's response to the baby's needs, is important because it is only when the two are brought together that the process of separating phantasy and reality can be commenced – a process we are all engaged upon for the rest of our lives. If the security and continuity of care is breached, then the baby experiences disintegration, a reverse of its growth.

As the baby becomes aware of its physical boundaries and its separateness, the difficult problem of the relationship between the internal and the external world moves to the foreground. The internal world, the world of phantasy, the world of creation, comes up against the often harsh world of external reality. There is a necessary disillusionment, which we all have to go through, as we learn that we cannot create the satisfaction of our needs; nevertheless, in our internal world we go on creating and our life consists of a process of creation and frustration. There is a third area in between, an area where our phantasy and the world of external reality come together: the transitional area. The clearest example of a transitional phenomenon is the *transitional object*: a child will sometimes become inseparable from a piece of the outside world, a cuddly toy, a piece of blanket, and any intervention by a parent to take the object, even to clean it, will create all sorts of trouble. Winnicott writes of such an article that it makes no sense to ask whether it came from the outside world or whether it was a product of internal phantasy. It is somehow both. The transitional area is the area of play, of creation out of external materials and internal phantasy. He sees it as the area which in adult life becomes art and religion, but also, pathologically, theft and fetishism.

As always with Winnicott's work, it is impossible to reproduce second-hand the subtlety with which he writes about the child's relationship to the transitional object, or the child in play. It is also impossible to present his account in the rigorous way that many sociologists would prefer: there is no real indication of where transitional phenomena might begin and end. It seems to me, in fact, that the transitional area does not begin and end. There is a sense in which all our perceptions and all our knowledge are suffused with our internal phantasies. Sometimes, when we are dealing with projective identification and splitting and projection, the outside world is engulfed by the internal world; in cases of denial, the opposite occurs from the point of view of the individual concerned, although that denial itself makes the external world part of the psychic world. For most of us, however, some distinction between internal and external is possible, and necessary for us to continue anything like a normal existence, but part of that normality is a transitional area. From a sociological point of view, what is interesting about this idea is that it complements points I have made earlier about events in the external world being taken up and given new meanings by our unconscious phantasies, but it points to such transformation of meaning in a less pathological sense.

As an example, I shall take my reaction to the American bombing of Libya in 1986. Initially, the agents were seen as internal objects, a punitive sadistic figure and a weak figure struggling for freedom. My reaction was one of incoherent anger – there was no thought of going on a demonstration, rather I wanted to hit some harmless American tourist on a train. This reaction was pathological. Calmer thought brought me back to the transitional area, where the events were still fused with the internal figures but I became able to distinguish the thoroughly irrational reaction from possible rational courses of action. I could play with ideas of the minimally effective protests, recognising that they were unlikely to have any effect on the events themselves, but might articulate a political position with which others might identify, and might add marginally to the possibility of political change. I could realise the greyness of both sides, as opposed to the black and white of my internal objects, and sort out a coherent argument against the action based on that greyness. Something had been created out of the combination of internal and external, without one swamping the other.

It must be remembered as well that theory, that sociology itself, has a place in the transitional area. Again there can, I think, be pathological forms of theorising in that the theory is constructed and worked out to satisfy, in phantasy, internal needs for, say, omnipotence or envious desires; it can also be a sort of playing in which the internal drives are less satisfied than exercised in an attempt to make new sense of the external world. The convention is to deny this internal reality.

## Concern and morality

For Winnicott there is an innate morality in the baby, an innate concern for others. One of the things that happens as the baby becomes aware of the outside world and the mother as a separate person is that he or she experiences two mothers. There is the mother-object, the mother the baby uses 'ruthlessly' to satisfy its desires; destruction is implied in this. Then there is the 'environment-mother', the mother who provides warmth and protection. The infant can make amends to the latter for the phantasised destruction of the former. We have to live with this sort of ambivalence, and tolerate it, throughout our lives in any sort of loving relationship. Winnicott maintains that no satisfactory social activity can be carried out that is not to some extent based on guilt at aggression.

It seems to me that Winnicott also has a wider and rather different conception of innate morality. This has something to do with personal integrity and, as often with Winnicott, I find it much easier to understand what he has to say than to explain it. He offers a dramatic example. He believes that infantile morality is fierce and involves a refusal to comply with any outside demand at the expense of a personal way of life; an infant may refuse to eat even to the point of death because it believes it is wrong to do so. In adult life we internalise external moralities, but perhaps the basic infantile morality remains in the form of a sense of integrity. It is an integrity which, I think, must be different for everyone, connected somehow with an internal world and a unique relation to an external world.

It seems to me that such integrity might assert itself as some sort of personal need rather than as an obedience to external moral rules. It seems to be there, for example, in the sense that some possible sexual relationships are wrong, even if there is a real attraction, and even if both partners are single and, as we put it, 'free'. It is perhaps also there in the discovery that we do not have to be loved by everyone, and that unsatisfactory and unnecessarily limiting relationships may be left behind. The interesting thing about this from a sociological point of view is just how much sociological explanations discount a sense of integrity and how much sociological theory denies its possibility. Any theory of socialisation or of social action which sees action as *only* produced by expectations or by position in the social structure cannot leave space for a sense of integrity. In this sense sociology is a discipline of the false self.

## *The false self*

It is not altogether fair to single out sociology as a science of the false self – the same can be true of any human science. The false self is common to all of us in everyday life: it is one of the compromises of maturity, a compliance with external demands. In pathological form it is established in the absence of the mother's 'reinforcement' of the baby's omnipotence. I put 'reinforcement' in inverted commas because it is not quite that, certainly not intentional. The good-enough mother responds to her baby's needs, and the baby experiences this as omnipotence, as if those needs actually produce the satisfaction. Winnicott uses the word 'implement'. In any case, the mother who is not good enough does not implement this omnipotence, but in Winnicott's terms 'substitutes her own gesture' with which the infant is expected to comply, giving the gesture meaning. It is, it seems, a reversal of the 'natural' process: instead of the mother giving meaning to the baby's gestures, the baby is expected to give meaning to the mother's.

The intellect is particularly important in the construction of a false self. The mother expects the baby to understand the situation and the baby complies, coming to experience itself as a mind, split off from the rest of the psyche and the body; sometimes the true self can seem completely lost. In the adult, Winnicott writes that the intellectual false self:

> is peculiar in that it very easily deceives. The world may observe academic success of a high degree, and may find it hard to believe in the very real distress of the individual concerned, who feels 'phoney' the more he or she is successful. When such individuals destroy themselves in one way or another, instead of fulfilling promise, this invariably produces a sense of shock in those who have developed high hopes of the individual. (1965: p.144)

Anybody who has worked in a university, or even had experience of student life, will recognise the poignancy of this situation and the number and variety of ways it applies to intellectual life. The important point as far as sociology is concerned, however, is that not only may the intellectual work itself be the product of a false self but only false selves will be seen. There is, I think, something like this going on behind the rationalist bias in sociology that I referred to in the Introduction.

### Destructiveness and anti-social behaviour

I shall end this account of Winnicott with a discussion of his account of what we might call the 'dark side' of human nature largely because this is where I part company with him. As I said earlier, he was reluctant to accept any such notion as the death instinct or an innate desire to destroy the good. Aggressiveness, he argued, is already there in our

motor abilities, a natural impulse to do things, and it becomes attached
to destructive phantasies, which, as far as I can understand him, he saw
as somehow naively natural, built in, say, to the absence of the mother,
something entailed in the *fort/da* game I discussed in relation to Lacan.
Beyond this, destructiveness, in the form of anti-social behaviour, is
the result of a deprivation of a good-enough environment. Winnicott
emphasises *deprivation*: the loss of a good-enough environment. The
result is that when things start going well they cannot be trusted and
are attacked. The absence of a good-enough environment from the
beginning creates a maimed, not necessarily destructive, person. This
distinction seems useful, but on the whole, Winnicott's understanding
of aggression tends towards the sociologistic, surprising in a theorist
who perhaps more than others recognises the importance of space in
the infant's development. It does not carry, as do many such arguments, Utopian implications. Winnicott is not implying the possibility
of a perfect environment, merely that it should be good enough;
nevertheless there is an implication of what I can only call the
possibility of the absence of evil from human life. He likened the
Kleinian idea to a version of original sin, and on the whole I think it is a
good analogy. But I like the idea of original sin, he does not. As I said
when I discussed Klein, I cannot really find a good theoretical
argument for the idea of a death instinct, but it does seem to be there;
religious ideas such as original sin do not come from nowhere, nor
simply from an environment that is not good enough. The real
evidence in support of my case lies in the centrality of the idea to
human thought, and whether we call the idea original sin, the death
instinct, envy or whatever, is of secondary importance. On top of this, I
think the clinical evidence is there too, but we are working at a
theoretical level where there are many mediations to be worked
through before we connect the theory with the evidence, and a great
deal must rest on intellectual rather than clinical interpretations.
Theoretically, I think, it has to be left as a mystery and, as I shall argue
later, there is a case to be made for retaining mysteries.

NOTE

1. For modern theory, the difficulties in Winnicott's conception of mothering are
   paralleled by those of his ideas about sexuality. He clearly thought it better that a
   person develop the sexuality appropriate to his or her body. In the sense of avoiding
   social and personal difficulties, this is probably true. Certainly socially, it is easier to
   be heterosexual than homosexual, and the social difficulties can generate personal
   difficulties or accentuate difficulties that might be there anyway. It seems to me that
   speculation around this issue, however, is not very useful. We can perhaps identify
   after the event why someone has opted, usually unconsciously, for an unconven-

tional form of sexuality, but to lay down, theoretically or clinically, rules for normal sexuality tends to be rather like laying down rules for the weather. It seems to me that we can regard sexuality as something produced in an area of freedom, and the onus is on society to allow for variations which are there in principle from the very beginning of life.

# REFERENCES AND FURTHER
# READING

INTRODUCTION

There are various accounts covering the range of object-relations theory.
I have found the following most useful:

Greenberg, J.R. and Mitchell, S.A. (1983) *Object Relations in Psychoanalytic Theory*, Cambridge, Mass: Harvard University Press.

Guntrip, H. (1961) *Personality Structure and Human Interaction*, London: Hogarth Press.

(1964) *Healing the Sick Mind*, London: Allen and Unwin.

Kohon, G. (ed.) (1986) *The British School of Psychoanalysis: The Independent Tradition*, London: Free Association Books.

For a recent original work, bringing together many ideas from the tradition, see:

Klein, J. (1987) *Our Need for Others and Its Roots in Infancy*, London: Tavistock.

A selection of major works from the school:

Balint, M. (1968) *The Basic Fault*, London: Hogarth Press.

Bowlby, J. (1971) *Attachment*, Harmondsworth: Pelican Books.

(1975) *Separation, Anxiety and Anger*, Harmondsworth: Pelican Books.

(1981) *Sadness and Depression*, Harmondsworth: Pelican Books.

(1988) *A Secure Base: Clinical Applications of Attachment Theory*, London: Routledge and Kegan Paul.

Fairbairn, W.R.D. (1952) *Psychoanalytic Studies of the Personality*, London: Tavistock with Routledge and Kegan Paul.

Guntrip, H. (1969) *Schizoid Phenomena, Object Relations and the Self*, London: Hogarth Press.


CHAPTER 8 MELANIE KLEIN: THE BALANCE OF LOVE
AND HATE

Melanie Klein's collected works are now available in several editions:

Klein, M. (1975) *Collected Works*. Vol. I: *Love, Guilt and Reparation and Other*

*Works*; Vol. II: *The Psychoanalysis of Children*; Vol. III: *Envy and Gratitude and Other Works*; Vol. IV: *Narrative of a Child Analysis*, London: Hogarth Press.
See also:
Mitchell, J. (1986) *The Selected Melanie Klein*, Harmondsworth: Penguin Books.

Among the secondary reading on Klein, Mitchell's introduction to *The Selected Melanie Klein* is useful, but see also:
Grosskurth, P. (1986) *Melanie Klein: A Biography*, London: Hodder and Stoughton.
Segal, H. (1964) *An Introduction to the Work of Melanie Klein*, London: Heinemann.
(1979) *Klein*, London: Fontana/Collins.

Also worth looking at are:
Bott-Spillius, E. (1988) *Melanie Klein Today: Developments in Theory and Practice*. Vol. I: *Mainly Theory*; Vol. II: *Mainly Practice*, London: Routledge and Kegan Paul.
Klein, M. *et al.* (eds) *Significance of Infantile Conflict in the Pattern of Adult Behaviour*, London: Tavistock.
Riviere, J. (1952) *Developments in Psycho-analysis*, London: Hogarth Press.

I mention in the text the Kleinian approach to symbol formation; see:
Segal, H. (1957) 'Notes on symbol formation', *International Journal of Psychoanalysis* 29.

I also mention in the text:
Bion, W.R. (1964) *Second Thoughts*, London: Heinemann Medical Books.

CHAPTER 9 D.W. WINNICOTT: SPACE AND MORALITY

Winnicott's own work:
Winnicott, D.W. (1957) *The Child and the Family: First Relationships*, London: Tavistock.
(1957) *The Child and the Outside World: Studies in Developing Relationships*, London: Tavistock.

Much of the above was brought together in:
Winnicott, D.W. (1964) *The Child, the Family and the Outside World*, Harmondsworth, Penguin Books.
(1965a) *The Family and Individual Development*, London: Tavistock.
(1965b) *The Maturational Processes and the Facilitating Environment*, London: Hogarth Press.

(1971a) *Playing and Reality,* London: Tavistock.

(1971b) *Therapeutic Consultations in Child Psychiatry,* London: Hogarth Press.

(1975) *Through Paediatrics to Psychoanalysis,* London: Hogarth Press.

(1978) *The Piggle,* London: Hogarth Press.

(1986) *Home is Where We Start From,* Harmondsworth, Penguin Books.

(1988) *Human Nature,* London: Free Association Books.

(1988) *Babies and Their Mothers,* London: Free Association Books.

There is comparatively little secondary work on Winnicott, although an immense amount employing his ideas. For fair accounts, see:

Chancier, A. and Kalmanoritch, J. (1988) *Winnicott and Paradox,* London: Routledge and Kegan Paul.

Davis, M. and Wallbridge, D. (1983) *Boundary and Space: An Introduction to the Work of D.W. Winnicott,* Harmondsworth: Penguin Books.

Phillips, A. (1988) *Winnicott,* London: Fontana.

# PART IV

## CONCLUSION

# 10

## THE LIMITS OF SOCIOLOGY

I have argued that the concepts of orthodox Freudian theory – instinct or drive theory – are too general to help us understand anything more than the broadest framework of the relation between individual and society. We can take from these approaches the conflict between instinct and civilisation, with its implication that each individual has to find some way of living with this conflict; and we can take the link that has been made between the role of the state, the father and personality structure. Neither of these, however, can provide us with the basis of a proper theory of society, or of the complexities of the individual psyche; they point only to some of the connections between the two.

Chapters 8 and 9 concentrate on internal processes, connecting with the social world primarily through the mother/child relationship. My argument is that in these internal processes, the largely unconscious phantasy world and the ways in which this internal world and the external world come together, inextricably, in a transitional and essential creative combination, we find the limits of sociological understanding. However, before looking at this in more detail, I want to argue that object-relations theory can provide an aid to sociological analysis that takes us closer to real human relationships and situations than do the more orthodox forms of Freudian theory. I shall start by looking at some recent feminist attempts to employ object-relations theory. They provide a useful contrast with the feminism of Juliet Mitchell that I have discussed in Part I. I shall also look at the more general processes of development in modern society that are of concern to Lasch and the Frankfurt School, again arguing that object-relations theory can give us a fuller understanding of what is happening. Finally, in this chapter, I want to explore the use of the approach in adding a dimension of understanding in the analysis of collective social movements and group behaviour. In all three areas, I shall be arguing that there are still limits to the analysis, and that these are the limits of any sort of sociological understanding. This will set the scene for the final chapter.


### MEN AND WOMEN

Nancy Chodorow puts the case for object-relations theory clearly: it offers a more complex view of society, based on the quality and extent of possible integration rather than a 'monolithic' conception of repression; it recognises that some part of the self, however small, is available for transformative activity. It offers the possibility of looking at intersubjectivity as both a social-historical and an interpersonal-psychological phenomenon:

> With a notion of primary sociality and intersubjectivity, with a theory that includes, in addition to sociality in a general sense, gender, generation and sexuality in a specific historical sense, with an account that sees life as a development and relational process, one could even begin to imagine not only liberated individuals, but individuals mutually engaged in a society built on liberated forms of social life. (1985: 312)

I have no real disagreement with Chodorow's case, but I think that when we move beyond programmatic statements such as this, the task becomes less easy. The limits of social analysis are greater than she imagines, and individual creativity, the space for individual action, is more problematic and conflict-laden. Here, I want only to look at the first difficulty, the limits of social analysis, and I shall do so by looking at her own work. I would emphasise what I said earlier when I discussed Chodorow's argument: that it seems to me that we still need instinct theory, both as a level of explanation, and in relation to the immediate experience of being governed by forces beyond our control.


### *Object-relations theory and femininity*

It is certainly the case that object-relations theory gives us a much more specific form of social analysis, which can be related to historically and socially variable family patterns and child-rearing practices, as well as to the specific features of each family. Chodorow's work as a sociologist is backed up by the work of two practising therapists, Louise Eichenbaum and Susie Orbach. I have already presented these arguments elsewhere (Craib, 1987), and I shall only summarise them here. While Chodorow gives a broad overview, Eichenbaum and Orbach present a rather more complex picture.

Their focus is not on the grand issue of sexuality *per se*, with personality structure simply derived from the oedipal model, as it is for Mitchell. Rather, it is on the different forms of early relationship which boy and girl babies have first with the mother and then with the father, and the way these relationships are internalised, in the course of development towards integration and relative independence, to produce different personality structures in adulthood. For both, but explicitly for Chodorow, the fact that women mother is of prime importance, preparing a little girl for mothering. Mothering entails certain requirements that are not necessarily, but have, in practice, come to be, socially seen and defined as feminine.

The argument is that the little girl is inhibited in her growth towards relative independence by a special identification which takes place between herself and her mother. This is neither left behind nor integrated in adulthood. Chodorow writes as if primary maternal preoccupation is somehow continued, and the adult daughter and mother will frequently feel 'the same' in quite fundamental ways. Eichenbaum and Orbach talk about a cycle, which, empirically, I have found very familiar, from the daughter identifying closely with her mother to attempting a complete emotional separation. Physical development towards relative independence can be taken as roughly the same for both sexes, but Chodorow's argument is that the little boy is pushed into psychic separation at a fairly early stage, while psychic separation is denied the little girl. Since mothering is work socially assigned to women, the father is almost always in some sense 'absent'; this may be literally and absolutely the case when we are talking about single parent families headed by women, through lesser degrees of absence, for example, in the case of families in which a divorced father has access, to what we might call 'normal absence' where a father might see his children briefly in the morning and evening, and at weekends.

The result is that the little boy becomes to some extent a substitute for the father. Chodorow argues that the relationship is sexualised from a very early stage, and gender identity becomes bound up with the process of individuation. The little boy comes to sense his masculinity as a vital part of his self-identity. Since the father is absent, the little boy finds it difficult to internalise a whole male person, with good and bad sides, strengths and weaknesses, and has to identify with an image of masculinity. She argues that, unlike femininity, masculinity often has to be consciously taught. The little girl, on the other hand, does not break free from the original identification with her mother.

The result is that in adult life the little boy has what she calls 'stronger ego boundaries' and a less complex internal object world. I am not too happy with this way of putting it. Ego-strength in psychoanalytic terms has to do with, among other things, the ability to experience strong emotions, and Chodorow is talking about the opposite: the man finds it difficult to feel empathy and tends to avoid strong emotions. Similarly, the complexity of the internal object world is less to do with gender than with the introjected objects, parents and siblings and later others. It is likely to be much the same in terms of complexity for both men and women. Instead, I tried to reconceptualise it in terms of a male fear of strong feelings, handled largely by projection. An example comes from Eichenbaum and Orbach: female dependence, they argue, rightly I think, is in fact a male myth, a result of projection. Dependence is a strong and dangerous feeling that men, by and large, try to avoid. It is clear from the above account than it is not allowed from an early developmental stage.

The female counterpart for Chodorow is weak ego boundaries, a strong and perhaps too ready ability to empathise, and a complex internal object world. The same sorts of objection can be raised to this description and I tried to reconceptualise it in terms of the dominant feminine defence being introjection. I think it is easier to understand this from Eichenbaum and Orbach's account. Their argument is that, in our society, women learn, usually unconsciously, that to be a woman involves subordinating their own needs to those of others. This makes the mother's identification with the little girl particularly difficult. The mother, having repressed her own needs, is faced by another female, another potential woman, who is only needy. She (the mother) is faced with the problem of satisfying the baby girl's needs and with teaching her to repress them. In fact, her daughter reflects back to her all those needy parts that she herself has repressed, and this produces an ambivalence: her needs must be met and they must be repressed. This reflects the ambivalence and fluctuation in the grown daughter's relationship to her mother. Thus the little girl, like the little boy, does not outgrow her psychic dependency as part of a 'natural' develop-ment, and has to repress it. Whereas the little boy does so by projection, the little girl introjects the needs of others, to the point where satisfying the needs of others is experienced as the satisfaction of her own needs. For Chodorow this reproduces the female role of mothering.

This, then, is the sort of analysis that object-relations theory can produce in relation to gender identity. Sexuality itself is less important than it is for Mitchell. Nor are we presented with an inevitable causal process. It is quite conceivable that, for all sorts of possible reasons, some men might grow up with a 'feminine personality', and vice versa. Rather, we are presented with a continuum, and by and large most men end up with a personality somewhere on the masculine side, and most women with a personality on the feminine side. One might suspect that in personality terms 'feminine men' and 'masculine women' might be homosexual, but there is plenty of everyday experience to indicate that this does not follow. The tie with sexuality as a sort of causal basis to personality structure that we find in Mitchell's work is broken.

A big advantage is that this is an approach which can take account of variations in child-rearing practices. The concepts employed allow not only for social and historical variations (different practices 200 years ago are likely to have produced different types of adult personality), they also allow for individual variations to be understood in terms of specific family structures and different individual personalities, in Winnicott's terms, perhaps, different environmental mothers. Instead of having to work at the abstract and universal level of the oedipal conflict, with a number of variations, we can go straight to specific child-rearing practices and experiences. We can therefore find a much more concrete form of politics from object-relations analysis. For both Chodorow, and Eichenbaum and Orbach, this politics involves men in mothering, in the early care of infants. This in turn brings us back to my discussion of Winnicott and it does offer the possibility of a critique of his work. It seems to me that we cannot get round the biological fact that women give birth, but this can, I suspect, be limited in its social consequences. One way of doing this is by involving men increasingly in child-care after the first months, and perhaps more as an emotional as well as a practical support during later pregnancy and the early months of life. In other words, the father can be added to the environment that provides continuity, a sense of boundaries and the space for the child's development. How we do that is still, I think, a difficult matter, for reasons which will become apparent shortly.

Now I want to turn to the limitations of this approach. The psychoanalytic theory employed here actually points directly to the nature of the limitations. I think the crucial issue is to be clear about the level of analysis at which we are working. The above discussion covers two levels and points to a third. The two levels that it combines are those of general social structures and general child-rearing practices and personality structures. It points towards the level of individual personality structure.

I think that one of the most important advantages of this type of analysis is that it leaves open the relationship between psychic and social structure, although at first sight this is not obvious. It would seem that, in our society, women generally have the type of personality that suits them for domestic work, caring and child-rearing; and men have the type of personality that suits them for work outside the home, which is often a matter of survival, struggle and competition. We could argue, therefore, that the psychological structures produced by child-rearing 'cause' the sexual division of labour in society. Alternatively, we could argue that (patriarchal) society produces the child-rearing practices that ensure its reproduction and survival. I think Chodorow gets closer to the second possibility, Eichenbaum and Orbach to the first.

I have spent a large part of this book trying to show that neither position is tenable, that society is the combination of a number of different causal processes. It is conceivable that one of these is the link between child-rearing practices and adult personality and the sexual division of labour but the link that exists is one of many other links and we cannot derive a total explanation from it. What we have is an account that fits with other accounts of other processes. Here lies one difficulty in what might be called 'the politics of fathering'. The fact that we are dealing with one process among many means that a change in child-rearing practices to involve the father need not have any significant effects on the distribution of power between men and women in the wider society, nor on the sort of personality required to operate effectively in that structure. The change would be in domestic life and in the depth and range of personal characteristics available to men and women. It would involve changes in career structures and work organisation, as I remarked earlier, but it does not follow that there would be a change in overall power-relations between men and women. It is conceivable that women's work would remain just that, and that men would hold on to the more powerful jobs. Similarly, we can imagine a society in which power is distributed more equally between the sexes, but which still maintains mothering as a strictly feminine role – either through the provision of wider child-care facilities than are at present available (staffed by women) or by allowing a larger number of women to remain childless, or perhaps through a reorganisation of career structures to enable women to mother and have careers.

I argued in my paper (1987) that these accounts of the development of femininity and masculinity should be taken as ideal-types in the Weberian sense, as rational reconstructions of a complex and contradictory reality. They are accounts of the ways men and women tend to act socially, in relation to others. Sociological analysis can show the fit between the typical behaviour patterns and other social processes, such as the sexual division of labour, but it does not follow that there is a causal relation between them. Now if we regard these theories of masculine and feminine personality structures as ideal-types, then we are taken towards the limits of this type of analysis. If they are rational reconstructions of a complex reality, that reality includes not only a number of other social structural processes but also a range of individual psychological processes that are contradictory in all sorts of ways.

I think clinical practice shows clearly that at an individual level we can find all sorts of complex cross-gender identifications. Every mother is in some specific, individual way masculine and every father feminine, and each will deal with those aspects of the personality in different ways. These will in turn be a reaction to the masculinity of their mothers and the femininity of their fathers. A perusal of almost any case-study establishes this. An ideal-type cannot cope with this specificity, nor should it. It is not the function of the sociologist to treat clinical evidence with the consideration and detail of the psychoanalyst, and if he or she were to do so, then sociology itself would become impossible, swamped by individual detail. Here we have the first limit to sociology, provided by the level of generalisation necessary to make sociological sense, to say something about general social processes and their relationship to the social structure in which we are all situated.

This limit is pointed to by object-relations theory in the way in which it draws attention to specific child-rearing practices and the specific organisation of the inner-object world. If cultural practices vary, then so do individual practices. Perhaps the limitation of sociological analysis is shown most clearly by the creative nature of psychotherapeutic practice, which Winnicott describes as taking place in the overlap of two play areas – that of the patient and that of the therapist. In social analysis, there is no room for play – the emphasis is, and must be, on coherence, rationality and causal relations.

The interesting question for sociology here is if and when these individual variations might affect general social processes and structures, perhaps by tranforming the effects of society on people in such a way as from the sociological point of view, their behaviour seems irrational and unpredictable; and whether these individual reactions, together or separately might actually transform social processes and structures.

### Object-relations theory and general social processes

Moving on from gender differences I now want to look at object-relations theory in terms of the even more general social and historical processes that were discussed in Chapter 6 in terms of more orthodox Freudian theory. The sort of criticism that I made of Freudian theory at this level will also apply to object-relations theory, but again with the proviso that the latter is capable of producing more specific analyses, partly because the complexity of its picture of the inner-object world allows more variations, partly because it is capable of taking into account specific features of the environment.

For orthodox Freudian theory the crucial variables were the super-ego and the state. A strong super-ego requires less state or social control of people's actions; the weaker the super-ego, the stronger the state has to be, the more dependent people become on the external agency, and consequently the weaker the super-ego becomes. In both cases the eventual aim is to repress, control and/or sublimate instinctual impulses which are seen as a major threat to social organisation or, possibly, as a source of social liberation. The development of modern industrial society over the past century is seen in terms of changes in family structure and relationships and corresponding changes in the state on the one hand, and personality structure on the other. The approaches that employ instinct theory take two directions. On the one hand, there is Marcuse's equation of social liberation and instinctual liberation, which I criticised in Part I; on the other, there is, at least implicitly, the view that we need to return to a comparatively rigid patriarchal authority within and outside the family, and an assumption that the irrational aspects of human behaviour can be eliminated. This is the approach I criticised in Chapter 6.

We can take as our starting point Lasch's argument that the narcissistic personality is in fact the appropriate personality for advanced industrial society; it is the personality structure that from the point of view of society enables modern technology and industry and finance to continue, and from the point of view of the individual offers the best chance of survival. This is a flat statement and one that implies exactly the tight, interlocked, functional/causal relationship between society and individual that I have been arguing against. However, it would follow from my earlier argument that if we drop the assumption of a causal relation, we can accept the move towards narcissism as one of several ways of being in the context of a combination of a number of different social processes: the increasing lack of moral responsibility and autonomy in the work situation, bureaucratisation, modern technology, the processes, well documented by Lasch and others, which have stripped the family of its functions and made childbirth and rearing the province of expert rather than general knowledge, the pluralisation of roles in everyday life that go with urban and industrial living, and the decline in manual skills in favour of more abstract skills.

It is possible to accept that this has to do with the weakening of parental and paternal roles and the strength of the super-ego and ego. Object-relations theory can take us beyond that, to look at the effects of these processes in terms of the development of the self. The weakening of the child–parent relationship in the socialisation process, and the pluralisation of roles can be seen as a fragmentation of individual experience. This theme has been dominant in sociological thought since the last century, different aspects appearing as alienation for Marx, anomie for Durkheim and rationalisation and disenchantment for Weber. In terms of psychoanalytic work, this real fragmentation of experience in the outer world corresponds to the earlier paranoid-schizoid position in the inner world. The external environment is impoverished in that it offers little in the way of support for integration and development, for the building of a self and an identity. Lasch's argument is that for Freud the problem was finding satisfactory ways of living with instinctual repression; now it is a matter of finding ways of living without such repression and he turns to Klein rather than Freud for an understanding of the inner world where instinctual repression is weakened. If he stayed with Freud I am not sure it would be possible to say anything more than that modern society allows, and perhaps alienates, greater instinctual satisfaction than it did a hundred years ago. The reality is much more complex.

The limit of this sort of analysis lies in the fact that it is again describing a general tendency. Just as we each have our own individual neuroses, so we have our own ways of living with narcissism. To say that there are impoverished materials available for building a self does not mean that a self, an identity, which allows more than survival, is impossible. The space which lies beyond sociological understanding is again the creative element in the activity of individuals and small groups. In practice, people can have any number of ways of establishing themselves in relation to others and to the outside world that bring them satisfaction; it could be a particular sort of work, a personal intimate relationship, the raising of children, one's own or others, a particular leisure activity, or some combination of any of them. The security of parental love and consistency of discipline is not impossible, although it might have to take different forms, and perhaps the more desirable psychic structure is not that governed by a strong super-ego, but one governed by a strong ego which can allow the strength of pre-oedipal desires and fears without necessarily acting on them.

What I am saying is that there is a range of freedom for an individual to construct a strong self; different and creative ways of living with narcissism. Erikson and Winnicott point respectively to religion and art as comparatively differentiated areas of adult life in which the feelings and experiences of the early stages of development may be expressed and satisfied. It might be that these areas can permeate other areas of adult life, that perhaps in small ways we can look at everyday life as an art, as opposed to a course of action, which a century ago would have been the more appropriate way. It must be remembered that any sort of society, in some sense or another, makes a satisfactory life difficult. The question has been, how does *this* society make life difficult and produce this particular range of problems? One can speculate that sufficient people can find sufficient satisfaction in their lives to make it worthwhile for them to continue in much the same way, refusing the possibilities both of subordinating themselves to a strong state or of revolution, or of madness; they can manage productively the potentially dangerous aspects of narcissism.

Although object-relations theory can give us a wider analysis, in terms of the whole self, it is, then, still very general, and it can point to the area of individual self-creation where social analysis cannot go. In this context, we can engage in a further contemplation of one of the paradoxes of my argument. I made the case that there was no necessary connection between the experiences of the oedipal stage and father–child relationships during this stage with the organisation and distribution of power in the wider society, or if there was such a connection then it was a sign of pathology. My point was that social organisation can be a matter of rational politics, child-rearing cannot. Yet when I dealt with those theories that use psychoanalysis to envisage a rational society, I argued that irrationality could not be left behind. It seems to me that the aim is to keep things in their proper place. Social organisation, the distribution of power between men and women, is a matter of rational debate; the irrationality must be worked out in the transitional area, the area of familial relationships where strong emotions are appropriate. Of course, this is actually what happens: each couple, involving whatever sex, achieves or fails to achieve those day-to-day compromises and innovations that help to make life bearable or positively pleasant or happy. Among the conflicts that have to be coped with or resolved here are those set up during the oedipal stage, and perhaps above all the conflict between envy of somebody close but different and love. Sociology can tell us about the patterns of marriage relationships; it cannot tell us about the individual colouring, flavour, strategies and arrangements, internal and external, by which we all make life more or less liveable.

## Collective processes

I want now to turn to a third area where I believe we can extend the scope of sociological analysis by means of object-relations theory, that of collective behaviour, or the part of it that is motivated by unconscious processes and relationships. I think there are two forms of analysis possible here: one is concerned with particular institutional frameworks and the way in which they develop as a result of unconscious processes; the second is concerned with rather more amorphous collective phenomena.

In the introductory chapter, I gave some idea of how unconscious processes might work in an institutional setting. My example there was my reacting to my boss as if he represented my father, and bringing into play all the feelings I might have had about my father. If we can take the institutional setting of work as a place where it is possible to project our internal world, then there will be times when all the various projections come into conjunction and lead to events and possibly changes in the institutional setting. Isabel Menzies' (1970) study of a teaching hospital is probably the finest example of this type, I suspect in part because the strength of the anxieties inherent in nursing make it especially open to psychodynamic study. If the institutional framework forces the repression of these anxieties rather than containing them, as good-enough parents might, then organisational problems are likely to develop.

The beginnings of a way of understanding unconscious group processes is provided by the work of Wilfrid Bion; it has a distinct Kleinian flavour and it provides a link with the sort of institutional analysis I have just discussed and with the more amorphous collective reactions of which I shall give examples shortly. Bion's central contribution was to identify what he called 'basic assumption groups'.

These can be seen as unconscious defences against rational understanding and self-guided action by a group. These possibilities are defended against precisely because they are risky: in any group there will be conflict in which each individual thinks he or she is at serious risk, and the ability to stand alone, to make one's own decisions and accept and deal with the consequences, remaining within a network of relationships upon which one might be dependent, and working co-operatively is always a hard-won ability, which I suspect none of us ever achieves completely.

One basic-assumption group which defends against these possibilities is the 'flight–fight' group. What happens is that the group might pick an external enemy or possibly an internal scapegoat, or it might divide against itself or its leader, the two sides arguing violently. In either case the group is avoiding an exploration of the real relationships within the group and an acceptance and dealing with those relationships. It is avoiding what is really going on because what is really going on is sensed as too painful or difficult. In Kleinian terms, what is involved is a projection of hostile, destructive feelings on to an individual or group who becomes an enemy, experienced as hostile and destructive. This enables the good feelings to be protected and preserved in the in-group. A second basic-assumption group is the dependency group, where the work is left to a group leader, who is expected to direct, instruct and take responsibility. The group regresses to an infantile dependency upon the mother, on the 'good breast', from which a bountiful supply of comforting food is expected. The third basic assumption group is something I found difficult to understand in the abstract, although it was easier after experiencing it in a group. This is the 'pairing group': two members of the opposite sex experience something like falling in love, or perhaps do fall in love. There is a general excitement among the rest of the group, who come to place their hope in this pair and their love. Bion suggests that the phantasy is that the union of the couple will produce a Saviour, a Messiah, who will relieve everybody of the burden of their 'sinfulness', the feelings they find dangerous and unpleasant.

I shall now, briefly, give a sociological example of each of these basic-assumption groups. The flight–fight group is fairly simple: it is a common-sense idea that an external enemy or a scapegoat is a useful weapon for those in power who want to maintain and increase that power, and that they will frequently find many subjects willing to place everything bad upon the enemy. If we take the First World War as an example, a flight–fight reaction seems to go some way to explaining the enthusiasm for fighting that outweighed what seems, from the perspective of eighty years further on, to be the rational self-interest of avoiding the horrors and insanities of the war. A dependency group is more difficult to find, but I think we might be witnessing one in modern Britain. Certainly, ten years ago, I, and many people on the left, would have predicted that a Conservative government, following the policies of the Thatcher government, would have had to face massive social unrest, and would probably have not survived its first term in office. In fact, it has been re-elected twice with large majorities, and the unrest, while there, has not been massive and has been suppressed. My speculation about what might be happening is that there is a complicated phantasy involving the projection of power on to the government, particularly on to Mrs Thatcher, and a contentment to live in awe of that power. For many people Thatcher's 'toughness' is simultaneously attractive and frightening. It is frightening because of the destructive feelings projected on to her; attractive because it relieves people of the responsibility to contribute to what might happen, as well as relieving them of their own destructive feelings. An example of a pairing is more difficult to find, but again I think there is an example in modern Britain: the interest and enthusiasm aroused by Royal weddings, and perhaps the Royal Family in general.

Now with all these examples, there are also structural explanations: the First World War can be seen as a product of economic competition, for example, and explanations at a cognitive level, in terms of the force of ideologies, nationalism, 'Thatcherism', etc., or even in terms of rational self-interest. All these explanations seem to me quite reasonable; the problem with each is that it leaves a space between what is being explained and the explaining factors; we might see it as the transitional area, the area of 'play'. Structural processes might have created the conditions for the First World War, but wars can be avoided, mutually satisfactory agreements arrived at. Ideologies do not have to take hold of people and drive them forward – there are plenty of examples of failed ideologies, even when conditions have been favourable to them. And finally, explanations in terms of rational self-interest, simply because they concern rational decisions, always leave a choice. Rationality does not imply determinism. The understanding of the unconscious mechanisms, and phantasies completes the other explanations.

These are examples of situations where psychoanalysis can add to a sociological understanding. Here, the limit of social analysis is the individual perception and unconscious phantasy, and the creative use of these and external materials in the transitional area. Where psychoanalysis can offer such specific insights it goes beyond the limits of sociology. There is always a dimension of unconscious meaning in people's perception of the external world. As well as the rational content to, for example, political commitment, there is also a relation to an individual's internal conflicts and neuroses (see Parin, 1985). This brings us back to the question of what happens beyond the limits of sociology, whether this dimension of meaning matters in our understanding of the world.

# 11

## BEYOND THE LIMITS

I feel that I am not very good at conclusions. Perhaps the model we often use for an argument, in a book or a paper, is based on sexual intercourse. A slow and steady build-up and a satisfying climax, followed by relaxation and basking in the warmth of the achievement. I find increasingly that I want to continue playing. Perhaps it is an effect of age. I have nothing startling to say: simply to point to the world of play, the world to which we can gain access through psychodynamic theory, and say to the sociologist that there is more to the world than is dreamt of in your theory. I shall say this at length in the first half of this chapter and then continue playing.

To begin with, I shall look at some of the things that happen in therapy and experiential groups, comparing a psychodynamic under-standing of these processes with various possibilities of sociological understanding, and trying to show the area of freedom, of play, that we can find here. Then I shall play with some of the phantasies and desires that might lie behind social analysis which implicitly or explicitly denies the existence of such an area. Finally, I shall look again at object-relations theory and try to tease out a critical dimen-sion, a view of the possibilities of social organisation which would allow individual space, beyond the ability to be rational.

Here we return to the central paradox or contradiction of my argument. I have argued that it is possible to conceive of a society that does not reproduce early, irrational perceptions as part of the social order – that, for example, the perceptions of the oedipal stage need not reappear as a male-dominated social organisation. I have also argued that these irrational perceptions must be a part of all our lives, and the conflicts they entail last on and must be dealt with, lived with in some way. The paradox is that we are both rational and irrational. Sociology too has to find ways of living with the irrational, allowing for the creative, the play areas in human life. This is something that cannot be understood simply as a product of society, language or discourse.

## Ordinary creativity

Erikson's aim is to understand how individuals can create something new and effective through their individual neuroses, which in turn can be seen as examples of a general neurosis. It seems to me that such creativity exists in every life, not on a world-changing scale, but as ways of living with general situations we all have to suffer, ways of making life more bearable for ourselves and the people we love. In every therapy group of which I have experience I have found myself respecting the ways in which patients have led often difficult and damaged lives, and their attempts at damage limitation, particularly in relation to their children and spouses. Theoretically, I have several times reiterated the source of this creativity: the compromises and balances of the internal object world, the dynamics of phantasy life and the transition area where these things come together with the external world and forge something different. I have several times asked the question, in what ways is this area important, if it is at all important to sociology?

I want to try to answer this question by some discussion of what occurs in a psychotherapy group, looking in turn at a number of different levels. To begin with, one gets a number of individuals. On the private market, these are self-selected; in the National Health Service they are referred via general practitioners and psychiatrists. The sociologist would immediately ask a number of questions about these people. In the case of the private group, I imagine the questions would have to do with self-selection: this makes it likely that the members would be fairly articulate, middle-class people who not only know about the existence of psychotherapy and what it might entail, but also know of ways of finding out about it, where to get it, and so on. In the case of the NHS, the questions would be concerned with the social distribution of 'mental illness' and of the diagnostic process (which many sociologists would see in terms of labelling theory) that led to people being identified as needing treatment and then referred for psychotherapy. These questions and answers would say something about society rather than the individuals. They would lead to conclusions, perhaps, about the social distribution of treatments – what sort of treatment is available to which social groups; it is often a criticism of psychoanalysis, for example, that it is best suited to an articulate, knowledgeable middle- and upper-class group who can afford it. There might also be conclusions about the social distribution, and therefore causation, of 'mental illness'. Depression, for example, or schizophrenia, seems to occur more frequently amongst underprivileged social groups. Others might talk about the labelling process, implying that patients are simply different from other people, perhaps not very different, but have fallen foul of relatives and the power of the medical and psychiatric professions, and internalised the role into which they have been put.

All these approaches seem to me to have something useful to say. Psychoanalytic therapy is a social institution and implicated in the class structure; our society does make it more likely that some sorts of people rather than others will succumb to what we call 'mental illness'; there is certainly a labelling process going on in diagnosis and treatment which might have little to do with the real unhappiness of the individual concerned. However, I have never met anybody as a client or patient who can be seen simply as the end-product of one or other of these factors. Certainly, there are people whose social conditions and work situation leave much to be desired, and who could cope better if these conditions were different; certainly, there are self-indulgent, narcissistic, middle-class clients part of whom would like nothing better than spending years talking about themselves without changing; and there are people who have been labelled, often in ways they do not like, whose difficulties have been misunderstood. But all such people have difficulties which go beyond these factors, an internal unhappiness, frustration or conflict which has made their lives, and/or the lives of those around them difficult.

Social factors, of course, appear in the therapy. One sees, for example, the effects of different types of socialisation, different class positions and different outside roles. These effects can appear at a cognitive level: people can come into a therapy group, say, with the political and social opinions that might easily be predicted from their social background. They enter with the different linguistic and cognitive abilities that are associated with different social classes and educational backgrounds. What becomes apparent after a while, however, is that the views and opinions are put to the service of, and often appear to be even the product of, a range of feelings – love, hate, envy, etc. – and will sometimes begin to change as the balance of these feelings change. Sometimes these views and opinions are used as more or less clear defences. I think of one man who held racist views, and who sociologically fell in to a grouping – a 'poor white' grouping – that might be expected to hold such a view. It was also clear, however, that these views were part of a way of relating to others that was habitual and very close to consciousness: it was a means by which he established himself as an outsider in any group, a hostile outsider. This in turn brought him the concern and attention, however unsatisfactory, that he felt he could not get in any other way. At the same time, the racism was a conscious expression of a paranoid phantasy about the world – a world of hostile and rejecting parts, which was how he experienced his internal world. In this way, his views were a defence against a recognition of that internal world by projecting it outside himself; eventually, it was a defence against full entry into the depressive position. Any constellation of political views can fulfil similar functions for the personality.

Sometimes this behaviour is part-cognitive, part-preconscious, and it can be a very strong defensive level. Often, it seems to me in training groups drawn from the 'caring' professions – social workers, health visitors, doctors, nurses – one is presented with something that Goffmann (1968) calls an 'institutional self'. This is something we all develop: a way of behaving and a way of being that is expected of us in a particular setting. It is more, I think, than playing a role: it is the adoption of a self in a way that is perhaps not consciously recognised. In the professions mentioned above, this role involves competence, lack of emotion, a sense of being able to cope, and often a sense of being well-adjusted, not sharing in the problems, let alone the madness of clients. A training group run along lines of psychoanalytic therapy is experienced as a challenge to this self. Members are asked to explore not only their difficulties and feelings of inadequacy, but also eventually their own madness. The institutional self emerges not only as something adopted to 'pass' in their everyday work, but as a systematic defence against a rage of internal feelings. Often, it emerges that the external, institutional, caring self depends upon a projection of internal damage and pain on to those cared for. There it can be built not only into a way of working but into a political and religious view of the world. In each of these examples the material supplied by the outside world is taken up and transformed by internal processes: what we have at the end is a combination that cannot be attributed to either.

The same transformation takes place for the general processes identified by object-relations theory and discussed in the last chapter. The self that is presented can be seen as the unconscious product of early socialisation, as outlined by Chodorow, and Eichenbaum and Orbach. Women often present the features of personality that they discuss, and so do men, although I do not think that even on a surface level these features are anything like universal. What always intrigues me about this is that, after a while, these personality features also emerge in the service of the normal range of feelings, or they begin to crumble and a range of 'non-gender, appropriate' feelings emerges. In fact, what begins to come out is the range of individual cross-identifications from early developments. Interestingly, the archetypes of what Winnicott calls, in capital letters, WOMAN – and its counterpart, which to the best of my knowledge he does not discuss, MAN – these remain, and often provide the focus of conflict; but the real people there, and their real relationships, display a wide variety of individual forms of bisexuality.

The same individual interpretive and creative process can be found in the usually unconscious group processes that I discussed earlier in terms of 'social movements' – the flight–fight group or the dependency group, for example. In some ways, these are the 'stuff' of group psychotherapy, the level at which one sees emerge very primitive feelings in universal human terms. At this level, too, very primitive family experiences are reproduced. Yet even here, there are important individual differences, important that is in understanding what is going on in the group and in terms of the therapeutic effectiveness of the group.

As an example, I shall employ a group in which rivalry, originally sibling rivalry, is close to the surface. Overtly, this will manifest itself in different ways: complaints, say, about the number of people in the group; resistance to the introduction of a new member should an old member leave; members feeling and expressing irritability with each other; comments about people who are absent; sometimes attempts to see the therapist alone. (All these things, incidentally, could signify something other than rivalry – in this case there will also be other signs which point to the rivalry, perhaps in the explicit content of what members talk about.) Each member in the group will have his or her own, very specific position in this competition. For one person, it will be experiencing themselves yet again as the unfavoured one, who can only get something remotely approaching a sign of love by misbehaviour; for another it will be the oppressive family meal where nothing approaching the truth can ever be spoken, and at which they must act, for fear of their existence, as a father or mother substitute to younger brothers and sisters; for a third, it will be the place where they must keep quiet about whatever they feel because father is ill; for a fourth it will be a matter of keeping quiet about a brother's deformity; for all, it will involve more or less suppressed aggression and guilt. And all will have developed their own particular way of dealing with this earlier experience which is, consciously or unconsciously, brought back to them.

The recognition and sharing of the common aspects are important, involving a recognition of the normality of these feared feelings; at the same time, unless the individual differences are recognised and explored, then the experience is unsatisfactory, partly because options are not explored and exposed, partly because individuality, if not explored, remains experienced as dangerous, shameful, frustrating or whatever; partly because it also feels like an absence of recognition, as if nobody cares. It is not just the differences of individual experiences that are important, but also of individual phantasies. The fear of showing hostility to siblings, for example, might for one person be a fear of being isolated, abandoned and lonely; for another it might be a fear of being lynched; for another, not just being destroyed, but of being destroyed in particularly nasty ways – 'I'll be eaten up', 'They'll tear me to pieces', and so on.

I suspect that where group interpretations are the only ones employed by the therapist, and where they are employed only sparingly and are concerned primarily with the most basic unconscious processes (this usually happens in groups run on the model supplied by Bion), the therapeutic effects are minimal. It seems to me that one of the aims of working with groups, an aim which cannot really be achieved in individual therapy, is to enable an individual to discover a way in which he or she can handle, at the same time, their need for and dependence on other people and their hostility and often hatred of others; the way in which they can understand themselves as part of a group, which they are all the time, throughout their lives, even if they are socially isolated, and as an individual separate and different from others; the way, if you like, in which they can discover their common humanity and their authentic individuality. Their common humanity is already there, waiting to be discovered; their discovery of their individuality is the creative process of the group.

In each of these cases I am talking about the combination of internal and external processes; what is difficult to describe is the process of the combination. If we have the raw materials and what has been made out of them, then we can superimpose a complex causal chain and imagine that we have explained what has happened. The real creativity at work is shown most clearly through the indeterminacy of the therapy and the development of the group, and the individual changes that take place. We can never be sure in advance what the internal world will make of the external world. It is here, beyond the limits of social analysis, that a creative life can perhaps be seen more clearly in therapeutic relationships, but it is there to some degree in everyday life as well.

One way of making this point is through the difficulties in constructing a causal explanation of 'mental illness'. Most sociological attempts acknowledge, or would have to acknowledge if pressed, that people react to similar situations in different ways: that, for example, not everybody subjected to stress reacts with symptoms that indicate mental or emotional problems. Similarly, not everybody who behaves oddly is labelled as 'schizophrenic' or even as 'ill'. If one increased the complexity of causal analysis by bringing in a psychodynamic understanding, say, the effects of a particular family background, there would be similar difficulties. Causal analysis implies relationships between general categories, but individuals react differently to similar situations. Faced with a way of being in the world and with others, the union of an inner object world with an outer world, it seems to me to be like the transitional object: it makes no sense to ask whether it originates in one or the other. It is an act of creation in between the two.

Of course, knowing the sociological and psychological antecedents of problems is useful. It aids the therapist's understanding, contributes towards his or her interpretations of transference, it helps situate the person on a broad map of understanding. However, it does not tell us how the therapy should proceed. If we take the obvious case of somebody with a clearly damaging background, for example, abandoned by a mother to a violent father, the cause is obvious. But knowing it does not help that person, nor does it tell the therapist what to do; the relationship with the patient is a creative one, if it is working properly, and effective interventions have to do with intuition and understanding rather than knowledge. The important issue is the way in which the external conditions have been taken in and phantasised, and the way in which they re-emerge in here-and-now relationships. The quality and complications of the transference can never be predicted in advance, but are created on the spot. Indeed, one could argue that the less space for this creative aspect, the greater the dangers of pathological breakdown. I do not intend to look in more detail at this area, but rather shall look at its implications for sociological analysis.

I began this book with a distinction between social action and social structure, arguing that perhaps the proper object of sociology was the latter. I want now to modify this position a little. Social structure, whether an underlying structure or a surface, institutional role structure, does affect individuals. In sociological terms, what goes on as social action can be seen in terms of ideology, beliefs, socialisation, institutional selves, role-playing, and so on. In terms of psychoanalysis the same phenomena can be seen as defence systems, false selves and more or less successful instinctual sublimation. We could say that both ways of seeing such phenomena are 'right', it is just that each sees it in a different context. I do not think this is sufficient, because in my account of what happens in a group, I was in effect saying that the internal dynamics actually outweigh the effect of the external, sociological dynamics. If people believe or act in a way that can be attributed to the effect of social forces, then it is only because the internal psychodynamics of the character structure allow them, or force them, to do so.

This means, for the sociologist, that we do not know what is happening, we can be surprised by what people do, the way things turn out. Discussing this recently with one experienced empirical sociologist, he suggested that people were only surprised by the world if they were daft enough to make predictions. He also made the point that many sociologists who write and think about methodology are not themselves always involved in much empirical work, and think and write as if prediction were possible. In the case of social theory, this implicit sociologism is even more powerful. The logic of my argument here is that sociology cannot predict and, more important, cannot move from the general to the particular, or can only do so if it remains concerned only with the level of the false self. To be *only* sociological is to turn partial, and often dangerous, aspects of the self into the whole of the self.

Another important consequence of ignoring this area is the political equivalent of a therapy group in which there are only group interpretations; it is implicit in any attempt to derive or implement a political theory based on social analysis alone, making the assumption that it is only the social that matters. I am not just talking about government policies, which often if not always have very different results from those expected, but also political organisations and movements. Any movement or party creates its own false self, adopted to a greater or lesser extent by its members. My experience of radical and socialist organisations is that the false self required is often exclusive of everything else. This, of course, limits the effectiveness of the party or the movement: if it can *only* draw on more or less rigid defence systems, and excludes the area of what might seem dangerous originality and creativity, its existence will become fixed. This seems to have been the case with far left organisations in England since the Second World War: membership may fluctuate, but the organisation remains basically static. The experience of many members of such groups is one eventually of being oppressed, not understood, restricted. I think this is true even for the larger, more open traditional political parties. A healthy politics cannot be the whole of life: it must often, in order to be healthy, take a second place to love, the importance of bringing up children, marital conflict, mourning, pleasure and hate. The sociologistic fallacy is to render these secondary, then invisible, or to invade the space where they occur with sociological explanations. In Britain, the history of sociology has intimate links with reforming and, for a while, revolutionary left-wing movements where such a fallacy dominates.

### THE SOCIOLOGISTIC ASSUMPTION

Just as everybody creates something out of their internal world, so does the sociologist create sociology. I have been critical throughout this book of 'sociologism', the assumption that everything that happens in the world can be explained in sociological terms, often preferably as part of a total, systematic theory. I think it is probably true that one has to think like this if one is going to be a sociologist, in order to develop a real commitment to the discipline. Such a starting point can, however, be subjected to rational criticism and modification: one can be a sociologist without thinking sociology is the whole world. My experience has been, however, that in practice, and often despite explicit statements to the contrary, the sociologistic assumption has played a considerable role in sociology. In 1970, Alvin Gouldner was able to speak of 'living for sociology' without anybody, as far as I know, suggesting that sociology was perhaps a rather sad thing to live for, compared, say, with love, or one's children, or pleasure, or whatever.

Where explicit disclaimers are made, they are often implicitly over-ruled. Thus in his theory of suicide, Durkheim makes the point that he cannot use the theory to tell who will commit suicide; it is an explanation of suicide rates. The explanation of who will commit suicide is the province of another human science. If we take him seriously, then he is not explaining either individual suicide or suicide rates, for these are made up of individual suicides and collective negotiations around the issue of whether or not a death is a suicide. Rather, he is analysing the social preconditions of suicide and suicide rates; as such, it seems to me he does a rather good job. When we look at the meanings that individuals and groups attach to these preconditions, his claims to explanation begin to look very inadequate.

My point has been that if the sociologistic assumption is not modified, we miss vital dimensions of what is happening in the world. Now I want to suggest that we can see some sociology as created out of an over-rigid defence system – not out of the creative areas of the unconscious and the transitional world, but out of attempts to avoid these areas. Elsewhere, I have discussed some of the psychodynamic processes that seem to exist in or underlie much theoretical work. Here I want to make some tentative suggestions about the psychodynamics of sociologistic thinking. I want to make them in a firm and polemical way.

To be a sociologist is often to engage in, implicitly or explicitly, a more or less immense, more or less manic denial of the internal world, an attempt to avoid an inner reality. The degree of denial can be measured by the strength of the dismissal of, say, psychological explanations. The accompanying phantasy is that the external world can, in principle, be controlled, even if we cannot do so at the moment. This brings relief from the messiness of internal conflict and the uncertainty and openness of the future that must be present if it is accepted that there is internal conflict and an area in which we have to create ourselves albeit from very limited materials.

Contempt for other people, which one often finds as part of the denial, may be disguised under abstract humanitarian ideals. Thus contempt is clearest in structural and deterministic theories of social life, where anything individual and different tends to be discounted, but it is also there in the assumption that social causation is the *most* important level in any causal complex. Even when we are forced into actions by things outside ourselves, we are still making something of them that needs to be understood if we are to be able to do anything about changing the situation. Working therapeutically with students, I often find that they express the feeling that the institution of their department does not care about them as people. Sociology students will sometimes go one step further than the others and talk about feeling oppressed and denied in certain vital ways.

Just as sociology often seems to imply that the external world may be brought under control, I suspect there is also the phantasy that bad experiences, dangerous feelings, aggressive feelings, actually destroy.

If such things can be accounted for by external situations, we do not have to take responsibility for our own destructiveness. Indeed, we can be 'good people' through our attempts to change the external sources of destructiveness. In the past, when sociology has sometimes gone hand in hand with radical politics, I have known people who have caused considerable pain to themselves and others by denying, for example, jealousy or greed; and it is unfortunate that radical politics often provide an apparently moral justification for envy.

Finally, I suspect there is the drive to construct and validate a false self – a self that is socially constructed and validated. The fear here is, I suspect, of isolation, abandonment as a result of being different from other people, and of avoiding an internal emptiness. Universities enable those of us with a highly intellectually defended false self to survive; where the social sciences are concerned, this survival is achieved by constantly reconstructing and reinforcing those defences.

It does not follow from this that sociologists are somehow 'wrong', that their work can be discounted. As the old joke goes: just because you're paranoid it doesn't mean they're not after you. Just because much sociology may be part of a rigid defence system does not mean that sociological analysis is wrong. However, it is better to know they are after you and to realise that you are no more than normally paranoid; then you can begin to do something about it realistically, without being driven by unconscious defences. If sociology could realise its limitations and allow for them, its insights would be more useful. Indeed, against a sociologically naive psychoanalyst I would argue for the importance of all forms of sociology, and suspect that the over-rigid defence at work in such a person amounts to a denial of the force of external reality.

Perhaps another way of making this point is that it is important to be creative, to risk being wrong, to play with ideas, as much in sociology as anywhere else. If we can recognise that we are only dealing with part of the world, then perhaps playing becomes possible. If we believe, consciously or unconsciously, that the world is in our hands, that we must be accurate and beyond criticism, that we must, at least potentially, be able to explain everything about what we are doing, then it becomes difficult to play. In play, we can also perhaps find a useful outlet for some of the less palatable aspects of our nature. My propositions about the unconscious dynamics behind sociological thought are certainly partly rooted in envy and considerable difficulty in losing the ideal object – the sort of totalising explanation that I once thought to be the province of sociology. I could repress such a reaction, or simply suppress it and stick to strictly rational considerations to make the same point. It is not nearly as satisfying as allowing envy a role and then modifying it.

## THE CRITICAL DIMENSIONS: MORALITY AND INTEGRITY

If there is anything further to say, then perhaps it is the same point directed at any way of conceiving, or attempting to organise, a world that does not recognise its own limitations. It is a political point and I find myself rather surprised when I start trying to fill out the practical details; it seems closer to some ideals of anarchism and some ideals of liberal democratic theory, and in the past I have not had all that much time for either approach. Here it seems the language of object-relations theory can be used to look at social organisation in a new light.

In the work of the Frankfurt School, the basis for the criticism of existing forms of social relations is a conception of what a truly rational society might be like. Some similar conception is necessary for any theory with critical dimensions. Few people have tried to look at the social implications of object-relations theory beyond a sort of common-sense social policy level. Mike Rustin (1984), for example, looks at the egalitarianism implied in the emphasis on feeling and feeling capacities, the chance of coming to grips with the biological basis of human behaviour, and the relevance, particularly of Klein's work, to methods of dealing with violence, and the way in which it goes beyond sympathy for deprivation and offers the possibility of bringing about change in the violent offender. Winnicott engages in a number of extended political speculations, all making the simplistic assumption that society is no more than a collection of individuals. If we make such an assumption, however, or if we just compare, say, socialist theory and Kleinian psychoanalysis I do not think we shall get very far. I am much more interested in drawing out the implications of Kleinian and object-relations theory for social organisation and then perhaps looking at the latter in terms of a comparison with socialism. I shall only be attempting the first half of this task here.

Object-relations theory offers an 'ideal', a developed self, sufficiently strong to allow and tolerate strong feelings, which will often be unpleasant feelings of dependence and anger, if not hatred, without acting immediately or blindly on these feelings. The self will have a reasonably firm sense of its own boundaries, an ability to test reality, and measure phantasy against reality and an ability to work creatively in an intermediate world between internal and external reality. It will not be a 'perfect' self. Anger and destructiveness will remain and sometimes be acted out as such. There will be internal conflict of varying degrees of strength from to time, and periods of comparative integration. There will be normal human misery and a capacity for happiness, should the world allow it. There will be failures and successes in creativity. As it stands, it is a fairly empty conception; one can say that it would be nice if people were like this, that on the whole it is better to tolerate a limited amount of bad behaviour in oneself and others than aim to eliminate it, and it is even better to be able to tolerate a range of strong and difficult feelings. It would also be nice if the sun shone every day during summer.

It can become a little firmer when we try to identify the forms of social organisation that allow the development of such a personality. In the first case they involve arrangements which allow good-enough mothering (and fathering) without creating disadvantages in other spheres of life for those who do become 'ordinary devoted parents'. Such arrangements clearly do not exist now. I think it also implies what we might call the continuation of parenting through school, perhaps with more real day-to-day involvement of parents with education, so that a full and complex, rather than a comparatively fragmented, external ego is there to be perceived and understood and internalised. Perhaps, also, some sort of wholeness, a general basis to specialist education, is implied.

In terms of wider institutions, the desirable balance seems to be that they should leave space enough for the individual to find his or her own creative position within them, but at the same time provide sufficiently firm boundaries to enable the individual to maintain a sense of identity. Davis and Wallbridge chose boundary and space as the title for their book on Winnicott and it seems to me that this can be transferred directly into a model of social organisation. We must assume reasonably equal material conditions for everybody, conditions which do not interfere with good-enough parenting; and a social space that does not take over vital functions from individuals or families, but at the same time does not leave individuals or families to fulfil these functions without support in a structurally disadvantaged situation. Another way of putting it is that there must be space for the irrational, and also for what we might think of as evil or bad. Winnicott says somewhere that the good thing about elections is that they enable people to get rid of governments for no good reason, presumably without the trauma or violence of revolution. I am not sure I agree with him, but I like the idea. There need to be ways in which we can do things for no good reason, and the possibility of recognising and living with our own greed and envy and aggression without expecting those who cannot live with them to carry all the responsibility – here is the link with Mike Rustin's comments about dealing with crime.

All this is extremely sketchy and abstract, but it indicates that we *can* find a critical social standard from object relations theory. Perhaps the good thing about it is that it does not generate a blueprint, but offers a critical standard: it enables us to see when things are not happening and leaves us free to create ways for them to happen.

That seems to be as far as it is possible to go here. It might be that the common-sense social policy implications are the most important. If sociologists need to recognise an area where they cannot legislate, then so should psychotherapists. The contribution of a different critical standard to public discussion is, in any case, no mean achievement. There is more to be said on a personal level; it is often the case that psychoanalysis can produce a model of maturity, or a morality, that, while laying claims to a rational basis along the lines I outlined in the Introduction, can also be experienced as a reinforcement of a punitive super-ego. I do not think what I am saying here avoids this. I imagine that a fair number of people who read my account of the 'ideal' self offered by object-relations theory wondered about themselves and how close they came to this ideal: some will feel criticised, some praised by it. Perhaps this is unavoidable – and should be unavoidable, since a world in which we did not strive after something some of the time would not be a very interesting place.

Yet this ideal is significant, it seems to me, because it leaves a place for what is bad. Envy, greed, aggression are repressed or suppressed but acknowledged, as is weakness, helplessness, depression and madness. It is also recognised that they cannot always be sublimated in some socially useful way. They exist and we have to find a way of living with them in ourselves and in other people – we must find some way of allowing them. Another way of putting it is that they are part of our integrity, our wholeness; the sense of self that is difficult to describe but which, Winnicott suggests in his dramatic example, a baby will die to protect. The morality which is related to this is a way of treating ourselves as well as other people. In fact, if repressed part of ourselves are often projected on to other people, then by allowing ourselves to have these parts, we are treating other people in a different way, not least by allowing them to be themselves as well.

I have picked up and used the word 'play' frequently in this chapter. It is in play that integrity, integration, is reached; perhaps better, it is through play that we can come as close to integrity as we can. Often in the psychoanalytic literature, the word 'work' or 'work through' is used to describe exactly the same experience. Work in this context is play, and perhaps the work is over when we realise we are engaged in a very serious form of play, going beyond a simple play on words, with all the absorption and creativity of a five-year-old and his or her Leggo. Building something up and knocking it down again. If our play is serious, then our creativity is sometimes destructive, and although the word has a pleasant ring to it, the result of creation need not be beautiful.

# REFERENCES AND FURTHER READING

For the use of object-relations theory in feminist analysis, see:

Chodorow, N. (1978) *The Reproduction of Mothering: Psychoanalysis and the Sociology of Gender*, Berkeley: University of California Press.

Eichenbaum, L. and Orbach, S. (1983) *What Do Women Want?*, London: Fontana.


For a critique of Chodorow's approach, see:

Elshtain, J.B. (1984) 'Symmetry and soporifics: a critique of feminist accounts of gender development', in Richards, B. (ed.) *Capitalism and Infancy: Essays on Psychoanalysis and Politics*, London: Free Association Books.


My discussion of masculinity:

Craib, I. (1987) 'Masculinity and male dominance', *Sociological Review* 35, pp. 721–43.


On psychoanalysis and modern society, see:

Hinshelwood, R.D. (1986) 'A dual materialism', *Free Associations* 4, pp. 36–50.


On psychoanalysis and groups and institutions, see:

Bion, W.R. (1961) *Experience in Groups*, London: Tavistock.

de Board, R. (1978) *The Psychoanalysis of Organisations*, London: Tavistock.

Foulkes, S. (1964) *Therapeutic Group Analysis*, London: George Allen and Unwin.

Hinshelwood, R.D. (1987) *What Happens in Groups: Psychoanalysis, the Individual and the Community*, London: Free Association Books.

Menzies, I.E.P. (1970) *The Functioning of Social Systems as a Defence Against Anxiety*, London: The Tavistock Institute.

Pines, M. (ed.) (1983) *The Evolution of Group Analysis*, London: Routledge and Kegan Paul.

(1985) *Bion and Group Psychotherapy*, London: Routledge and Kegan Paul.

In the text I also mention:
Davis, M. and Wallbridge, D. (1983) *Boundary and Space: An Introduction to the Work of D.W. Winnicott*, Harmondsworth: Penguin Books.
Parin, P. (1985) 'Freedom and Independence', *Free Associations* 3, pp. 65–79.

For an understanding of the range of sociological approaches to mental illness, see:
Brown, G.W. and Harris, T. (1978) *The Social Origins of Depression: A Study of Psychiatric Disorder in Women*, London: Tavistock.
Cochrane, R. (1983) *The Social Creation of Mental Illness*, New York: Longman.
Goffmann, E. (1968) *Asylums*, Harmondsworth: Penguin Books.
Gouldner, A.W. (1971) *The Coming Crisis of Western Sociology*, London: Heinemann.
Miles, A. (1988) *Women and Mental Illness: The Social Context of Female Neurosis*, Hemel Hempstead: Harvester Wheatsheaf.
Scheff, J. (1966) *Being Mentally Ill: A Sociological Theory*, New York: Aldine.

In the text, I also draw attention to Durkheim's theory of suicide; it is useful to read in juxtaposition:
Durkheim, E. (1975) *Suicide: A Study in Sociology*, London: Routledge and Kegan Paul.
Douglas, J.D. (1967) *The Social Meanings of Suicide*, Princeton, N.J.: Princeton University Press.

I also refer to my own paper:
Craib, I. (1987) 'The pscychodynamics of theory', *Free Associations* 10, pp. 32–58.

And Michael Rustin's work:
Rustin, M. (1982) 'A socialist consideration of Kleinian psychoanalysis', *New Left Review* 131, pp. 71–96.
    (1984) 'Psychoanalysis and social justice', *Free Associations*, pilot issue, pp. 98–112.

# INDEX

sexual object and sexual aim, 39–42
sexuality, 5–6, 24–5, 32–4, Chapter 3
    *passim*, 61, 124–8, 166–7n, 176–7
sociology, *see* psychoanalysis and sociology
sociology of mental illness, 188–95
structural linguistics, 116–18
structuralism, 50–1
super-ego, 3–4, 21, 23, 26, 32, 36, 43–4,
    47, 57–8, 75, 102–16, 136, 142, 149,
    180, 181, 182; *see also* fathers

transference and counter-transference,
    92–4, 96, 100
transitional phenomena, 161–95, Part IV
    *passim*

unconscious, 3–7, 41, 75, 100, 117,
    118–20, 142–3, 156, 163, 183,
    185–6
unconscious phantasy, 142–3
Utopia and utopianism, 34–7, 99–100

Wallbridge, D., 155, 156, 199
Weber, M., 114, 181
Will, D., 13n
Winnicott, D.W., 84, 100, 137, 153,
    Chapter 9 *passim*, 179, 182, 190,
    198, 199
Wollheim R., 13n, 17

Zaretsky, E., 112